ALTERNATIVES *to* ECONOMIC GLOBALIZATION

⟦ *A Better World Is Possible* ⟧

~

A REPORT OF THE
INTERNATIONAL FORUM ON GLOBALIZATION

REPORT DRAFTING COMMITTEE:

John Cavanagh, Co-Chair   Jerry Mander, Co-Chair
Sarah Anderson   Andrew Kimbrell
Debi Barker   David Korten
Maude Barlow   Sara Larrain
Walden Bello   Helena Norberg-
Robin Broad   Hodge
Tony Clarke   Simon Retallack
Edward Goldsmith   Vandana Shiva
Randall Hayes   Victoria Tauli-Corpuz
Colin Hines   Lori Wallach

BK

BERRETT-KOEHLER PUBLISHERS, INC.
San Francisco

Berrett-Koehler Publishers, Inc.
235 Montgomery Street, Suite 650
San Francisco, CA 94104-2916
Tel: (415) 288-0260   Fax: (415) 362-2512
www.bkconnection.com

Ordering Information

Quantity sales. Special discounts are available on quantity purchases by corporations, associations, and others. For details, contact the "Special Sales Department" at the Berrett-Koehler address above.
Individual sales. Berrett-Koehler publications are available through most bookstores. They can also be ordered direct from Berrett-Koehler: Tel: (800) 929-2929; Fax: (802) 864-7626; www.bkconnection.com
Orders for college textbook/course adoption use. Please contact Berrett-Koehler: Tel: (800) 929-2929; Fax: (802) 864-7626.
Orders by U.S. trade bookstores and wholesalers. Please contact Publishers Group West, 1700 Fourth Street, Berkeley, CA 94710. Tel: (510) 528-1444; Fax: (510) 528-3444.

Berrett-Koehler and the BK logo are registered trademarks of Berrett-Koehler Publishers, Inc.

Printed in the United States of America

Berrett-Koehler books are printed on long-lasting acid-free paper. When it is available, we choose paper that has been manufactured by environmentally responsible processes. These may include using trees grown in sustainable forests, incorporating recycled paper, minimizing chlorine in bleaching, or recycling the energy produced at the paper mill.

LIBRARY OF CONGRESS CATALOGING-IN-PUBLICATION DATA
Alternatives to economic globalization : a better world is possible /
Alternatives Task Force of the International Forum on Globalization ;
drafting committee, John Cavanagh . . . [et al.].
    p.   cm.
Includes bibliographical references and index.
ISBN 1-57675-204-6
1. International economic relations.
2. Globalization.
3. Economic development.
I. Cavanagh, John.
II. International Forum on Globalization. Alternatives Task Force.
HF1359 .A547   2002
337—dc21   2002026007

FIRST EDITION

07 06 05 04 03   10 9 8 7 6 5 4

Project management, design, and composition: BookMatters, Berkeley
Copyedit: Sandra Beriss; Proofreading: Ann Foley; Index: Ken DellaPenta

ALTERNATIVES *to* ECONOMIC GLOBALIZATION

Contents

TWO
TEN PRINCIPLES FOR SUSTAINABLE SOCIETIES
54

THREE
THE COMMONS:
WHAT SHOULD BE OFF-LIMITS TO GLOBALIZATION?
79

FOUR

THE CASE FOR SUBSIDIARITY:
BIAS AWAY FROM THE GLOBAL TOWARD THE LOCAL

105

FIVE

CORPORATE STRUCTURE AND POWER

121

SIX

ALTERNATIVE OPERATING SYSTEMS

151

Acknowledgments

It is an extraordinary undertaking to reach consensus among nineteen individuals about anything, let alone about concrete ideas on how to build sustainable societies. It was possible only because of the many years of collaboration and friendship among the authors, especially as part of the International Forum on Globalization (IFG), which provided the creative space to explore ideas and possibilities, and work them through to completion. Each of the drafters contributed ideas, writings, and responses to others' offerings. From 1999 to 2002, the Alternatives Task Force of the IFG met four times and on other occasions in smaller subgroups. Typical of consensus processes, not every contributor agrees completely with every other one, or with every idea in these pages. But all are in agreement on the overall direction of the arguments, and with the overwhelming majority of points. It has been an inspiring process for all of us.

The authors would like to offer special thanks to David Korten and Sarah Anderson who, in the final months of preparation on this document, worked tirelessly to help refine, edit, and clarify many parts of the manuscript. Others who contributed greatly to the discussions or gave feedback on particular parts of the report include Agnes Bertrand, Brent Blackwelder, Victor Menotti, Anuradha Mittal, David Morris, Mark Ritchie, and Steve Shrybman. And for extremely useful feedback on the manuscript and editing ideas, thanks also to Peter Berg, Ernest Callenbach, Paul Hawken, and Michael Shuman. Suzanne York of the IFG provided important research at many stages, and Elizabeth Connor did a magnificent job processing and coordinating the flows of information and drafts among all the far-flung participants.

We also offer our acknowledgement and heartfelt thanks to IFG board member and cofounder Martin Khor and the Third World Network. No individual or organization has contributed more to our collective thinking and analysis before and throughout this process. Many of us think of Martin as our Paul Revere for his ability to warn us well in advance of crucial new developments in the World Trade Organization and other trade bodies, and to steer us toward viable alternative strategies. We are indebted to him.

Finally we thank Steve Piersanti and his tremendous team at Berrett-Koehler, whose enthusiasm, professionalism, and good ideas have made this a better book. We also wish to thank our excellent copyeditor Sandra Beriss.

FOR THE DRAFTING COMMITTEE:
John Cavanagh, Washington D.C.
Jerry Mander, San Francisco
July 31, 2002

A NOTE ON SOURCES

Readers will note that we have not used footnotes in this book. Key sources are indicated within the flow of the text, and all sources can be found in the "Sources" section on page 243. All URLs cited in this book were confirmed on September 9, 2002.

Introduction

THIS BOOK, *Alternatives to Economic Globalization,* is an offshoot of an ongoing dialogue among associates of the International Forum on Globalization (IFG). IFG is best known for its contribution to building public awareness about the nature and consequences of corporate globalization, and for its resistance against the forces of global corporate rule. The authors of this volume believe that the ultimate success of citizen movements depends on their becoming more proactive in creating the world that can be.

The immediate priority is to frame the issues, recognizing that to arrive at a consensus among even a few people—let alone millions—is a far more complex and difficult task than building agreement on what we oppose. That which we oppose is immediate and concrete. Along with billions of our fellow humans, we live and breathe the consequences of corporate globalization and share the great pain it inflicts on humanity and the earth.

Any vision we may craft of an alternative future is less certain. It holds many possibilities and is always a work in progress. Citizen movements that are addressing globalization have no governing body, official ideology, or charismatic leader with a mandate to speak for the whole. We are brought together by our shared belief that there is a human capacity for cooperation, compassion, creativity, and responsible choice that will make a better world possible, even though it is all too often suppressed by the culture and institutions of corporate globalization. We are learning together as we join in common cause to turn possibility into reality.

In preparing this report, we have tried to remain true to what we sense to be the larger consensus unfolding within these movements. Yet we are aware that any effort to articulate positions for a movement so diverse is necessarily subject to discussion and debate. Therefore, we have sought patterns and points of convergence in the movement. But in the end the observations and conclusions we offer here represent mainly our personal views at this particular moment in history and in our own evolving understanding.

Global Resistance

Over the past decade, millions of people have taken to the streets in India, the Philippines, Indonesia, Brazil, Bolivia, the United States, Canada, Mexico, Argentina, Venezuela, France, Germany, Italy, the Czech Republic, Spain, Sweden, the United Kingdom, New Zealand, Australia, Kenya, South Africa, Thailand, Malaysia, and elsewhere, in massive demonstrations against the institutions and policies of corporate globalization. Often the mainstream media has done more to mislead than to inform the public on the issues behind the protests. Thomas Friedman, foreign affairs columnist for the *New York Times*, is typical of pundits who characterize the demonstrators as "ignorant protectionists" who offer no alternatives and do not merit serious attention. Many in the media have tried to reduce the complex issues involved to a simplistic contest between "protectionism" and "openness," or between "anarchy" and "an orderly democratic process." In North America and Europe, those involved in the protests are dismissed as spoiled children of privilege—selfish, ill-informed malcontents who would end trade and international cooperation.

Anyone who makes even the smallest effort to find out why millions of people from virtually every nation and walk of life have taken to the streets finds these simplistic characterizations to be untrue. As for the charge of being anti-poor, the largest protests are in low-income countries, and most of those involved are themselves poor. The charges of isolation and xenophobia are equally uninformed; the resistance against corporate globalization is global in scope and is dedicated to international cooperation to achieve economic justice for every person on the planet. As for the charge of being anti-trade, many of the movement's leaders are actively involved in the promotion of *fair* trade—in contrast to the often exploitative *free* trade they oppose—as a means of improving the economic conditions of poor people and their communities.

In fact, the resistance is grounded in a sophisticated, well-developed critique set forth in countless publications and public presentations, including, among many others, documents available from the International Forum on Globalization (IFG) and numerous books and articles by IFG associates. The critique is also available in the publications of a thriving independent media that tells the stories and communicates the opinions that the mainstream media so often ignores or dismisses. These independent information sources are gradually expanding public awareness and enlarging the constituency for transformational change, but they have not yet reached sufficient critical mass to force a reframing of the terms of the political debate still dominated by corporate media and interests.

The claim that the protestors offer no alternatives is as false as the other claims. In addition to the alternatives described in books, periodicals, conferences, and individual articles and presentations, numerous consensus statements have been carefully crafted by civil society groups over the past two decades that set forth a wealth of alternatives with a striking convergence in their beliefs about the underlying values human society should serve. In 2001 and 2002, tens of thousands gathered in Porto Alegre, Brazil, for the first and second annual World Social Forum, titled "Another World Is Possible," to carry forward this process of popular consensus building toward a world that works for all.

Perhaps the most obvious and straightforward alternative advocated by civil society is simply to place a moratorium on the negotiation of new trade agreements. More ambitious proposals—such as those presented in this volume—center on redirecting global, national, and local priorities toward the task of creating healthy, sustainable human societies that work for all.

Although many of the protests have centered on opposition to trade agreements, global civil society does not oppose trade. Humans have engaged in trade since the beginning of time and as long as two or more members of the species survive will surely continue to do so. What the protesters reject is the use by corporate interests of international trade *agreements* to circumvent democracy in their global campaign to strip away social and environmental protections that ordinary people have struggled for decades—even centuries—to put in place.

The issue is governance. Will ordinary people have a democratic voice in deciding what rules are in the best interests of society? Or will a small ruling elite, meeting in secret and far from public view, be allowed to set the rules that shape the human future? If the concern of the decision makers is only for next quarter's corporate profits, who will care for the health and well-being of people and the planet?

These are increasingly serious questions for a great many people who live with the violence and insecurity that spreads through the world in tandem with growing inequality, an unraveling social fabric, and the collapse of critical environmental systems. It is this reality of social and environmental disintegration that has brought millions of people together in a loose global alliance that spans national borders to forge what may be considered the most truly global and inclusive social movement in human history.

Different Worlds

The corporate globalists who meet in posh gatherings to chart the course of corporate globalization in the name of private profits, and the citizen movements that organize to thwart them in the name of democracy, are separated by deep differences in values, worldview, and definitions of progress. At times it seems they must be living in wholly different worlds—which, in fact, in many respects they are. Understanding their differences is key to understanding the nature and implications of the profound choices humanity currently faces.

Corporate globalists inhabit a world of power and privilege. They see progress at hand everywhere, because from their vantage point the drive to privatize public assets and free the market from governmental interference spreads freedom and prosperity around the world, improving the lives of people everywhere and creating the financial and material wealth necessary to end poverty and protect the environment. They see themselves as champions of an inexorable and beneficial historical process toward erasing the economic and political borders that hinder corporate expansion, eliminating the tyranny of inefficient and meddlesome public bureaucracies, and unleashing the enormous innovation and wealth-creating power of competition and private enterprise.

Corporate globalists undertake to accelerate these trends as a great mission. They seek public policies and international agreements that provide greater safeguards for investors and private property while removing restraints to the free movement of goods, money, and corporations in search of economic opportunity wherever it may be found. They embrace global corporations as the greatest and most efficient human institutions, powerful engines of innovation and wealth creation that are peeling away the barriers to human progress and accomplishment everywhere. They celebrate the World Bank, the International Monetary Fund, and the World Trade Organization as essential and beneficial institutions for global governance engaged in the great work of rewriting the rules of commerce to free the market and create conditions essential to economic growth.

Corporate globalists subscribe to this worldview like a catechism. They differ among themselves mainly in their views of the extent to which it is appropriate for government to subsidize private corporations or provide safety nets to cushion the fall of the losers in the market's relentless competition.

Citizen movements see a very different reality. Focused on people and the environment, they see a world in a crisis of such magnitude that it threatens the fabric of civilization and the survival of the species—a world of rapidly growing inequality, erosion of relationships of trust and caring, and failing planetary life support systems. Where corporate globalists see the spread of democracy and vibrant market economies, citizen movements see the power to govern shifting away from people and communities to financial speculators and global corporations dedicated to the pursuit of short-term profit in disregard of all human and natural concerns. They see corporations replacing democracies of people with democracies of money, replacing self-organizing markets with centrally planned corporate economies, and replacing diverse cultures with cultures of greed and materialism.

In the eyes of citizen movements, these trends are not the result of some inexorable historical force but rather of the intentional actions of a corrupted political system awash in corporate money. They see the World Bank, the IMF, and the World Trade Organization as leading instruments of this assault against people and the environment.

Ironically, the citizen movements seek many of the things the corporate globalists claim to offer but in fact fail to deliver: democratic participation, economies comprising enterprises that provide good jobs and respond to the real needs and preferences of their customers, a healthy environment, an end to poverty. However, where the corporate globalists seek a competitive global economy ruled by megacorporations that owe no loyalty to place or person, citizen movements seek a planetary system of economies made up of locally owned enterprises accountable to all their stakeholders. Citizen movements work for economic justice for all, international cooperation, vibrant cultural diversity, and healthy, sustainable societies that value life more than money.

Citizen movements recognize that corporate globalists *cannot* deliver on their promises because the narrow and shortsighted financial imperatives that drive their institutions are antithetical to them. Many corporate globalists may act with the best intentions, but they are blinded by their own financial success to the costs of this success for those who have no place at the table, including future generations.

Corporate globalists generally measure progress by indicators of their own financial wealth, such as rising stock prices and indicators of the total output of goods and services available to those who have the money to pay. With the exception of occasional cyclical setbacks in Latin America and elsewhere and declining per capita incomes in the poorest African countries, these indicators generally perform well, confirming in the eyes of corporate globalists their premise that their program is enriching the world. (We do note that in July 2002, as this book was about to go to press, the main U.S. stock market indexes fell by over 5 percent in a week.)

In contrast, citizen movements measure progress by indicators of the well-being of people and nature, with particular concern for the lives of those most in need. With the exception of the highly visible pockets of privilege enjoyed by corporate globalists, these indicators are deteriorating at a frightening pace, suggesting that in terms of what really matters, the world is rapidly growing poorer.

⌒

The U.N. Food and Agriculatural Organization (FAO) reports that the number of chronically hungry people in the world declined steadily during the 1970s and 1980s but has been increasing since the early 1990s. The U.S. Department of Agriculture estimates that by 2008 two-thirds of the people of sub-Saharan Africa will be undernourished, and 40 percent will be undernourished in Asia.

In a world in which a few enjoy unimaginable wealth, two hundred million children under age five are underweight because of a lack of food. Some fourteen million children die each year from hunger-related disease. A hundred million children are living or working on the streets. Three hundred thousand children were conscripted as soldiers during the 1990s, and six million were injured in armed conflicts. Eight hundred million people go to bed hungry each night.

This human tragedy is not confined to poor countries. Even in a country as wealthy as the United States, 6.1 million adults and 3.3 million children experience outright hunger. Some 10 percent of U.S. households, accounting for 31 million people, do not have access to enough food to meet their basic needs. These are some of the many indicators of a deepening global social crisis.

On the environmental side, a joint study released in September 2000 by the United Nations Development Program (UNDP), the United Nations Environment Program (UNEP), the World Bank, and the World Resources Institute assessed five ecosystem types—agricultural, coastal, forest, freshwater, and grassland—in relation to five ecosystem services—food and fiber production, water quantity, air quality, biodiversity, and carbon storage. It found that of these twenty-five ecosystem-service combinations, sixteen had declining trends. The only positive trend was in food and fiber production by forest ecosystems, which has been achieved by an expansion of industrial forest monocropping at the expense of species diversity.

Human activity—in particular, fossil fuel combustion—is estimated to have increased atmospheric concentrations of carbon dioxide to their highest levels in twenty million years. According to the Worldwatch Institute, an environmental think tank, natural disasters, including weather-related disasters such as storms, floods, and fires, affected more than two billion people and caused in excess of $608 billion in economic losses worldwide during the decade of the 1990s—more than the previous four decades combined. Three hundred million people were displaced from their homes or forced to resettle because of extreme weather events in 1998 alone.

It becomes more imperative to rethink human priorities and institutions by the day. Yet most corporate globalists, in deep denial, reiterate their mantra that with time and patience corporate globalization will create the wealth needed to end poverty and protect the environment.

Citizen movements counter that the policies and processes of corporate globalization are destroying the real wealth of the planet while advancing a primitive winner-takes-all competition that inexorably widens the gap between rich and poor. They reject as absurd the argument that the poor must be exploited and the environment destroyed to make the money necessary to end poverty and save the planet.

Many citizen movements embrace the present imperative for transformational change as an opportunity to lift humanity to a new level of possibility—the greatest creative challenge in the history of the species. Yet experience leads them to conclude that the institutions with the power to provide the leadership are neither inclined nor suited to doing so. Nor is there realistic cause for hope that leaders who are lavishly rewarded by the status quo and hold steadfastly to the view that there is no alternative will suddenly experience an epiphany.

The challenge of providing leadership to create a just and sustainable world thus falls by default to the hundreds of millions of extraordinary people in an emerging global civil society who believe a better world is possible—and who are forging global alliances that seek to shift the powers of governance to democratic, locally rooted, human-scale institutions that value life more than money. Although the most visible among them are those who have taken to the streets in protest, equally important and even more numerous are those struggling to rebuild their local communities and economies in the face of the institutional forces aligned against them.

Economic Democracy

The current and future well-being of humanity depends on transforming the relationships of power within and between societies toward more democratic and mutually accountable modes of managing human affairs that are self-organizing, power-sharing, and minimize the need for coercive central authority. *Economic* democracy, which involves the equitable participation of all people in the ownership of the productive assets on which their livelihood depends, is essential to such a transformation because the concentration of economic power is the Achilles heel of *political* democracy, as the experience of corporate globalization demonstrates.

The defining political struggles of the twentieth century centered on a choice between socialism and capitalism. Both centralized the power of ownership in unaccountable institutions, the state in the case of socialism and the corporation in the case of capitalism. Both worked against the classic liberal economic ideal of self-organizing markets—markets in which communities organize themselves to respond to local needs within a framework of democratically determined rules.

Although rarely noted, economic democracy is as essential to the efficient function of economies as sound public regulation. Because today's markets respond only to money, they are overly attentive to the wants of the rich and neglect the most basic needs of the poor. Economic democracy is also a necessary foundation of individual, community, and national economic self-determination—the right to determine one's own economic priorities and the rules of one's economic life—because it helps secure a political voice for each person.

At the same time, there are real and often difficult trade-offs to be considered in the choice between local, national, and global rule making. For example, civil society has a strong commitment to raising social and environmental standards everywhere. To this end, some activists call for setting universal labor, health and safety, and environmental standards, possibly enforced with trade sanctions. They correctly point out that allowing different standards in an open, competitive global economy inevitably puts competitive pressure on everyone to lower their standards.

But others note that it is invariably the strong nations who advocate for uniform standards because they hold the power to impose self-serving rules of their own choosing on weaker nations. Furthermore, uniform international standards not only violate the democratic right to self-determination but also fail to take into account differing local conditions and preferences. Those on this side of the argument call for measures to secure the right of nations and even localities to adopt standards of their choosing appropriate to their circumstances, as long as they do not shift the burden of their decisions onto others.

Both positions reflect valid concerns. The differences relate in part to the extent of the priority given to economic self-reliance. The less the self-reliance of a community or nation, the greater its external dependence and the greater the need for globally uniform rules to avoid a downward pressure on standards everywhere. By the same token, the greater the self-reliance of a community or nation, the greater the scope for local flexibility and adaptation to local circumstances. Dialogue on these trade-offs in the IFG has led to a consensus tilt in favor of self-reliance and local self-determination.

~

The concern for local self-reliance and self-determination has important implications for global governance. For example, in a self-reliant and localized system, the primary authority to set and enforce rules rests with the national and local governments of the jurisdictions to which they apply. The proper role of international institutions is to facilitate the coordination of national policies on matters where the interests of nations are inherently intertwined—global warming, for example.

Of course, a democratic commitment to self-determination means that ultimately it is left up to the people of every nation—if not every indigenous group or local community—to decide the extent to which they will integrate their own economy with the economies of other nations. The people of different countries will likely reach different decisions. The international interest is properly confined to assuring that these decisions are made democratically, that economic relationships among countries are just and balanced, that no country builds up unpayable debts to the rest of the system, and that each national economy is secure against predatory interventions from foreign nations and corporations.

There is certainly a need for international institutions to facilitate cooperative exchange and the working through of inevitable competing national interests toward solutions to global problems. These institutions must, however, be transparent and democratic and support the rights of people, communities, and nations to self-determination. The World Bank, the IMF, and the World Trade Organization violate each of these conditions to such an extent that the authors of this book recommend that they be decommissioned and new institutions built under the authority of a strengthened and reformed United Nations. These new institutions would be responsible for freeing Third World nations from the burden of unpayable international debts, helping all nations bring their international trade and investment accounts into balance with the global system, and working with national governments to establish the public accountability of corporations with operations that span national borders.

Momentum for Change

Less than a decade ago, the claims of corporate globalists of the inevitability of their cause were credible to many. Talk of economic alternatives seemed little more than bravado. Today, although corporate globalization remains a formidable force, it no longer seems quite as invincible, nor discussion of alternatives quite as fanciful. Public consciousness of the pervasive abuse of corporate power has fueled the growth of a powerful opposition movement.

For example, secret negotiations toward a multilateral agreement on investment (MAI) under the Organization for Economic Cooperation and Development (OECD) were exposed and ultimately ended. U.S. president Clinton was twice denied the "fast track" authority he sought, which would have allowed him a free hand in negotiating trade agreements with minimal congressional debate and no amendment. (A Republican Congress finally did grant this authority to President George W. Bush in 2002, by three votes.) Efforts to launch a new round of trade negotiations at the 1999 WTO ministerial meeting in Seattle were disrupted, and the WTO was forced to expose its undemocratic nature by moving its 2001 ministerial meeting to Qatar, a remote monarchy where public protest is ruthlessly suppressed. In April 2000, police shut down much of Washington, D.C., to secure a World Bank– IMF meeting from protestors demanding the decommissioning of these institutions and the cancellation of Third World debt. A subsequent meeting of IMF and World Bank directors in Prague closed a day early, and a planned meeting in Barcelona was canceled. In 2001, pharmaceutical corporations were forced to make concessions allowing greater use of low-cost generic drugs in poor countries. Increasingly, protestors and members of the Group of 77—a formal intergovernmental body of over 130 of the world's poorest countries—find themselves aligned in a common cause.

The evolving alliance of civil society organizations brings together union members, farmers, landless peasants, people of faith, women's organizations, youth organizations, small business owners, artisanal producers, economic justice organizers, prison reform advocates, environmentalists, AIDS and other health activists, politicians, independent media organizations, civil servants, the homeless, peace and human rights organizations, gay and lesbian groups, intellectuals, consumer advocates, and even a few corporate CEOs of every age, religion, race, and nationality. It is the product of a largely spontaneous awakening of millions of people to the reality that their future and the future of their children depends on exercising their democratic right to participate in the decisions that shape their future.

Unified by a deep commitment to universal values of democracy, justice, and respect for life, this alliance functions with growing effectiveness without a central organization, leadership, or defining ideology. It also takes different forms in different settings.

In India, activists seek to empower local people through the democratic community control of resources under the banner of a millions-strong Living Democracy movement. In Canada, hundreds of organizations have joined together to articulate a citizens' agenda that seeks to wrest control of governmental institutions back from corporations. In Chile, coalitions of environmental groups have created a powerful Sustainable Chile proposal that seeks to reverse that country's drift toward free markets and reassert popular democratic control over national priorities and resources. The focus in Brazil is on the rights of workers, the poor, and the landless. In Bolivia, a mass movement of peasants and workers has successfully blocked the privatization of water. In Mexico, the Mayan people have reignited the spirit of Zapata in a movement to confirm the rights of indigenous people to land and resources. French farmers have risen up in revolt against trade rules that threaten to destroy small farms. The construction of new highways in the United Kingdom has brought out hundreds of thousands of people who oppose this desecration of the countryside to meet globalization's relentless demand for ever more high-speed transport.

These are only a few examples of the initiatives and actions in defense of democratic rights that are occurring around the world. Some are purely local; others are national or international. All are linked together in common rejection of the illegitimate power and false promises of global corporations and a proactive commitment to revitalize democracy at local, regional, national, and global levels. Each contributes to an emerging vision of the healthy, just, and sustainable society that humanity has the means to create. Each adds its voice to a growing global chorus proclaiming the right of "We the people of planet earth" to create such a society.

This volume discusses many of these alternative proposals as well as initiatives on the ground. Some are short-term and address the debates of the moment; others are long-term and spell out new rules and institutions to advance sustainable societies. Martin Khor of the Malaysia-based Third World Network offers an excellent framework for understanding the interactions of these different kinds of alternatives work (in Box A).

BOX A: COMMENTARY—CONFLICTING PARADIGMS

By Martin Khor, Third World Network

Let me put forward two conflicting paradigms that civil society is now facing and which require that we make some difficult choices about how we advance our work. The first paradigm involves the choice to work in the system of globalization, which we feel we are trapped in. If we do work within that system, we begin by asking: "Are the rules of the game fair, particularly to the weaker partners, or are they being twisted and manipulated by the strong partners in order to keep the weaker countries down?" If the latter, then we should fight for the reform of the rules of the game so that they can be more fair. We should monitor and be aware where the rules of the game go against the weak and the poor. In this first paradigm, we will be working and arguing within the parameters of the system and trying to tinker with it, because we may conclude that there is no choice, at least in the short run. And this may be an approach pragmatic people will take who are involved in, say, survival for the next five years or ten years.

But we realize that even as we work in that system and make it more fair for all the participants, that system may not last very long because of ecological limits. In other words, if we continue to emphasize high growth, but the growth is more equitably shared and the poor are made to come out better, still the whole system of industrialism goes on. So the debate is whether the textile mills should continue to be in London and provide jobs for British workers with high standards of living and security or whether they should be transferred to Bangladesh where child labor is exploited. But maybe it's better for the child laborer to be exploited than to be out of a job, and dead. It's that kind of debate that we may be entering into within this first paradigm. Is it fair for the Bangladeshi to be exploited in a factory or should he remain unexploited; should his labor standard go up? If his labor standard goes up he may lose his job because the factory may move back to London and the London worker will have the job.

So then the issue becomes this: maybe the factory shouldn't exist in London or Bangladesh either because industrialism is bad, perhaps industrial-

CONTINUED

BOX A: CONTINUED

ism is incompatible with the long-term survival of the world. This is the basis of the second paradigm—that this debate over North-South is irrelevant because in twenty or thirty years the whole system will blow up anyway. So, in the second paradigm, we work for Gandhi-style, community-based, self-reliant family units of production, trading mainly within the community and the region and only making occasional exchanges with the rest of the world, as needed.

Now if you are working within this second paradigm, you might say, "I don't want transnational corporations. I will use any methods to kick them out, and I will go back to emphasizing local production." So, if we are working from this second paradigm we would certainly come out with different policy conclusions than if we were working from the first paradigm, which is for fairer trade, fairer economic relations.

The debate on whether worker rights and environmental rights should be addressed in trade agreements is really contained in that first paradigm, while at the same time we must remember there is that second paradigm. But sometimes we borrow ideas from that second paradigm to buttress our arguments for the first paradigm, and vice versa, and we get confused. So as we work and debate which initiatives make sense, we should be explicit as to whether we are arguing from the first or the second paradigm.

Let us be clear that the real world is moving ahead in the first paradigm. Some of us may be fighting from within that paradigm to point out where

there are inequities, where there are double standards, and where there must be fairer terms of exchange, and so forth. I personally often work in the context of the first paradigm, whereas emotionally I really belong to the second one. So if we ask if we should trade with the rest of the world, we must make it very clear what our assumptions are and which paradigm we are proceeding from. Because at the end of the day, it is better if we can infuse the second paradigm into the first paradigm as a kind of transition.

For example, as we grapple with trade and environment under the first paradigm, we would do well to ask how we make the globalized system more environmentally sustainable as a transition toward the second paradigm. And to do it in such a way that the poor do not suffer and the costs of adjusting are borne by the rich.

I believe that for now we must always try to work in both paradigms. In this sense, we can devise a system that moves toward environmental sustainability in a socially equitable manner that will reduce income inequalities, resolve the poverty problem, but at the same time solve the environmental problem. Can trade mechanisms, systems of prices and products, and other things be devised so that we have this transition toward Paradigm Two? This is one of our greatest challenges.

SOURCE: Martin Khor, "Commentary." In John Cavanagh, ed., *South-North: Citizen Strategies to Transform a Divided World.* San Francisco: International Forum on Globalization, November 1995.

IFG Alternatives Process

The International Forum on Globalization's inquiry into alternatives to corporate globalization was initiated in January 1999, nearly a year before the Seattle confrontation between global civil society and the World Trade Organization. Some thirty IFG Board members and key associate members have since been writing papers and holding regular meetings to develop consensus on a framework for positive change. This volume is our interim report.

Chapter 1 presents a critique of the institutions, theory, and practice of corporate globalization and the argument for why they must be replaced by institutions, theory, and practice that serve and nurture life and democracy.

Chapter 2 outlines ten organizing principles for healthy, just, democratic, and sustainable societies. They provide a guiding framework for the creative work of institutional restructuring and rule making that lies ahead.

Chapter 3 discusses the special nature of common resources like water, which are an inheritance essential to life, and explains why allowing them to be privatized, monopolized, and allocated solely on the basis of ability to pay and without regard to equity and the public interest is morally and environmentally unacceptable.

Chapter 4 makes the case for shifting decision-making power from the global to the local and outlines some of the ways in which that can be accomplished.

Chapter 5 examines the processes by which global corporations have established themselves as the dominant ruling institutions of the planet and outlines specific steps to alter corporate structure, limit their power, and hold them accountable to the public interest.

Chapter 6 draws lessons from exploratory initiatives in the practice of living democracy being advanced by a variety of movements in both the North and the South. In particular, it outlines alternative operating systems in energy, transportation, agriculture, and manufacturing.

Chapter 7 argues for replacing the triumvirate of the World Bank, the IMF, and the World Trade Organization with new institutions to be created under the authority of the United Nations. These institutions would have mandates to support and assist the transition to a cooperative planetary system of local economies that exchange information, technology, culture, and goods in a framework of mutual, democratic accountability.

Chapter 8 offers some concluding reflections.

We present this report with an awareness of the complexity of the issues and the trade-offs involved. We also recognize that the serious discussion of alternatives and practical proposals is a relatively new undertaking in civil society. Thoughtful and intelligent people may disagree on many points—just as many of us who shared in the authorship of this volume disagree in some ways. Our purpose is to stimulate further dialogue and debate toward a more refined vision and statement. We plan to distribute this volume among many thousands of citizen and policy groups engaged with these issues on all continents to invite their input. We envision a three-year process that will include meetings in every region among interested groups to advance dialogue and consensus building toward a revised and expanded report that we hope will take the discussion to a new level of sophistication and concreteness.

We invite your participation as well.

CHAPTER ONE

A Critique
of Corporate Globalization

THE ALTERNATIVES OFFERED in this report grow from the widespread damage inflicted by corporate globalization over the past five centuries as it passed from colonialism to imperialism to postcolonial export-led development models. Since World War II, the driving forces behind economic globalization have been several hundred global corporations and banks that have increasingly woven webs of production, consumption, finance, and culture across borders. Indeed, most of what we eat, drink, wear, drive, and entertain ourselves with today are the products of global corporations.

These corporations have been aided by global bureaucracies that have emerged over the last half-century, with the overall result being a concentration of economic and political power that is increasingly unaccountable to governments, people, or the planet and that undermines democracy, equity, and environmental sustainability.

~

Advocates like to describe economic globalization as a long-term, inevitable process, the result of economic and technological forces that have simply evolved over centuries to their present form. They describe these forces almost as if they were uncontrollable, like forces of nature; they say that it's utopianism to believe things could be otherwise. To accept this inevitability, as most governments, academics, and mainstream media tend to do, would mean that no resistance is possible. But on the evidence of the hundreds of thousands of people who have demonstrated in Seattle, Quebec City, and various European capitals, in India, Japan, and Brazil, in Mexico, the Philippines, New Zealand, Argentina, the United Kingdom, and elsewhere, it should already be obvious that such passivity is no longer the norm.

It is true that global trade activity and concepts like free trade have existed for centuries in various forms. Although earlier versions were very different from the modern one in scale, speed, and form, the social and environmental outcomes have always been similar.

Modern globalization is not an expression of evolution. It was designed and created by human beings with a specific goal: to give primacy to economic—that is, corporate—values above all other values and to aggressively install and codify those values globally. In fact, the modern globalization era has a birthplace and a birth date: Bretton Woods, New Hampshire, July 1944. That was when the world's leading corporate figures, economists, politicians, and bankers met to figure out how to mitigate the devastation of World War II and prevent another Great Depression. They decided that a new centralized global economic system was needed to promote global economic development. This, they said, would prevent future wars, reduce poverty, and help the world rebuild.

The conferees at Bretton Woods saw themselves as altruists, though many had a large financial stake in the outcome. They decided that the ideal instrument to keep the pieces together would be the global corporation, supported by new bureaucracies and new rules of free trade. Out of the Bretton Woods meetings came the World Bank (originally called the International Bank for Reconstruction and Development) and the International Monetary Fund. Later came the General Agreement on Tariffs and Trade (GATT), which eventually gave birth to the World Trade Organization. (For more on these institutions, see "Bureaucratic Expressions of Economic Globalization" later in this chapter.) Other expressions of the model include the North American Free Trade Agreement (NAFTA), the European Union's Maastricht Agreement, the proposed Free Trade Area of the Americas (FTAA), and others.

Together these instruments are bringing about the most fundamental redesign of the planet's social, economic, and political arrangements since the Industrial Revolution. They are engineering a power shift of stunning proportions, moving real economic and political power away from national, state, and local governments and communities toward unprecedented cen-

tralization of power for global corporations, bankers, and the global bureaucracies they helped create, at the expense of national sovereignty, community control, democracy, diversity, and the natural world.

The good news is that all of this can be reversed or revised, if with
difficulty. And the central purpose of this document is to help us move that
process forward.

I. Key Ingredients of the Globalization Model

Economic globalization—sometimes also referred to as *corporate globalization*
or *neoliberalism*—has several key features:

- Promotion of hypergrowth and unrestricted exploitation of environmental resources to fuel that growth
- Privatization and commodification of public services and of remaining
  aspects of the global and community commons
- Global cultural and economic homogenization and the intense promotion of consumerism
- Integration and conversion of national economies, including some that
  were largely self-reliant, to environmentally and socially harmful export-
  oriented production
- Corporate deregulation and unrestricted movement of capital across
  borders
- Dramatically increased corporate concentration
- Dismantling of public health, social, and environmental programs
  already in place
- Replacement of traditional powers of democratic nation-states and local
  communities by global corporate bureaucracies

We begin with a review of some of these features of the economic globalization model.

HYPERGROWTH

The first tenet of the globalization design is to give primary importance to
the achievement of ever more rapid, never-ending corporate economic
growth—hypergrowth—fueled by the constant search for access to new

resources, new and cheaper labor sources, and new markets. This is why there is such excitement about China joining the experiment, as it offers all three: labor, resources, and markets. To achieve hypergrowth, the emphasis is on the ideological heart of the model—free trade—accompanied by deregulation of corporate activity. The idea is to remove as many impediments as possible to expanded corporate activity. In practice, such impediments are usually environmental laws, public health laws, food safety laws, laws pertaining to workers' rights and opportunities, laws permitting nations to control investment on their own soil, and laws attempting to retain national control over local culture. Viewed as obstacles to corporate free trade, such laws are open to challenge by new trade and investment agreements. As a result, while corporations are deregulated and freed,

---

BOX B: PUBLIC INTEREST LAWS AS "IMPEDIMENTS" TO FREE TRADE

By Debi Barker and Jerry Mander, International Forum on Globalization

A major goal of the Bretton Woods institutions is to remove impediments, including public interest regulations, that might restrict corporate access to markets, labor, and resources.

WTO tribunals have an impressive record for challenging democratically created laws and standards, particularly environmental protections. The WTO's very first ruling was against the U.S. Clean Air Act, which set high standards against polluting gasoline. The act was found noncompliant with WTO trade rules and had to be softened.

Other controversial rulings have targeted other issues:

• The U.S. Marine Mammal Protection Act (particularly the provision that protects dolphins otherwise killed by industrial tuna fishing)
• The sea turtle protections under the Endangered Species Act
• Japan's ban on imports of fruit products carrying dangerous invasive species
• The European Union's ban on imports of U.S. beef injected with biotech growth hormones

Although only governments may submit WTO complaints, global corporations are almost always the driving force. In one of the most appalling examples, the U.S. government acted on behalf of Chiquita to challenge the European Union's preferential treatment of banana imports from former colonies.

CONTINUED

nation-states and local governments are harshly regulated and constrained, making it far more difficult for them to protect local jobs, identity, and tradition as well as national sovereignty and the natural world. (See Box B.)

Advocates of globalization like to argue that the beneficiaries of all this growth will be the poor because the increased wealth will "trickle down" to them. But as we will discuss later, all evidence shows that the opposite is true. The benefits of hypergrowth mainly trickle *up*.

PRIVATIZATION AND COMMODIFICATION

A second tenet of the design is to push toward privatization and commodification of as many noncommodified nooks and crannies of existence as

---

BOX B: CONTINUED

There is also a secondary chilling effect from this process. For example, the government of Guatemala cancelled a public health law that had forbidden infant formula companies, notably Gerber, from advertising their products as being healthier than breast milk. And Canada cancelled its ban on the import of MMT, a fuel additive that can damage nervous systems. In both cases the reasons were threats of suit under trade regimes. In the Gerber case the U.S. threatened a suit in the WTO. In the Canadian case, Ethyl Corporation threatened to sue Canada under NAFTA's investor-state provision—likely to be expanded in the FTAA agreement—which allows corporations, for the first time, to sue sovereign governments, not in domestic courts but in international tribunals. The Ethyl threat alleged an illegal "expropriation" by Canada because Canada's environmental safety law diminished the firm's fu-ture profits. A similar case has been brought against the U.S. government over a California ban on another dangerous fuel additive.

The net effect is that the whole process produces a mutual ratcheting downward of environmental, labor, or health standards in all countries. It's a kind of "cross-deregulation," a way that corporations can get their own governments to destroy laws in other countries, just as they pressure for deregulation domestically.

Advocates love to call it *free* trade, but what they really mean is freedom for global corporations but suppression of the freedoms for communities or nations to regulate or otherwise maintain primary values, like the environment, health, culture, jobs, national sovereignty—and democracy.

SOURCE: Debi Barker and Jerry Mander, *Invisible Government*. San Francisco: International Forum on Globalization, 1999.

possible. This too is necessary to expand the terrain for economic activity and profit. The conversion process now includes formerly pristine elements of the global commons—elements that have until now always been far outside the trading system and that most of us have always assumed would remain the inalienable right of all human beings to retain in a noncommodified form. For example, the genetic structures of our bodies, and of all life, are now becoming "enclosed" as part of the commodity trading system through biotechnology, with the process greatly assisted by WTO rules on intellectual property rights. Similarly, indigenous seeds, developed and freely shared by agricultural communities for thousands of years, are now subject to long-term monopoly ownership by global corporations through patenting. Recent protests against the WTO's TRIPs (Trade-Related Intellectual Property Rights agreement) by farmers in India and by AIDS victims in Africa and elsewhere who are trying to get relief from high-priced patented medicines, have begun to focus a new light on some appalling aspects of this issue.

There is also a similar pressure to privatize freshwater—rivers, lakes, streams—probably the most basic element of sustenance, always considered a part of the commons. These too may soon be converted into part of the global trade system. All of these and others are being rapidly privatized and commodified as part of the globalization project to bring even more raw material—more territory (geographic and biological)—into play for corporate access, investment, development, and trade. (See chapter 3, "The Commons," for more on these issues.)

Alarmingly, the privatization process is now also taking place in the realm of public services. Corporations argue that government is invariably bureaucratic, inefficient, and self-serving in contrast to the so-called efficiency, dynamism, and consumer responsiveness of the private sector. Thus, public services should be left to them. They make this argument even though they operate on an entirely different hierarchy of values than do governments. Privatization of public services is now an important part of both the new FTAA agreement and the General Agreement on Trade in Services (GATS) within the WTO. Those negotiations involve changes in many services that were until recently reserved for governments, like public broadcasting, public education, public health, water delivery and treatment, sewage and sanitation services, hospitals, welfare systems, police, fire, social security, railroads, and prisons. These may all soon be commodified, privatized, opened to foreign investment and domination, and eventually available only to those people who will be able to pay commercial rates for them. We could wind up with Mitsubishi running social security, Bechtel controlling the world's water, Deutschebank running the jails (and maybe the parks), Disney running the British Broadcasting Corporation, Merck running the Canadian health care system. It sounds far-fetched, but the threat is real.

There is also the commodification of money itself. Right now, the overwhelming majority of global transactions under the free trade system are not in goods and services but are financial. Money itself is a commodity for speculation. Modern information technology has made it possible to shift unimaginably large sums of money instantaneously across borders, anywhere in the world, without any controls on the transactions, by the stroke of a computer key. This has already had terrible destabilizing effects on many countries and was one of the precipitating causes of the 1997–98 financial crisis that began in Asia.

ECONOMIC AND CULTURAL HOMOGENIZATION

The third tenet of economic globalization is to integrate and merge the economic activity of all countries into a homogeneous model of development—a single, centralized supersystem. Countries with cultures, economies, and traditions as varied as those of India, Sweden, Thailand, Kenya, Bhutan, Bolivia, Canada, Russia, and close to two hundred others are all meant to adopt similar tastes, values, and lifestyles. They are to be served by the same few global corporations, the same fast-food restaurants, hotel chains, and clothing chains; wear the same jeans and shoes; drive similar cars; receive the same films, music, and television shows; live in the same kind of urban landscape; and engage in the same kind of agricultural and industrial development schemes, while carrying the same personal, cultural, and spiritual values—a *global monoculture*. This trend is already visible to any traveler. Every place is becoming more and more like every other place. Cultural diversity is going the way of biodiversity.

Such a homogeneous model serves the efficiency needs of the largest corporations, which can act on a global plane, duplicating their production and marketing efforts on an expanded terrain and achieving the many efficiencies of scale that go with borderlessness. It's like the standard gauge railway of another era or, in today's terms, like computer compatibility. Among the primary purposes of the global trade agreements and bureaucracies is to make rules that ensure there are no blockages in the flow, that global corporations can move freely in all countries, and that economic homogenization and integration are accelerated.

EXPORT-ORIENTED TRADE AND INVESTMENT

Corporate globalization favors orienting all national economies to export, lifting barriers to foreign investment, and removing all restraints on the free flow of speculative money across national borders. These preferences encourage production for sale to other countries over domestic sale, foreign ownership over domestic ownership, and financial speculation. These activities favor global corporations and financiers but leave people everywhere dependent for their livelihoods on the actions of absentee owners over whom they have no influence.

The underlying theoretical rationale for export-oriented production centers on the theory of *comparative advantage*. According to this theory, every country should produce only those products over which it has a relative advantage; thus, some countries now specialize in single crops like coffee, sugarcane, forest products, or high-tech assembly. Theoretically, they can meet their other needs by using the earnings from these specialized exports to buy goods and services over which others have an advantage.

Comparative advantage is a crucial component of globalization theory. It facilitates the replacement of diverse local or regional economic systems, including systems that may currently emphasize successful diversified, small-scale, industrial, artisanal, and agriculture systems that feature many small producers using mostly local or regional resources and local labor for local or regional consumption. The goal is to substitute large-scale monocultural export systems.

Going back to the mid-twentieth century, many countries of the world actively tried to do the *opposite* of specialization: they diversified their industrial and agriculture systems precisely in order to recover from a colonial period during which huge monocultural systems, such as pineapple planta-tions, coffee plantations, banana plantations, or, more recently, industrial assembly work were imposed on them. Once independent, the governments of many of these countries concluded that this kind of imposed special-ization left them extremely vulnerable to political decisions abroad and to the shocks and whims of the market and commodity-pricing systems. As a result, they were sometimes unable to purchase necessities like health prod-ucts and food, energy, and basic industrial needs. Naturally, they sought self-sufficiency in these items. Their preferred system was sometimes called *import substitution*, or simply *national self-reliance*. It was intended to help countries regain some degree of control over their domestic economies.

After Bretton Woods, and especially during the 1980s, the World Bank and the IMF put tremendous pressure on these countries to abandon self-reliance, a term that came to be synonymous with isolationism and protec-tionism. The World Bank and the IMF pressured these countries to open their borders to private investments by global corporations in a position to produce on the large scale appropriate for the export model. It became impossible for these countries to gain any financial aid from the bank or the IMF unless they submitted to structural adjustment programs (SAPs)—in other words, unless they redesigned their domestic systems to emphasize exports. The pressure worked. But after converting so much production to export, these same countries found that they were still subject to restrictions on imports by the wealthy countries. Many poor countries are now sorry they accepted the system and are joining the resistance to it.

Why did the World Bank and the IMF push so hard to achieve these goals? Here's the crux of the matter: *systems that emphasize local or regional self-reliance are extremely subversive to free trade, economic globalization, and hyper cor-porate growth.* These all depend on maximizing the number and scale of economic transactions. Local and regional production for regional con-sumption is the archenemy of globalization because it operates on an inher-ently smaller scale, and there are fewer steps in the process.

There is far less opportunity for global corporations if local populations or countries can satisfy their needs internally or regionally than if eco-nomic activity is designed to move back and forth across oceans, exporting, importing, or reworking it and then exporting it again, with thousands of ships passing each other in the night. That's what builds global economic growth and provides opportunities for global corporate operations. But alas, it's also what destroys the environment fastest and makes countries dependent on external forces they cannot control.

Ironically, free trade theorists often invoke the names and theories of Adam Smith and David Ricardo in defense of these destructive export-oriented policies. Yet Smith had an explicit preference for small, locally owned enterprises. And Ricardo's theory of comparative advantage assumes that capital is immobile, confined inside national borders—a far cry from the current rules and theories.

Converting diverse local economies into export trade systems benefits global corporations but makes individuals, communities, and nations dependent and vulnerable. Society, communities, and the environment would all be better off if international institutions and agreements emphasized aiding local and national self-sufficiency rather than export production.

The agriculture sector is a prime example of the social and environmental problems of the export-oriented development model. Even in today's computer age, nearly half of the world's population still lives directly on the land, growing food for their families and communities, primarily staples and other mixed crops. These farmers replant with indigenous seed varieties and use crop rotation and community sharing of resources like water, seeds, and labor. Such systems have kept them going for millennia. But local systems are anathema to global corporations. So companies like Monsanto, Cargill, and Archer Daniels Midland are leading a chorus of corporate, government, and bureaucratic statements—often expressed in millions of dollars worth of advertising—that small farmers are not "productive" or "efficient" enough to feed a hungry world.

Nearly all the investment rules of the WTO and the big banks—and many more now being proposed—strongly favor global corporations and monocultures over local diverse farming for self-sufficiency. So where tens of thousand of small farmers once grew food to eat, giant corporations and global development schemes are converting the land to single-crop luxury monocultures run by absentee landlords.

Furthermore, these companies do not grow food for the local people to eat. Instead, they favor high-priced, high-margin luxury items—flowers, potted plants, beef, shrimp, cotton, coffee—for export to the already overfed countries. As for the people who used to live on these lands and grow their own foods, they are rapidly being removed. And because the corporate systems feature machine-intensive production, there are few jobs. Thus, the people who used to feed themselves become landless, cashless, homeless, dependent, and hungry. Communities that were once self-sustaining disappear; still-intact cultures are decimated. This is so even in the United States, where few family farmers are still in business.

Other environmental problems intrinsic to the shift to export include loss of biodiversity from emphasizing single crops for export and heavy use of pesticides. Where indigenous Filipinos, for example, once grew thousands of varieties of rice, a few varieties now account for the bulk of production, and the other varieties are disappearing. Mexico has lost more than 75 percent of its indigenous maize varieties. According to the Food and Agriculture Organization (FAO), the world has already lost up to 75 percent of its crop diversity because of the globalization of industrialized agriculture.

There are also external costs of industrial agriculture. Hailed as more efficient than small-scale farming, this is a kind of efficiency that ignores the costs of air, water, and soil pollution, toxic rivers, dead fish. Many public health problems from food-borne diseases are directly attributable to factory farming systems: infections from salmonella, *e. coli,* and *listeria* as well as Mad Cow disease, hoof and mouth disease, and others.

Finally, industrial agriculture brings the social costs of taking care of all the farmers who lose their livelihoods through this system; together, social and environmental costs rise into the billions of dollars. If you take all these external costs into account, does it make any sense to call this system "efficient"?

Indeed, farmers are rapidly becoming the leaders of international resistance to globalization in many parts of the world. We have seen mass protests by rice farmers in Japan, Thailand, and the Philippines. There have been huge protests against Cargill, Kentucky Fried Chicken, and Monsanto in India, with millions of people on the streets. And a few years ago, a French farmer named José Bové drove his tractor into a McDonald's restaurant in France. Bové was protesting "bad food," he said, as well as the entire industrial agricultural system, the corporate takeover of small farms for export monocultures, and the destruction of traditional farming in France.

BENEFICIARIES OF ECONOMIC GLOBALIZATION

One might give the benefit of the doubt to the architects of this global experiment. Perhaps they actually believed that the system would produce the kind of rapid growth that would truly benefit the poor and the environment. We have certainly heard them repeat the homily over and over: "A rising tide will lift all boats." We continue to hear it from the heads of the WTO, the World Bank, and most countries' leaders, including President George W. Bush. But is it true?

BOX C: INTRINSIC ENVIRONMENTAL CONSEQUENCES OF TRADE-RELATED TRANSPORT

By Jerry Mander, International Forum on Globalization,
and Simon Retallack, The Ecologist

The central feature of an export-oriented production model is that it dramatically increases transport and shipping activity. In the half-century since Bretton Woods, there has been about a twenty-five-fold increase in global transport activity.

As global transport increases, it in turn requires massive increases in global infrastructure development. This is good for large corporations like Bechtel, which get to do the construction work: new airports, seaports, oil fields, pipelines for the oil, rail lines, high-speed highways. Many of these are built in areas with relatively intact wilderness, biodiversity, and coral reefs, or they are built in rural areas. The impact is especially strong now in South and Central America, where there have been tremendous investments in infrastructure development in wilderness regions, often against great resistance from native communities like the U'wa

in Colombia, the Kuna in Panama, and many different groups in Ecuador. The problems also occur in the developed world. In the United Kingdom a few years ago, there were protests by two hundred thousand people against huge new highways jammed through rural landscapes so that trucks could better serve the global trading system. Both the indigenous protestors and the rural English were protesting the same thing—the ecological destruction of their region to serve globalization.

Increased global trade increases fossil fuel use as well, contributing to global warming. Ocean shipping carries nearly 80 percent of the world's international trade in goods. The fuel commonly used by ships is a mixture of diesel and low-quality oil known as "Bunker C," which is particularly polluting because of high levels of carbon and sulfur. If not consumed by ships, it

CONTINUED

The problems begin with the assumption that hypergrowth can continue forever. How can exponential growth possibly be sustained, given the limits of a finite planet? Where will the resources—the minerals, the wood, the water, the land—come from to feed hyperexpansion without killing the planet and ourselves? The world's limits are already in view. How many cars and refrigerators can be built and bought? How many roads can cover the land? How many fish can be vacuumed from the sea before species disappear and ecosystems fail? How much pollution can the world survive? What about global warming, toxic dumping, ozone depletion?

BOX C: CONTINUED

would otherwise be considered a waste product. The shipping industry is anticipating major growth over the next few years; the port of Los Angeles alone projects a 50 percent increase over the next decade.

Increased air transport is even more damaging than shipping. Each ton of freight moved by plane uses forty-nine times as much energy per kilometer as when it's moved by ship. A physicist at Boeing once described the pollution from the takeoff of a single 747 like "setting the local gas station on fire and flying it over your neighborhood." A two-minute takeoff by a 747 is equal to 2.4 million lawnmowers running for twenty minutes.

Ocean pollution from shipping has reached crisis levels, and there have been direct effects of these huge ships on wildlife and fisheries. Even more serious, possibly, is the epidemic increase of bioinvasions, a significant cause of species extinction. With the growth of global transport, billions of creatures are on the move. Invasive species, brought by global trade, often outcom-

pete native species and bring pollution or health crises. In the United States, the emergence of the West Nile virus where it never existed before is due to increased transport activity. So is the spread of malaria and dengue fever.

Ocean shipping also requires increased refrigeration—contributing to ozone depletion and climate change—and an increase in packaging and the wood pallets used for cargo loading; these are little-noted but significant factors in increased pressure on global forests.

Global conversion of agriculture from diverse, small-scale local farms to giant, chemical-intensive industrial production for *export* markets has also brought terrible environmental destruction to lands and waters across the planet. (See also chapter 6.)

The central point is this: if you are going to design a system built on the premise that dramatically increased global trade and transport is good, you are guaranteed to bring on these kinds of environmental problems. They are *intrinsic* to the model.

There's another important question: Who actually benefits from this system? It's not the farmers who are driven from their own lands and made into
homeless, jobless refugees in both the South and the North. It's not the
urban dwellers who must deal with masses of displaced people jamming
into cities looking for jobs. It's not the workers caught in downward wage
spirals in both the North and the South. It's not indigenous peoples facing
hordes of corporate invaders seeking the last resources. And it's surely not
nature.

The actual beneficiaries are obvious. They are the exact opposites of
those whom the advocates claim. In the United States, for example, during
the period of most rapid globalization—the 1990s—the top corporate executives of the largest global companies made salaries and gained options in
the many millions of dollars (often in the hundreds of millions), while real
wages of ordinary workers barely rose. Sarah Anderson and John Cavanagh
of the Institute for Policy Studies report that American CEOs were paid on
average 458 times more than production workers in 2000, up from 104
times in 1991. The Economic Policy Institute's 1999 report by Lawrence
Mishel and others says that median hourly wages are actually down by 10
percent in real terms over the previous twenty-five years. And in the industry that led our recent boom—the computer industry— where some people
famously made fortunes, 80 percent of assembly and production workers
are temporary workers, earning $8 an hour with no benefits and no unions.

As for lifting the global poor, the U.N. Development Program's 1999
Human Development Report revealed that the gap between the wealthy and the
poor within and among countries of the world is growing steadily larger. It
blamed inherent inequities in the global trade system for this situation. Even
the U.S. Central Intelligence Agency concurred. In its *Global Trends, 2015*
report, the CIA maintained that globalization will create "an even wider gap
between regional winners and losers than exists today. [Globalization's] evolution will be rocky, marked by chronic volatility and a widening economic
divide . . . deepening economic stagnation, political instability, and cultural
alienation. [It] will foster political, ethnic, ideological, and religious extrem-
ism, along with the violence that often accompanies it." Such is already the
degree of wealth concentration that the world's 475 billionaires are now
worth the combined income of the bottom half of humanity.

The economic clout of global firms is equally staggering. As Sarah

Anderson and John Cavanagh of the Institute for Policy Studies report, the combined sales of the top two hundred firms grew faster than overall global economic activity between 1983 and 1999, reaching the equivalent of close to 30 percent of world GDP. Yet these firms employ only three-quarters of 1 percent of the global workforce. As they continue to grow larger and more globalized, they continue to replace workers with machines or to buy up competitors and eliminate duplicate jobs. Such economies of scale are intrinsic to the free trade, globalization design, just as environmental pollution is intrinsic to export-oriented trade. Large-scale mergers and consolidations—bigness—produce fewer jobs, not more jobs. Indeed, the ideologies and rules of economic globalization have destroyed the livelihoods of millions of people while eliminating basic public services.

It is true that there are isolated instances where some improvement has been achieved in Third World countries. The Bretton Woods institutions often trumpet these examples. But it is also true that the benefits of this growth have usually been short-lived. Furthermore, nearly all of it goes to the elites in these countries and to the chief executives of the global corporations at the hub of the process.

Let's look at the so-called poster children of free trade, the Asian Tigers: Taiwan, South Korea, Singapore, and Malaysia. In these countries, improvement has come not by assiduously following the dictates of the Bretton Woods institutions but often by doing the opposite of what they prescribe. Asian countries that have had some brief successes in developing their own economies did not cut all their tariffs as demanded by globalizing institutions, permit foreign entry without controls, or eliminate existing support for domestic businesses, local economies, and local agriculture. Instead, those countries first developed the ability to take care of their basic needs internally, rather than totally converting to an export-based production system.

By at first resisting the economic model pushed by Bretton Woods, some countries managed to stay free of the volatility of export markets. But when they finally succumbed to pressure from the IMF and the World Bank, they found their glory days quickly ending.

Indeed, most poor countries have never enjoyed much benefit from globalization. After three decades of strong doses of IMF and World Bank medicine and less than a decade of WTO policies, many have seen that globalization is a false promise. The policies are not designed to benefit them but to benefit rich industrial countries and their global corporations. For this reason, many of the poor nations of the world—notably from the Caribbean and Asia—held firmly together in opposition to the WTO in Seattle in 1999 and only reluctantly agreed to further trade talks in Doha, Qatar, in 2001.

So much for the rising tide that lifts all boats. Clearly it lifts only yachts. (See also Box D.)

Hundreds of thousands of people are now convinced that it doesn't need to be this way; there is nothing inevitable about it. Globalization is driven by a set of rules and self-interested institutions that can be changed— if we have a democracy.

At its root, economic globalization is really an experiment, an economic model promoted by people who most benefit from it. As for the charge that we are utopian, obviously the globalizers have got things backwards. To keep arguing as they do—that a system that homogenizes global economic activity and culture to benefit corporations, removes power from communities and puts it into global bureaucracies, marginalizes and makes homeless millions of farmers and workers, and devastates nature can survive for very long—*that* is utopianism. It's not going to work. It's far better that we seek other solutions.

THE ROLE OF THE MEDIA

Signs of the instability and unfairness of the globalization experiment are in view everywhere. Sadly, however, they are poorly reported. When the mainstream media does report a few crises created by globalization, it fails to help the public grasp that these crises are all rooted in the same problem— corporate globalization itself. Here are some examples.

- We read about environmental problems such as changes in the global climate, the melting polar ice cap, or habitat destruction. We read about ozone depletion, ocean pollution, or wars over oil, and soon we will probably read about wars over water supply. But rarely are these grave matters linked to the imperatives of global economic expansion now accelerated by free trade, the overuse of resources, and the consumer

BOX D: GLOBAL ECONOMIC APARTHEID

By Robin Broad, American University, and John Cavanagh, Institute for Policy Studies

A careful analysis of social and economic data from the United Nations, the World Bank, the IMF, and other sources offers a shocking picture of trends in the global economy and the gap between rich and poor countries. There are two ways to measure what is happening economically between North and South. The first is to measure which is growing faster, and therefore whether the gap between them is growing or shrinking. The second is to measure financial resource flows between the two.

On the first issue the picture is clear: the North-South gap widened dramatically in the decade after 1982 as the Third World debt crisis drained financial resources from poor countries to rich banks. Between 1985 and 1992, Southern nations paid some $280 billion more in debt service to Northern creditors than they received in new private loans and government aid. Gross national product (GNP) per capita rose an average of only 1 percent in the South in the 1980s (in sub-Saharan Africa it fell 1.2 percent), while it rose 2.3 percent in the North.

Situating the lost decade of the 1980s within a longer time period reveals similar trends for some regions. According to the United Nations Development Program, per capita incomes in Africa were one-ninth of those in Northern countries in 1960; they had fallen to one-eighteenth by 1998. Per capita incomes in most of the rest of the developing world (Latin America and the Caribbean, and South Asia) remained at about one-tenth of Northern levels at the beginning and end of these four decades. Only in East Asia have developing countries closed the gap with the North.

Likewise, a look at various resource flows between North and South is instructive. Despite the perception of an easing of the debt crisis, the overall Third World debt stock swelled by around $100 billion each year during the 1990s (reaching $2.4 trillion in 2001). Southern debt service (which reached $331 billion in 2000) still exceeds new lending, and the net outflow remains particularly crushing in Africa. Although it is true that a series of debt reschedulings and the accumulation of arrears by many debtors have reduced the net negative financial transfer from South to North over the last few years, the flows remain negative.

Part of the reason why some analysts now argue that the debt crisis is no longer a problem is that since the early 1990s these outflows of debt repayments have been matched by increased inflows of foreign capital. Here too, however, a deeper look at disaggregated figures underlines the disconcerting reality. According to World Bank figures, roughly half of the new foreign direct investment by global cor-

CONTINUED

BOX D: CONTINUED

porations into the South in 1992 quickly left those countries as profits. In addition, foreign investment flows primarily to only ten to twelve Third World nations that are viewed as new profit centers by Northern corporations and investors. According to World Bank figures, more than 70 percent of investment flows in 1998 went to just ten of the so-called emerging markets: China, followed by Brazil, Mexico, Singapore, Thailand, Poland, Argentina, South Korea, Malaysia, and Chile.

The inescapable conclusion is that the North-South economic gap is now narrowing for about a dozen countries but continues to widen for well over one hundred others. Hence, without a major shift in policy, the world of the twenty-first century will be one of economic apartheid. There will be two dozen richer nations, a dozen or so poorer nations that have begun to close the gap with the rich, and approximately 140 poor nations slipping further and further behind.

As U.S. firms have shifted from local to national and now to global markets over the past half-century, a new division of winners and losers has emerged in all countries. The book *Global Dreams,* by Richard Barnet, cofounder of the Institute for Policy Studies, and John Cavanagh, chronicles how powerful U.S. firms and their counterparts from England, France, Germany, and Japan are integrating only about one-third of humanity (most of those in the rich countries plus the elite of poor countries) into complex chains of production, shopping, culture, and finance.

Although there are enclaves in every country that are linked to these global economic webs, others are left out. Wal-Mart is spreading its superstores throughout the Western Hemisphere; millions in Latin America, though, are too poor to enjoy anything but glimpses of luxury. Citibank customers can access automated teller machines around the world; the vast majority of people nevertheless borrow from the loan shark down the road. Ford Motor Company pieces together its new "global car" in Kansas City from parts made all over the globe; executives in Detroit worry about who will be able to afford it.

Thus, although on one level the North-South gap is becoming more pronounced for most Third World countries, on another these global chains blur distinctions between geographical North and South. These processes create another North-South divide: the roughly one-third of humanity who make up a "global North" of beneficiaries in every country, and the two-thirds of humanity from the slums of New York to the favelas of Rio who are not hooked into the new global menu of producing, consuming, and borrowing opportunities in the "global South."

SOURCE: Adapted and updated from Robin Broad and John Cavanagh, "Development: The Market Is Not Enough." *Foreign Policy* 101, Winter 1995–96.

lifestyle that's being promoted worldwide by television and its parent—
advertising.

- The financial crises in Asia in 1997 to 1998 and in Argentina in 2001 to
2002 were often reported as being caused by incompetence, inefficiency,
corruption, and cronyism in the countries involved. The gigantic bailout
by the International Monetary Fund in Asia was made to seem like a
beneficent act of charity toward our underprivileged, dysfunctional
Asian friends, who had not yet achieved our own higher ethical standards. Rarely was it acknowledged that the money did not go to the citizens of those countries but rather was used to bail out the international
bankers who caused the problem in the first place through reckless lending that created artificial economic bubbles. Nor did the popular media
describe the role of currency speculators in the Asian crisis. Under the
new rules of global free trade and deregulation, there are no controls
over the massive movement of funds across borders, into countries, and
back out of them. Since the advent of global computer networks, currency speculators have been able to move unimaginably huge amounts of
money instantaneously and invisibly from one part of the globe to
another, thus destabilizing currencies and countries and forcing nations
to seek the radical solution of an IMF bailout. (We call it a "casino economy" when countries cannot control the rapid entry and exit of billions
of speculator dollars.) If countries do make rules to slow down the
process—as have done Malaysia, Chile, and China—they are often
ridiculed by the economic establishment and the media as well.
- The mainstream media does report on the anti-immigrant backlash,
whether led by a Pat Buchanan in the United States, a Jean-Marie Le Pen
in France, or a Joerg Haider in Austria. But it neglects to mention the role
of the international trade agreements in making life at home impossible
for those who migrate. Elsewhere we mention NAFTA's role in destroying the self-sufficient corn-farming economy of Mexico's Mayan people.
In India, Africa, and Latin America, megadevelopment schemes have displaced millions of indigenous people and small farmers to make way for
gigantic dams and other development projects. The result is that more
people join the landless, jobless urban masses.
- Terrible new diseases such as Ebola, Mad Cow disease, *e. coli* infection,
and, lately, the West Nile virus outbreak in the U.S. are thoroughly

reported. But the connection between the outbreaks and the new mobility that disease vectors are provided by global transport and development is rarely mentioned. The news stories also leave out the link to factory farming practices and the globalization of industrial agriculture.

- We read about the appalling performance of Enron Corp. as it led the process of energy deregulation, cheated its own workers while paying bonuses to its top executives, and gave intimate advice to the U.S. president and vice president about energy policy and government appointments. What the popular media has not fully explained are the ways in which Enron directly benefited from global bureaucracies like the World Bank, which gave structural adjustment loans to poor countries, often on the condition that those countries hire firms like Enron with that money to build domestic infrastructure and drive their economies. The World Bank gave with one hand and took back for its friends with the other. Nor did we read much about how Enron's behavior was not unique; it is typical of the behavior of global corporations, and it is built into their structure. Like other aspects of globalization, the problem is systemic.

- We also read stories about the assaults on the last indigenous tribes in the Amazon, Borneo, and the Philippines. Insufficiently reported are the root causes—the need on the part of the globalization process for more water or forests or oil or genetic resources in areas where indigenous people have lived for millennia and the equally desperate need to try to convert self-sufficient people into consumers. This too is part of the globalization process: the homogenization of conceptual frameworks, the mono-culturalization of peoples and lands, the utter uniformity of the development model everywhere on earth.

All of these subjects are treated by the mainstream media as if they were unrelated. This is a disservice to an insecure public that is trying to figure out what is going on. People are not being helped to understand that dozens of major issues—overcrowded cities, unusual weather patterns, the growth of global inequality, the spread of new diseases, the lowering of wages as profits and CEO salaries soar, the elimination of social services, the destruction of the environment—are all part of the same global process. They are of one piece, a fabric of connections resulting from the world's new economic arrangement, all in the cause of an economic ideology that cannot serve social or ecological sustainability.

II. Bureaucratic Expressions of Economic Globalization

Creating a world that works for all must begin with an effort to undo the enormous damage inflicted by the free trade economic policies that so badly distort economic relationships among people and countries. The thrust of those policies is perhaps most dramatically revealed in the structural adjustment programs imposed on low- and intermediate-income countries by the International Monetary Fund and the World Bank. Structural adjustment requires governments to do the following:

- Cut government spending on education, health care, the environment, and price subsidies for basic necessities such as food grains and cooking oils.
- Devalue the national currency and increase exports by accelerating the plunder of natural resources, reducing real wages, and subsidizing export-oriented foreign investments.
- Liberalize (open) financial markets to attract speculative short-term portfolio investments that create enormous financial instability and foreign liabilities while serving little, if any, useful purpose.
- Increase interest rates to attract foreign capital that has fled its home country, thereby increasing bankruptcies of domestic businesses and imposing new hardships on indebted individuals.
- Eliminate tariffs and other controls on imports, thereby increasing the import of consumer goods purchased with borrowed foreign exchange, undermining local industry and agricultural producers unable to compete with cheap imports, increasing the strain on foreign exchange accounts, and deepening external indebtedness.

THE WORLD BANK

According to its charter, the World Bank was created "to assist in the reconstruction and development of territories of member nations by facilitating the investment of capital for productive purposes" and "to promote the long-range balanced growth of international trade." The World Bank was originally intended to focus on financing the post–World War II reconstruction of Europe, using capital subscribed by member governments as guarantees against which it could borrow in international financial markets at favorable rates and then lend out for development projects. When Europe showed little interest in mortgaging the future of its economy to foreign bankers, the World Bank set about marketing its loans in the newly independent former colonies. At first, that too proved a hard sell. So the bank invested in training and education to indoctrinate scores of Third World bureaucrats and economists in an economic ideology that equates development with export-led economic growth fueled by foreign borrowing and investment—the basic fallacy that remains a cornerstone of its policy today.

Originally, the loans were used to finance infrastructure projects and imports beyond the means of the country's export earnings. Eventually, ever-larger new loans were needed just to service payments of interest and principle due on previous loans. The more the borrowing, the greater the need for still larger loans, and borrowing became something of an economic addiction. Aside from a handful of citizen watchdog groups, few paid attention to the burden these loans placed on domestic economies when the time came to repay.

During the 1970s, OPEC sharply increased oil prices and hence the cost of energy imports. Northern banks, awash with OPEC deposits, lavished loans on Third World countries—often with the encouragement of the World Bank. Soon the costs of debt service exceeded repayment capacity by such a wide margin that there was a threat of a global financial crisis. Beginning with Mexico in 1982, the IMF and the World Bank swung into action with structural adjustment as their primary response. Together they reoriented national economies to focus on debt repayment and to further open their resources, labor, and markets to foreign corporations. "Adjusted" countries came under great pressure to increase the export of their natural resources and the products of their labor, become more import dependent, and increase foreign ownership of their economies. Once the countries accepted these conditions, the IMF and the World Bank rewarded them with still more loans, thus deepening their indebtedness—rather like a fireman pouring gasoline on a burning house to stop the blaze.

The results have been disastrous not only in human and environmental terms but also in economic terms. In 1980, the total external debt of all developing countries was $609 billion; in 2001, after twenty years of structural adjustment, it totaled $2.4 trillion. In 2001, sub-Saharan Africa paid $3.6 billion more in debt service than it received in new long-term loans and credits. Africa spends about four times more on debt-service payments than it does on health care.

In recent years, the World Bank has provided hundreds of billions of dollars in low-interest loans to subsidize the efforts of global corporations to establish control over the natural resources and markets of assisted countries. Corporations in the energy and agriculture sectors have been among the main beneficiaries. Often World Bank–financed roads, power plants, and electrical grids were built primarily to serve the global corporations establishing operations in the service area of the loan-financed facilities, rather than to serve the local populations. Indeed, as documented by the Institute for Policy Studies, the World Bank has become the major contributor to global greenhouse gas emissions through fossil fuel projects that primarily benefit global corporations. Regional development banks such as the Asian Development Bank (ADB) and the Inter-American Development Bank have generally copied the World Bank's model.

THE INTERNATIONAL MONETARY FUND

The International Monetary Fund (IMF) was originally created to work with member nations to implement measures to ensure the stability of the international financial system and correct balance-of-payments maladjustments. By the early 1980s, however, it took a different course. Rather than helping governments avoid currency crises, it has persistently pressured them to abandon the regulation of cross-border trade and financial flows, resulting in massive trade imbalances and reckless financial speculation.

IMF-sanctioned policies helped attract huge inflows of foreign money to what were called the "emerging market economies" of Asia and Latin America in the form of loans and speculative investment. As Walden Bello and Martin Khor have documented, the rapid buildup of foreign financial claims set the stage for the subsequent financial meltdown in Mexico in 1994 and in Asia, Russia, and Brazil from 1997 to 1998. This is why: When it became clear that the huge financial bubbles the inflows had created could not be sustained and that claims against foreign exchange could not be covered, speculators were spooked and suddenly pulled out billions of dollars. Currencies and stock markets went into a free fall. Millions of people fell back into poverty. Then the IMF stepped in with new loans to bail out the foreign banks and financiers involved—leaving it to the taxpayers of the devastated economies to pick up the bill once the loan payments came due. In many instances, at IMF insistence, uncollectible private debts were converted into public debt.

Over the last two decades, structural adjustment programs were imposed by the World Bank and the IMF on close to ninety developing countries, from Guyana to Ghana. The objective of SAPs went beyond debt repayment or attainment of short-term macroeconomic stability, seeking nothing less than the dismantling of protectionism and other policies of government-assisted capitalism that their theorists judged to be the main obstacles to sustained growth and development.

Two decades after the first structural adjustment loan, the bank states that it has formally abandoned the entire program, replacing it with what it calls the "Comprehensive Development Framework." The new paradigm, according to a statement of the Group of Seven Finance Ministers and Central Bank Governors, has the following elements:

- Increased and more effective fiscal expenditures for poverty reduction, with better targeting of budgetary resources, especially on social priorities in basic education and health
- Enhanced transparency, including monitoring and quality control over fiscal expenditures
- Stronger country ownership of the reform and poverty reduction process and programs, involving public participation
- Stronger performance indicators that can be monitored for follow-through on poverty reduction
- Assurance of macroeconomic stability and sustainability, and reduction of barriers to access by the poor to the benefits of growth

What brought about this shift in plans? Clearly, it was spectacular failure that could no longer be denied at the pain of totally losing all credibility. With dozens of countries under "adjustment" for over a decade, even the World Bank had to acknowledge that it was hard to find a handful of success stories. In most cases, as Rudiger Dornbusch of the Massachusetts Institute of Technology put it, structural adjustment caused economies to fall into a hole wherein low investment, reduced social spending, reduced consumption, and low output interacted to create a vicious cycle of decline and stagnation rather than a virtuous circle of growth, rising employment, and rising investment, as originally envisaged by the World Bank–IMF theory.

With much resistance from the bank's entrenched bureaucracy, President James Wolfensohn moved slowly to distance the bank from hard-line adjustment policies and even convinced some of his staff (grudgingly) to work with civil society groups to assess SAPs in the so-called Structural Adjustment Program Review Initiative (SAPRI). For the most part, however, the change of attitude did not translate into changes at the operational level because of the strong internalization of the structural adjustment approach among bank operatives.

Although self-doubt began to engulf the World Bank, the IMF plowed confidently on. Lack of evidence of success was interpreted to mean simply that a government lacked political will to push adjustment. Through the establishment of the Enhanced Structural Adjustment Facility (ESAF), the IMF sought to fund countries over a longer period in order to institutionalize more fully the desired free-market reforms.

It was the Asian financial crisis that finally provoked the IMF to make some cosmetic changes. In 1997–98, it moved with grand assurance into Thailand, Indonesia, and Korea with its classic formula of short-term fiscal and monetary policy cum structural reform in the direction of liberalization, deregulation, and privatization. This was the price it exacted from governments for financial rescue packages that would allow them to repay the massive debt incurred by their private sectors. Instead, a short-term crisis turned into a deep recession as governmental capacity to counteract the drop in private-sector activity was destroyed by budgetary and monetary repression. If some recovery is now discernible in a few economies, it is widely recognized as coming in spite of rather than because of the IMF.

For a world that had long been resentful of the IMF's arrogance, this was the last straw. In 1998–99, criticism of the organization rose to a crescendo. Criticism went beyond the IMF's stubborn adherence to structural adjustment and its serving as a bailout mechanism for international finance capital to its being nontransparent and unaccountable. Its vulnerable position was exposed during the recent debate in the U.S. Congress over a G-7 initiative to provide debt relief to forty poor countries. Legislators depicted the IMF as the agency that had caused the debt crisis of the poor countries in the first place, and some called for its abolition within three years. Said representative Maxine Waters: "Do we have to have the IMF involved at all? Because, as we have painfully discovered, the way the IMF works causes children to starve."

In the face of such criticism from legislators in the IMF's most powerful member, Clinton administration treasury secretary Larry Summers claimed that the IMF-centered process would be replaced by "a new, more open and inclusive process that would involve multiple international organizations and give national policymakers and civil society groups a more central role."

What does this mean? Is structural adjustment dead, and have the Bretton Woods institutions seen the light? The fact is, in the case of the IMF, as well as that of the World Bank and the Asian Development Bank, jettisoning the paradigm of structural adjustment has left them adrift, in the view of many critics, with the rhetoric and broad goals of reducing poverty but without an innovative macroeconomic approach. James Wolfensohn and his ex-chief economist Joseph Stiglitz talk about "bringing together" the "macroeconomic" and "social" aspects of development, but World Bank officials cannot point to a larger strategy beyond increasing lending to health, population, nutrition, education, and social protection to 25 percent of its total lending. The ADB is even more of a newcomer in the antipoverty approach, and a recent strategy paper is long on laudable goals. But even ADB insiders agree that it breaks no new ground in macroeconomic innovation. Most at sea are IMF economists, some of whom openly admitted to NGO representatives at the September 1999 IMF–World Bank meeting that so far the new approach was limited to relabeling the Enhanced Structural Adjustment Facility the Poverty Reduction Facility, and that they were looking to the World Bank to provide leadership.

It is not surprising that in such circumstances the old paradigm would reassert itself. For example, the IMF told the Thai government—already its most obedient pupil—to cut its fiscal deficit despite a very fragile recovery, and it pushed Indonesia to open its retail trade to foreign investors despite the consequences of higher unemployment. Similarly, technocrats of the ADB made energy loans contingent on the Philippine government's accel-

BOX E: ARGENTINA AND THE IMF

By Sarah Anderson, Institute for Policy Studies

Perhaps more than any other country in Latin America, Argentina embraced the free market economic model promoted by the IMF and the World Bank. Beginning in the early 1990s, the government lifted barriers to trade and investment. With strong backing from these two institutions, it also liberalized financial markets, privatized everything that wasn't nailed down, and tied its own hands further by pegging the value of its currency to the U.S. dollar.

The tying of the peso to the dollar initially had broad public support because it braked a runaway inflation rate. However, according to Jerome Levinson, former general counsel of the Inter-American Development Bank, this arrangement was "merely the neoclassical model's reliance on the market carried to its logical extreme." Policymakers lost all discretionary authority, while the financial markets determined the level of economic activity. When the value of the U.S. dollar began to rise in the mid-1990s, things began to fall apart. Argentine exports lost competitiveness and industry began to decline, causing a jump in unemployment. As revenues fell, the government turned to the IMF for help in meeting its loan payments. In return, the IMF demanded deep cuts in public spending that further cut domestic demand and stoked social unrest.

Although Argentina's abandonment of the currency peg in early 2002 was a significant factor in its economy's collapse, other free market reforms exacerbated the problems. Once trade barriers and capital controls had been lifted, the government was powerless to address the looming trade deficit and the flight of capital. The privatization of public assets led to reduced access to services for the poor and middle class. Millions of Argentines lost health coverage as private international insurers pressured providers to cut costs. Argentine banks were sold to foreign firms, which cut back lending to small and medium enterprises, a previously important source of employment. Stripped of protections, private employers were pressured to become "lean and mean" in the global economy. They laid off workers in droves and, along with the IMF, lobbied for a labor law reform in April 2000 that further weakened the power of Argentine unions. All of this fueled the anger that exploded in the riots in December 2001—in which more than twenty-five people died—that brought about the country's political and economic crash.

In the end, the IMF never admitted any wrongdoing. It claimed there was nothing wrong with the overall model. Instead, it blamed Argentina's collapse on excessive public spending and the currency peg, which it initially supported and helped sustain but then claimed was a purely homegrown policy.

erating the IMF-promoted privatization of the National Power Corporation, even though consumers are likely to end up paying more to the seven private monopolies that will succeed the state enterprise. "It's the old approach of deregulation, privatization, and liberalization, but with safety nets," is the accurate description of one Filipino labor leader much consulted by the multilateral institutions.

THE GATT AND THE WORLD TRADE ORGANIZATION

The World Trade Organization (WTO) has emerged as the third pillar of the Bretton Woods system.

A very healthy debate was launched after World War II about the need for a global trade and investment institution that could help generate full employment, protect worker rights around the world, and protect against what were then referred to as "global cartels"—small groups of corporations that gained too much power over a sector. These broad-based goals were enshrined in a Havana charter that proposed the formation of an International Trade Organization (ITO). Rejected by the U.S. Senate on the grounds that its broad mandate would compromise U.S. sovereignty, only one element of the ITO, the General Agreement on Tariffs and Trade (GATT), was created instead, with the more narrow goal of reducing tariffs in goods and services and setting a handful of broad trade principles.

World trade grew dramatically following World War II, under the guidance of the GATT. While initially limited to this trade expansion mandate, the GATT evolved into an institution that promoted corporate rights over human rights and other social and environmental priorities.

In the early 1980s, economists and politicians, powered by the so-called Reagan Revolution and the Thatcher and Kohl ascendancies in Europe, began planning a new but dramatically different GATT negotiating round. Their goal was to expand the GATT disciplines to bind signatory governments to a set of multilateral policies regarding the service, government procurement, and investment sectors; to establish global limits on government regulation of environmental, food safety, and product standards; to establish new protections for corporate intellectual property rights granted in rich countries; and to have this broad panoply of one-size-fits-all rules strongly enforced over every level of government in every signatory country.

This agenda was translated into the Uruguay Round of GATT negotiations, a transformational undertaking pushed largely by U.S.-based global corporations and their allies in the U.S. government. When completed in 1994, the Uruguay Round replaced the old GATT trade contract with a new institution, the World Trade Organization. The WTO was given a built-in enforcement system more powerful than that of any previous treaty. This system, with closed tribunals of trade bureaucrats who determined if a country's laws exceeded the constraints set by the new rules, included automatic, permanent trade sanctions against any country refusing to comply with WTO demands. In short, the WTO took on the role of implementing globally much the same policy agenda that the World Bank and the IMF had already imposed on most of the Third World.

Proponents of the WTO argue that it is needed to regulate trade, prevent trade wars, and protect the interests of poor nations, but its actions tell a different story. (See Box B for a list of some of the most controversial WTO rulings on environmental protections.) WTO panels have also ruled against Canada's cultural protections, which taxed U.S. magazines. India has been told it must change its national constitution because WTO rules do not allow it to provide its people with inexpensive generic drugs since it is considered unfair to foreign drug companies that profit handsomely from branded products. The WTO even takes for itself responsibility for determining whether it is permissible to label such products so consumers will know what they are buying and can assess the risks accordingly.

Given the claim that the WTO protects the poor and prevents trade wars, the 1999 WTO "banana wars" decision is especially revealing. Europeans were told by the WTO that they could not give import preference to bananas produced by two hundred thousand members of small banana farmer cooperatives located in the Caribbean because it was unfair to two giant U.S. agribusiness corporations, Chiquita and Dole, which grow bananas in Central America and control half the world's banana trade. When Europe refused to end its preference, the WTO sanctioned a retaliatory move by the United States to impose 100 percent tariffs on a wide variety of European exports. Thus, in a single case, the WTO struck down a preference for the poor and sanctioned a trade war.

Specifically, the WTO has served primarily U.S. government and corporate interests over developing-country and civil-society interests. Just as it was the United States that blocked the founding of the International Trade Organization in 1948 when it felt that this would not serve its position of overwhelming economic dominance in the postwar world, so it was the United States that became the dominant lobbyist for the comprehensive Uruguay Round and the founding of the WTO when it felt that more competitive global conditions had created a situation where its corporate interests now demanded an opposite stance.

Just as it was the threat of the United States in the 1950s to leave GATT if it was not allowed to maintain protective mechanisms for milk and other agricultural products that led to agricultural trade's limited coverage in GATT rules, so it was U.S. pressure that brought agriculture fully under the GATT-WTO system in 1995. The reason for Washington's change of mind was articulated quite candidly by then–U.S. Agriculture Secretary John Block at the start of the Uruguay Round negotiations in 1986: the "idea that developing countries should feed themselves is an anachronism from a bygone era. They could better ensure their food security by relying on U.S. agricultural products, which are available, in most cases, at much lower cost." Washington did not just have developing country markets in mind but also Japan, South Korea, and the European Union.

It was the United States that pushed to bring services under WTO coverage with its assessment that in the new burgeoning area of international services, particularly financial services, its corporations had a lead that needed to be preserved. It was also the United States that pushed to expand WTO jurisdiction to the Trade-Related Investment Measures (TRIMs) and Trade-Related Intellectual Property Rights (TRIPs) mentioned earlier. The first sought to eliminate countries' ability to shape foreign investment policies to ensure national benefits. For instance, TRIMs targeted domestic laws regulating internal cross-border trade of product components among TNC subsidiaries, which developing countries had passed in order to develop new domestic industries. TRIPs was designed to consolidate the U.S. advantage in the cutting-edge, knowledge-intensive industries.

It was again the United States that forced the creation of the WTO's formidable dispute-resolution and enforcement mechanism after being frustrated with what U.S. trade officials considered weak GATT efforts to enforce rulings favorable to the United States. As Washington's academic point man on trade, C. Fred Bergsten, head of the Institute of International

Economics, told the U.S. Senate, the strong WTO dispute settlement mechanism serves U.S. interests because "we can now use the full weight of the international machinery to go after those trade barriers, reduce them, get them eliminated."

In sum, it has been Washington's changing perception of the needs of its economic interest groups that has shaped and reshaped the international trading regime. It was not global necessity that gave birth to the WTO in 1995 but rather the U.S. government's assessment that the interests of its corporations were no longer served by a loose and flexible GATT. In the course of the 1990s, what had been a U.S. idea spread to become the mantra of the wealthiest countries, then known as the G-7 (the United States, Japan, Germany, France, the United Kingdom, Italy, and Canada). From the free-market paradigm that underpins it to the rules and regulations set forth in the different agreements that make up the Uruguay Round to its system of decision making and accountability, the WTO is a blueprint for the global hegemony of the largest corporations based in the richest nations.

But what about the developing countries? Is the WTO a necessary structure—one that, whatever its flaws, brings more benefits than costs and therefore merits efforts at reform? When the Uruguay Round was being negotiated, there was considerable lack of enthusiasm for the process by the developing countries. After all, these countries had formed the backbone of the United Nations Conference on Trade and Development (UNCTAD; for more on this organization see chapter 7), which, with its system of one-country—one-vote and majority voting, was, they felt, an international arena more congenial to their interests. They entered the Uruguay Round greatly resenting the policy of the large trading powers to weaken and marginalize UNCTAD in the late 1970s and early 1980s. However, they had been promised that the WTO's multilateral rules and enforcement would stop the unilateral bullying by more powerful nations on trade matters.

Yet as the WTO began operations, it became evident that the imbalance in economic power had not been remediated. WTO rules were enforced only when countries spent millions of dollars to bring a case, and then the rules were enforced with trade sanctions. Many developing countries began to realize that they had signed away their right to employ a variety of critical trade measures for development purposes. In contrast to the loose GATT framework, which had allowed some space for development initiatives, the comprehensive and tightened Uruguay Round was fundamentally antidevelopment. This is evident in the following: in signing on to the WTO, Third World countries committed to ban all quantitative restrictions on imports and reduce tariffs on many industrial imports, and they promised not to raise tariffs on all other imports. In so doing, they effectively gave up the use of trade policy to pursue domestic objectives. The route that the newly industrializing countries (NICs) had taken to industrial status through the policy of import substitution was now removed.

The antidevelopment thrust of the WTO accord is made even more manifest in the TRIMs and TRIPs agreements. NICs like South Korea and Malaysia made use of many innovative mechanisms, such as trade-balancing requirements that tied the value of a foreign investor's imports of raw materials and components to the value of its exports of the finished commodity, and "local content" regulations that mandated a certain percentage of the components that went into the making of a product to be sourced locally.

These rules did indeed restrict the maneuvering space of foreign investors, but they were successfully employed by the NICs to marry foreign investment to national ventures. They enabled these countries to raise income from capital-intensive exports, develop support industries, and bring in technology, while still protecting local entrepreneurs' preferential access to the domestic market. TRIMs makes these mechanisms illegal.

Proposals under consideration for future WTO action include expanding existing WTO prohibitions regarding trade in goods that forbid any public policies that give preference to local over foreign investors (including banking, media, and other service sectors) or to local over foreign suppliers. Also on the agenda are constraints on initiatives to protect national food security by shielding local farmers from foreign competition, to protect forest and water resources from exploitation by foreign corporations, and to regulate speculative movements of international money. Other WTO proposals would open the way to privatizing public services, such as public schools and health care, under the ownership of global corporations.

The WTO rules and enforcement system is regularly used by corporations and their allied governments to attack measures taken by governments to protect the health, safety, and culture of their people and to preserve the environment. Yet under WTO rules, governments take ever stronger steps to protect the profits and property rights of corporations and financiers.

(continued on page 52)

BOX F: THE HYPOCRISY OF THE NORTH IN THE WTO

By Martin Khor, Third World Network

There is perhaps no arena in which the United States and the other richest industrial countries fail more to practice what they preach than trade policy. For two decades, through their own dictates as well as through the World Bank, the IMF, the GATT, and now the WTO, they have uniformly preached that liberalization of Southern markets is essential. Just as consistently, they have failed to practice this dictum at home.

The old GATT system dealt with trade in goods. There were imbalances even in that system. For example, the largest economic sectors and export sectors of most developing countries are agriculture and textiles. Both still employ millions in the industrial countries, and both have been highly protected in most of these countries for decades.

Beginning in 1986, governments began the famous Uruguay Round negotiations that transformed the GATT into the WTO in 1995. At the core of the negotiations was a proposed tradeoff. Developing countries would agree to a series of new issues in the WTO (services, intellectual property, investment measures) that would make the system more imbalanced and more intrusive (as the system moved from its traditional concern with trade barriers at the border to greater involvement with domestic economic and development structures and policies). In turn, the developing countries were promised, the Uruguay Round would open up Northern markets for agriculture and textiles.

The North has insisted that the South keep its side of the bargain but has failed to deliver on its own promises. The developing countries have been under great pressure to liberalize their rules on imports and foreign investments as fast as possible from the industrial nations, the international financial institutions, regional trade arrangements with developed countries, and the WTO. Implementing their obligations under the WTO agreements has brought many problems for developing countries. Here are some examples:

- The prohibition of investment measures and subsidies has made it harder or impossible for the state to encourage and promote the domestic sectors.
- Import liberalization in agriculture threatens the viability and livelihoods of small farmers whose products face competition from cheaper imported foods, many of which are artificially cheapened through massive subsidy.
- The effects of a rigorous intellectual property rights regime include exorbitant prices for medicines and other essentials, patenting by Northern corporations of biologi-

CONTINUED

BOX F: CONTINUED

cal materials originating in the South, and higher costs for and lower access by developing countries to industrial technology.

- Increasing pressures on developing countries to open up their services sectors, which could deny the poor access to essential services.

These measures threaten to stop developing countries from industrializing, upgrading technology, developing local industries, protecting small farmers, achieving food security, and fulfilling health and medicinal needs.

The developing countries' problems arise from the structural imbalances and weaknesses of several WTO agreements. They have compiled a lengthy list of their problems of implementation and proposals for addressing them, and submitted these in the WTO. There has been progress on very few of the implementation problems. Some are on the post-Doha work program along with many other topics. The attitude of the developed countries seems to be that the developing countries entered into legally binding commitments and must abide by them or make new concessions to change them. Such an attitude does not augur well for the WTO, for it implies that the state of imbalance will remain, and if developing countries pay twice or pay three or four times, the imbalances will become worse and the burden even heavier.

The new WTO rules also pose problems for the public in the rich countries, including the high cost of medicines and other consumer products due to patenting, and the threats to public services and management of natural resources such as water, as a result of services liberalization. The regional NAFTA agreement has also generated a host of problems and controversies, including corporations suing the state for expropriating their future profits as a result of measures on health and environmental or other grounds.

Meanwhile, the industrial nations have largely failed to deliver on their pledges to open up their own economies in agriculture and textiles. In most Northern countries, these sectors remain closed. In agriculture, tariffs on many items of interest to developing countries are prohibitively high (some tariffs are over 200 to 300 percent). Domestic subsidies in OECD countries have actually risen from U.S. $275 billion (annual average for base period 1986–88) to $326 billion in 1999, according to OECD data published in 2000. The increases in permitted subsidies more than offset the decrease in subsidy categories under the agriculture agreement.

In textiles and clothing, only very few items that the developing countries export have been taken off the quota lists of Northern countries, even though more than half of the ten-year implementation period has passed. According to a submission at the WTO in June 2000 by the International Textiles and Clothing Bureau, only a few quota restrictions (13 out of 750 by the United States, 14 out of 219 by the European Union, 29 out of 295 by Canada) had been eliminated. Given this record, it is doubtful that the designated quotas will be removed by 2005.

In early 2002, the United States announced that it would be imposing tariffs of up to 30 percent on some of its steel imports in order to protect its domestic steel industry. This decision sent shock waves around the world, because it signifies the rise of unilateral protectionist actions in the world's richest country.

Developing countries are asked to bear for a little while the pain of rapid adjustment, with assurances that it will surely be good for them after a few years; whereas the developed countries that advocate this policy ask for more time for themselves to adjust in agriculture and textiles (and other products) that have been protected for many decades.

The fact that rich countries still argue that they need more time to protect their weak or uncompetitive sectors should make them sympathetic to the developing countries' increasing complaints that import liberalization and other obligations have damaged their societies. But the governments of rich countries refuse to admit the truth of the matter and resist the demand of citizen groups and many Southern governments to change the system.

At the November 2001 Doha, Qatar, WTO ministerial meeting, developing countries raised many of these implementations issues. Instead, the largest developed countries pushed very hard to have the WTO expand its negotiating and rule-making mandate, including into new areas such as investment, competition policy, government procurement, and trade and the environment.

This attempt at expansion was strongly resisted by most of the developing countries (including regional groupings), which argued that (a) they were not yet ready to enter negotiations or consider agreements on these issues; (b) they did not adequately understand the implications of the proposed issues; and (c) from the limited understanding they did have, they were very concerned that new agreements in these areas would add to their already heavy obligations and further restrict their development policy options and constrain or reduce their development prospects. The Doha meeting ended with confusing language on both the implementation concerns of the developing nations and the desire for new issues by the developed countries. There is certainly no consensus in the WTO on how to move forward.

Although the WTO presumes to impose a one-size-fits-all set of rules constraining the public interest policies of WTO member nations, it does nothing to limit the excesses of global corporations and financial speculators—two priority regulatory needs. Instead, it regulates national and local governments to prevent them from regulating international trade and investment. In short, it regulates governments to protect corporations.

PROPOSALS

The Bretton Woods institutions have a distorted view of economic progress and relationships. Their embrace of unlimited expansion of trade and foreign investment in order to achieve economic growth suggests that they consider the most advanced state of development to be one in which all productive assets are owned by foreign corporations producing for export; the currency that facilitates day-to-day transactions is borrowed from foreign banks; education and health services are operated by foreign corporations on a for-profit, fee-for-service basis; and almost everything that local people consume is imported. When placed in such stark terms, the absurdity of this ideology becomes obvious. It also becomes clear who is served by such policies. Rather than enhancing the life of people and the planet, they consolidate and secure the wealth and power of a small corporate elite.

Harvard economist Dani Rodrik has pointed out that relevant data demonstrate that trade and investment liberalization do not necessarily bring increased economic growth or prosperity. They do, however, contribute to serious imbalances in the global economy, including alarming growth in inequality both inside and between nations. Alternative models that emphasize domestic production for domestic markets and that direct trade and foreign investment to the service of national needs hold greater promise.

Author William Greider has pointed out another, less noted imbalance that is encouraged by trade and investment liberalization—rapid expansion of production combined with the suppression of wages so that most workers cannot afford to buy the products they produce. As a result, there is a substantial surplus of production today. The world has dealt with this by looking to the United States as the buyer of last resort. For more than two decades, the United States has been buying far more from others than it sells to them and paying for the difference with money borrowed from foreign investors, primarily the Japanese. This actually puts the United States into a financial position similar to that of Asia, Russia, and Brazil just before their financial collapses in 1997 and 1998. On the other side of this troubling equation, we find country after country exporting goods and resources to support needless consumption in the United States while their own people lack the financial means to obtain even the most basic necessities.

Trade theory gives great importance to keeping international trade and payment accounts in balance if the exchange is to be mutually beneficial and economic relations are to be reasonably stable. British economist John Maynard Keynes, one of the chief architects of the Bretton Woods system, took this idea quite seriously. In 1942, he pointed out that we "need a system possessed of an internal stabilizing mechanism, by which pressure is exercised on any country whose balance of payments with the rest of the world is departing from equilibrium in either direction, so as to prevent movements which must create for its neighbors an equal but opposite want of balance."

Ironically, one of the IMF's original responsibilities was to help nations keep their international accounts in balance. Yet current policies of the World Bank, the IMF, and the WTO not only ignore this principle but set in place conditions that prevent nations from honoring it. The result is imbalance, instability, inequality, and deprivation.

In the current economic system, liberalizing trade and investment and enhancing international competitiveness are seen as the means to growth, which, in turn, is seen as the key to prosperity and democracy. The following chapter outlines the principles of an alternative system that proposes democracy and rights as the means toward sustainable communities, dignified work, and a healthy environment.

CHAPTER TWO

Ten Principles
for Sustainable Societies

ON A RAINY DAY in late November 1999, environmentalists dressed like tur-
tles marched arm-in-arm with Teamsters down the city streets in what has
become known as the Battle of Seattle, an extraordinary event that dead-
locked WTO negotiators and brought that powerful agency's momentum to
a standstill. These unlikely partners were joined by tens of thousands of
others—students, religious activists, women's rights activists, family farmers,
health activists, indigenous people, and economic justice organizers from
many countries—in what was baptized the Seattle Coalition.

In sifting through the thousands of pieces of literature produced by
these formerly disparate groups, we found that a fascinating pattern
emerged. Certain words cropped up time and again as core principles, no
matter the particular group or specific country in which the organization
was based.

Almost all the authors of this volume were in Seattle, first at a giant
International Forum on Globalization teach-in, organized in Seattle's sym-
phony hall, and then on the streets. We all remarked on this commonality
in core principles.

The term *democracy* was perhaps the most common thread linking all the
groups, with different groups affixing different adjectives to try to give the
word a deeper meaning: *living democracy, participatory democracy, new democracy, people's democracy*. After democracy, *ecological sustainability* came next,
again often described in related terms. Most groups now also suggest *localization* and *subsidiarity* as key principles opposed to *globalization*.

As we pored over the documents and manifestos distributed in Seattle and elsewhere, we found that ten terms were repeated most often as organizing principles, and we began to understand the basis for the movement that has alternately been described as "anti–corporate globalization" or "pro–global justice." It is this growing commonality among principles that allows this set of disparate groups with thousands of separate leaders and hundreds of different significant issues to be called a *movement*.

These principles stand in stark contrast to those that guide economic globalization, which are narrow and serve the few at the expense of the many and the environment. Economic growth has been the central goal of the IMF, the World Bank, and the GATT, as well as its successor, the WTO. Expanding international trade and investment flows has been viewed as an end in itself.

As chapter 1 explained, the governing ideology of the past half-century has been that unfettered trade and investment will bring prosperity, which will bring democracy. This ideology has guided the declarations of U.S. presidents from Harry Truman to George W. Bush, as well as the policy pronouncements of most leaders the world over, particularly since the 1980s. The persistent mantra of corporate and government leaders alike has been that to remain competitive in a global economy governments must cut regulations and encourage the most favorable climate for foreign investment, often at the cost of worker rights and environmental integrity. In the words of Council of Canadians chair Maude Barlow, "Stateless corporations have given rise to corporate states."

The time has come to create healthy, sustainable societies that work for all. Healthy, sustainable societies vest power in institutions that measure their performance by their contribution to the long-term well-being of people, community, and nature, and distribute power equitably among all of society's stakeholders. Such societies are measured by their essential qualities, primarily the well-being of all their people. Each sustainable community and nation seeks to achieve sufficient self-reliance in meeting basic needs—including food, shelter, clean water, energy, education, health, political participation, and culture—to assure the livelihoods, civil liberties, and sense of meaning and identity of each of its members.

Ten Core Principles for Sustainable Societies

To achieve truly sustainable societies, all international, national, and regional economic policy rules and institutions should be designed to conform to the ten basic principles that are enunciated below.

I. NEW DEMOCRACY

The rallying cry of the amazing diversity of civil society that converged in Seattle was the simple word *democracy*. Democracy flourishes when people organize to protect their communities and rights and hold their elected officials accountable. For the past two decades, governments have transferred much of their sovereignty into the hands of global corporations. The authors of this volume advocate a shift from governments serving corporations to governments serving people and communities, a process that is easier at the local level but vital at all levels of government.

We use the terms *new democracy* and *living democracy* in part because *democracy* is equated in many minds with elections alone. As vital as fair elections are to democracy, we want to focus more attention on the dynamic processes initiated by civil society organizations around the world to instill new energy and meaning into democratic movements. In some countries, primarily in the Southern Hemisphere, these movements focus on winning community control over natural resources. In other countries, mainly in the North, they are striving to refocus government agendas on a citizens' agenda of rights.

Accountability is central to living democracy. When decisions are made by those who will bear the consequences—such as when a community democratically decides how to manage forests immediately around its homes on the watershed it depends upon for flood control and water—they are likely to give a high priority to the sustained long-term health of those forests because their own well-being and that of their children is at stake. This is not the case if the management decisions are in the hands of a foreign corporation whose directors live thousands of miles away and, furthermore, face a legal mandate to maximize short-term return to shareholders. The shareholders, in turn, may not even know they hold shares in this particular company, let alone the location of its forests. These circumstances lead directors to consider only the immediate profit that clear-cutting the trees will bring; they will neither see nor bear the costs of the flooding, mudslides, and disruption of local water supply that this choice will inflict on others. When health, labor, and environmental standards and the rules of foreign trade and investment are shaped by corporate lobbyists in secret negotiations in distant cities, those who will profit are well represented, but those who bear the costs are not at the table, and their interests carry no weight.

The principle of new democracy means creating governance systems that give those who will bear the costs the vote when decisions are being made. It also means limiting the rights and powers of absentee owners and assuring that those who hold decision-making power are liable for the harms their acts bring to others. The dominant institution of the global economy—the publicly traded, limited liability corporation—violates both of these conditions by institutionalizing an extreme form of absentee ownership and by insulating the shareholders in whose name the corporation acts from liability for the harm these acts may inflict on others. It is an institutional form poorly suited to the needs of sustainable societies.

BOX G: CITIZENS' AGENDA IN CANADA

By Tony Clarke, Polaris Institute

"All great social movements have been fired by a fierce imagination," declared a participant in the 1998 citizens' inquiry that was held across Canada in the wake of the collapse of the OECD negotiations for a multilateral agreement on investment (MAI).

The behind-closed-doors negotiations on the MAI at the OECD headquarters in Paris during the late 1990s had become a flash point for citizen activists in Canada. More than any other set of issues since the U.S.-Canada Free Trade Agreement and its sequel, NAFTA, the MAI had come to symbolize the massive resistance to, and the failures of, corporate globalization. When the Canadian government refused to heed the lessons of the MAI defeat in 1998, the country's largest public interest organization, the Council of Canadians, seized the moment.

Working in collaboration with some forty other national organizations, the council organized a series of public hearings in fall 1998 in eight Canadian cities. The series, called "The MAI Inquiry: A Citizens' Search for Al-

CONTINUED

ternatives," was conducted by a panel of commissioners including individuals who were both well-known in the country and knowledgeable about globalization issues.

In preparation for the hearings, a *Citizens' Handbook,* designed to stimulate imagination about alternative ways to organize the global economy, was widely circulated. Highlighting the need to reorganize the global economy in terms of the three Rs of democracy—rights, rules, and responsibilities—the handbook included a citizens' report card to evaluate the performance of institutions like the WTO, the IMF, and the World Bank. While hundreds of civil society groups made submissions to the commissioners as they traveled across the country, thousands of individual citizens filled out and handed in their report cards.

During the public hearings, witness after witness emphasized the need for new organizing principles as the basis for transforming the global economy. These organizing principles included the following:

- *Recognizing people's fundamental democratic rights* as enshrined in the U.N. Declaration of Human Rights and the international covenants on economic, social, and cultural rights and on civil and political rights
- *Protecting the common good and heritage* affecting the lives and rights of all people, such as food security, labor standards, environmental safeguards, cultural integrity, public services, vital resources, and basic human rights
- *Building sustainable local communities,* where greater priority is put on employing local resources and people to produce goods and services for local and regional communities within ecological limits
- *Restoring the political sovereignty of governments,* such as the powers to determine economic, social, and environmental objectives for national development and the capacity to ensure that transnational corporations meet these priorities
- *Reasserting the democratic control of citizens* through new forms of participatory democracy whereby citizens become effectively involved in international policymaking on trade, investment, and finance

As the final report of the citizens' inquiry demonstrated, there is no shortage of imagination when it comes to reorganizing the global economy to serve the democratic rights of people and ensure the survival of the planet. No blueprint or platform for transforming the global economy was laid down before the hearings. Instead, people were encouraged to come forth as individuals and groups to present their own ideas and proposals for discussion and debate. Through this process, a variety of creative initiatives emerged:

- *Harnessing transnational corporations* and making them more accountable by requiring a more rigorous screening process on their operations
- *Renegotiating trade agreements* like NAFTA and the WTO by reopening the contentious areas but, if no satisfactory changes result, proceeding to invoke the abrogation clause
- *Reregulating foreign investment* to serve objectives and priorities for national development
- *Controlling speculation in financial markets* by adopting "speed bump" measures to regulate the inflows and outflows of capital
- *Curbing the threat of capital flight* by governments developing a more creative negotiating strategy with transnational corporations and encouraging strategic use of workers' pension funds as an alternative source of capital

In short, the citizens' inquiry provided the grounds for people to come together and begin reclaiming democracy and the commons through a process of outlining proposals for transforming the global economy. For most participating citizen activists, this is an important part of building a new democracy movement in Canada and around the world.

But the Council of Canadians soon realized that this was not a one-shot endeavor. Building a citizens' agenda is an ongoing process. Nor is it sufficient to focus energy on the global economy without at the same time developing proposals and strategies to change the structures of economic policymaking and governance at national and local levels. What's more, developing a citizens' agenda for social transformation should not be confined to the membership of one organization alone. To be effective, the process must be carried out in a broad alliance with a variety of civil society organizations and groups.

Accordingly, the council set up a task force to design and implement a three- to five-year plan of action to build a citizens' agenda for social transformation in Canada. The plan focused on developing an agenda for transformation on three tracks: local, national, and international. The council has not developed this citizens' agenda process in a vacuum. On the contrary, steps have been taken to learn from the experiments that have taken place in other countries, such as the Sustainable Chile project, the Via Panchayat movement in India, and the peoples' budget process that has been instituted by the metropolitan government in Porto Alegre, Brazil. In this way, the citizens' agenda is meant to be stimulated by, and contribute to, the building of a global civil society movement.

2. SUBSIDIARITY

Economic globalization entails first and foremost the delocalization and disempowerment of local communities and economies. Yet a high percentage of people on earth still survive through local, community-based activities: small-scale farming, local markets, local production for local consumption. This traditional system has enabled these people to remain in control of their economic and food security, and it also maintains the viability of their communities and cultures. Even in developed countries, most livelihoods have traditionally been connected to local economic production. Economic globalization is rapidly dismantling this, favoring instead economies based on export with global corporations in control. This brings destruction of local livelihoods, local jobs, and community self-reliance.

It is necessary to create new rules and structures that consciously favor the local and follow the principle of subsidiarity—that is, whatever decisions and activities can be undertaken locally should be. Whatever power can reside at the local level should reside there. Only when additional activity is required that cannot be satisfied locally should power and activity move to the next higher level, that of region, nation, and finally the world. Site-here-to-sell-here policies and the grounding of capital locally should be codified. Economic structures should be designed to move economic and political power downward, toward the local rather than in a global direction. (In Europe, calls by IFG members and others that globalization be replaced by greater emphasis on protecting and rebuilding local economies has had its first political success. United Kingdom Green members of the European Parliament were elected in 1999 on a manifesto that called for a "protect the local, globally" route to localization.)

Subsidiarity respects the notion that sovereignty resides in people. In other words, legitimate authority flows upward from the populace through the expression of their democratic will. Thus, the authority of more distant levels of administration is *subsidiary*, or subordinate, to the authority of more local levels, which allow a greater opportunity for direct citizen engagement. Decisions are properly made as close to the level of the individuals who will bear their consequences as feasible. Most of the affairs of self-reliant local economies are properly left to local people and institutions;

issues such as global warming that demand collective action on a global scale necessarily require a greater involvement from global institutions.

The principle of subsidiarity recognizes the inherent democratic right to self-determination of people, communities, and nations as long as its exercise does not infringe on the similar rights of others. This right is properly secured through (a) the local and national ownership and control of resources and productive assets; (b) local and national rule-making authority in a system in which more central levels of authority support the local in achieving self-defined goals; and (c) local and national self-reliance in meeting essential needs with local and national resources to the extent feasible. Greater local ownership, political authority, and self-reliance mean less external dependence and vulnerability to exploitation—and the reduction or elimination of winner-takes-all competitive struggles for jobs, markets, money, and physical resources that are central to the global economic system. It does not, however, mean isolation. Sustainable societies are good neighbors that reach out to engage in cooperative, peaceful, and mutually beneficial relationships with all people through trade, cultural exchange, and the sharing of information and technology.

The principle of subsidiarity is so central to sustainable societies that chapter 4 of this volume is dedicated to the subject, spelling it out in some detail and offering a glimpse of the rich debate about this issue.

3. ECOLOGICAL SUSTAINABILITY

Economic activity has to be ecologically sustainable. It should allow for meeting the genuine needs of people alive today without compromising the ability of future generations to meet theirs, and without diminishing the natural diversity of life on earth or the viability of the planet's natural life-support systems.

Economic globalization is intrinsically harmful to the environment because it is based on ever increasing consumption, exploitation of resources, and waste disposal problems. One of its primary features, export-oriented production, is especially damaging because it is responsible for increasing global transport activity, fossil fuel use, and refrigeration and packaging, while requiring very costly and ecologically damaging new infrastructures such as ports, airports, dams, canals, and so on. It also accelerates conversion to industrial-style agriculture with corresponding increases in pesticides, water and air pollution, and biotechnology. Combined with many other wasteful aspects of global trade, these phenomena are powerful contributors to the problems of global climate change, loss of habitat, and unprecedented pollution.

If the planet is to support generations to come, it is vital that an alternative economic system be built that is rooted in the principle of ecological sustainability.

A healthy natural environment requires an acceptance that the planet's living systems are the foundation of life. Therefore, sustainable societies consider environmental health to be as important as the health of people and communities. Especially conscious of their responsibility to future generations, they take care to ensure that (a) rates of renewable resource use do

---

BOX H: SUSTAINABLE CHILE

Ten years ago, Augusto Pinochet was forced out of power through a plebiscite, and Chile began rebuilding a more democratic government. However, the new democratically elected leaders in Chile have largely continued to support policies that contribute to an inequitable and unsustainable society. Although Chile is often cited as a model of macroeconomic success, a number of Chilean NGOs, academics, and civil society groups continue to raise serious questions about what this "success"— based on the authoritarian implementation of neoliberalism—has meant for the environment, the poor, and the common good.

In response to growing concerns, the Institute for Political Ecology, the National Network for Ecological Action, and the University Bolivariana began the Sustainable Chile project in 1997. Over the course of a year and a half, the project coordinated with a number of civil society groups, churches, and academics to articulate a citizens' agenda for a sustainable Chile based on social equality, environmental sustainability, and strengthened democracy. In addition, more than five hundred civil society leaders represented their communities in workshops held in a number of Chilean cities, in which they elaborated on regional diagnostic studies of sustainability problems facing their regions and formulated concrete proposals to address the issues.

Throughout this process, participants articulated the ways in which poverty, inequality, unequal distribution of wealth, exploitation of natural resources, pollution, and limited demo-

CONTINUED

not exceed their rates of regeneration; (b) rates of consumption or irretrievable disposal of nonrenewable resources do not exceed the rates at which renewable substitutes are phased into use; and (c) rates of pollution emission into the environment do not exceed the rate of their harmless assimilation. Compromising any of these conditions puts the well-being of future generations at risk. (See also chapter six.)

4. COMMON HERITAGE

There exist common heritage resources that constitute a collective birthright of the whole species to be shared equitably among all. We believe that there are three categories of common heritage resources.

The first category includes the water, land, air, forests, and fisheries on

---

BOX H: CONTINUED

cratic institutions represent serious threats to sustainability in Chile. The citizens' agenda expresses these concerns and priorities of Chilean civil society and proposes a number of remedies, ranging from redistributing income, reducing military spending, reforming national environmental and fishing laws, and stabilizing copper production to reforming the 1980 constitution, written by the Pinochet regime, abolishing an amnesty law designed to ensure impunity for human rights violators and creating a national youth program. The agenda also includes proposals for protecting indigenous lands and waters, such as by creating a national registry of indigenous lands and water sources and national oversight mechanisms for land and water concessions, offering tax exemptions to indigenous owners of water sources, and ratifying

ILO Convention 169 on the protection of indigenous rights.

The process of elaborating the citizens' agenda brought together diverse groups throughout Chile and thus strengthened civil society. The agenda is intended to serve as a basis for further discussion and dialogue among citizens and politicians throughout Chile. Sustainable Chile project organizers hope that it will not only contribute to a public debate but also be used as a tool to mobilize the social and political will to put their proposals into action to establish a new Chilean society based on sustainability. Similar exercises have been conducted in Brazil, Uruguay, and Argentina (in 2002) under the Sustainable Southern Cone program.

SOURCE: Adapted from *For a Sustainable Chile: A Citizen's Agenda for Change.* Santiago: Sustainable Chile Program, 1999.

which everyone's life depends. The second includes the culture and knowledge that are collective creations of our species. Finally, more modern common resources are those public services that governments perform on behalf of all people to address such basic needs as public health, education, public safety, and social security, among others. All of these common heritage resources are under tremendous strain as corporations seek to privatize and commodify them.

Together, these three categories of resources form the foundation of all real wealth. After all, without them there is neither life nor civilization. Healthy societies acknowledge and reward individual contributions to increasing the useful productivity of natural resources or expanding humanity's common pool of culture and knowledge. At the same time, they recognize that no individual created the natural wealth of the planet or the whole of any underlying body of knowledge.

Where property rights to common heritage resources are used to secure the livelihood rights of individuals, it is recognized that any right to the use of a common heritage resource carries a corresponding moral obligation to act as its steward on behalf of all. Similarly, the accumulation of such rights must not infringe on the birthright of others to their equitable share in the common inheritance. Efforts by persons or corporations to monopolize ownership of an essential common heritage resource, such as water, a seed variety, or a forest, and exclude the needs of others should be deemed unacceptable.

Our belief that these categories of common heritage resources should be treated differently in the global economy opens up a vast and fascinating debate over how to manage them. Chapter 3 of this volume is devoted to that debate.

5. DIVERSITY

A few decades ago, it was still possible to leave home and go someplace where the architecture was different, the landscape was different, and the language, lifestyle, dress, and values were different. Today, farmers and filmmakers in France and India and millions of people elsewhere are protesting to maintain that diversity. Tens of thousands of communities around the world had perfected local resource management systems that worked but are being undermined by corporate-led globalization. Yet cultural, biological, social, and economic diversity are central to a dignified, interesting, and healthy life.

Diversity is key to the vitality, resilience, and innovative capacity of any living system. So too for human societies. The rich variety of the human experience and potential is reflected in *cultural diversity*, which provides a sort of cultural gene pool to spur innovation toward ever higher levels of social, intellectual, and spiritual accomplishment and creates a sense of identity, community, and meaning. (See Boxes I and J.) *Economic diversity* is the foundation

(continued on page 70)

BOX I: CULTURAL DIVERSITY
The Right of Indigenous Peoples to Remain Different and Diverse

By Victoria Tauli-Corpuz,
Indigenous Peoples' International Center for Policy Research and Education

There are still some three hundred million indigenous people on the earth. We represent more than five thousand distinct cultures and six thousand languages. According to the United Nations Environment Program, indigenous peoples account for a majority of the world's remaining cultural diversity.

But economic globalization presents a grave threat to our continuing existence, just as much as it threatens the biodiversity of our forests and fields. Globalization is really a continuation of the colonization we were subjected to for five hundred years. In the past, swords and guns were used to quell our resistance and take our lands. The colonizers also used government laws and institutions, schools, and churches to make our ancestors despise our cultures and deny our identities. Today the forces of globalization continue to regard our rights, our political systems, our economic systems, and our culture and knowledge systems as backward, unrealistic, and romantic. But the true explanation for the aggression toward us is that we occupy the last remaining places on earth where resources abound and biodiversity and cultural diversity thrive. Our continued existence stands in the way of their "progress."

The indigenous worldview respects Mother Earth and reveres the sacredness of life. We believe in reciprocity with nature and in sharing nature's gifts among peoples and generations. Ours is a collective identity with collective ownership of forests, waters, and lands. These are antithetical to individualism, private property, modernization, and global capitalism.

For indigenous peoples, keeping

CONTINUED

BOX I: CONTINUED

our territorial or ancestral lands is the most important thing; it determines our identity. This is where our ancestors walked and learned everything that they left for us. This is where we have forged our relations with nature and created social bonds with each other. This is why we resist cultural homogenization and globalization.

Pressures to take our lands and resources have led to conflagrations worldwide. Because of the trade-liberalizing rules of the WTO, corporations are rapidly invading our communities. The U'wa in Colombia are fighting oil development on their lands; the pygmies in Rwanda and Burundi are battling logging concessions; the Igorot, Mangyan, and Lumad in the Philippines are fighting mining on ancestral lands. The Penans of Sarawak, the Cree of Canada, and the Mapuche of Chile are all fighting World Bank dam projects. And these are only a few examples.

Yet our minerals, logs, waters, and biodiversity are not enough for them; now they also want our collective knowledge and our human genes. Corporations are all over native lands, prospecting for seeds we have developed or for our knowledge of the cosmetic and pharmaceutical properties of forest plants. They take this knowledge home and patent our plants. This "biopiracy" even extends inside our bodies to our gene structures: they are surreptitiously collecting blood samples from our people without telling us why. They call it the Human Genetic Diversity Project, but we call it the Vampire Project. Biopiracy is legitimized by the WTO's Trade-Related Intellectual Property Rights agreement, which confirms the rights of individuals and corporations to patent life forms in defiance of our traditional beliefs and practices.

Our ancestors told us that land is sacred, that animals and plants are our relatives, and that it is our duty to ensure that they are defended for the next generations. Our resistance to these efforts to homogenize us must be supported—our right to self-determination and our right to be allowed to remain different and diverse. Legal instruments that conflict with our indigenous values, cosmologies, lifestyles, and customary laws should not be imposed on us from any outside body. These are not decisions for the WTO or the IMF or the World Bank. We fight for the right to define ourselves and to maintain our continued existence as indigenous peoples on our own ancestral lands.

One important way in which we are fighting to protect ourselves is by urging member states of the U.N. Commission on Human Rights to adopt the U.N. Draft Declaration on the Rights of Indigenous Peoples. But even more important is to raise the awareness of indigenous peoples all over the world about our rights as distinct peoples. All forty-five articles of the declaration are equally critical, but I will highlight just a few of them:

- Indigenous peoples have the right to self-determination. By virtue of this right, we freely determine our political status and freely pursue our economic, social, and cultural development (Article 3).
- We have the collective and individual right to maintain and develop our distinct identities and characteristics, including our right to identify ourselves as indigenous and to be recognized as such (Article 8).
- We have the right to practice and revitalize our cultural traditions and customs. This includes the right to maintain, protect, and develop the past, present, and future manifestations of our cultures, such as archeological and historical sites, artifacts, designs, ceremonies, technologies, visual and performing arts, and literature, as well as the right to restitution of cultural, intellectual, religious, and spiritual property taken without our free and informed consent or in violation of our laws, traditions, and customs (Article 12).
- We have the right to maintain and develop our political, economic, and social systems, to be secure in the enjoyment of our own means of subsistence and development, and to engage freely in all our traditional and other economic activities. Those who have been deprived of their means of subsistence and development are entitled to just compensation (Article 21).
- We have the right to maintain and strengthen our distinctive spiritual and material relationship with the lands, territories, waters, coastal seas, and other resources that we have traditionally owned or otherwise occupied or used, and to uphold our responsibilities to future generations in this regard (Article 25).
- Indigenous peoples are entitled to the recognition of the full ownership, control, and protection of our cultural and intellectual property. We have the right to special measures to control, develop, and protect our sciences, technologies, and cultural manifestations, including human and other genetic resources, seeds, medicines, knowledge of properties of fauna and flora, oral traditions, literature, designs, and visual and performing arts (Article 29).
- We have the right to our traditional medicines and health practices, including the right to protect vital medicinal plants, animals, and minerals (Article 24).
- We have the right to own, develop, control, and use the lands and territories, including the total environment of the lands, air, waters, coastal seas, sea ice, flora and fauna, and other resources we have traditionally owned, occupied, and used. This includes the right to the full recognition of our laws, traditions, and customs, land tenure systems, and institutions for the development and management of our re-

CONTINUED

BOX I: CONTINUED

sources. States should provide protective measures to prevent any interference with, alienation of, or encroachment upon these rights (Article 26).

- Indigenous peoples have the right to determine and develop priorities and strategies for the use of our lands, territories, and other resources, including to require that states obtain our free and informed consent prior to the approval of any project affecting these, particularly in connection with the development, utilization, or exploitation of mineral, water, and other resources (Article 30).
- We have the right to the recognition, observance, and enforcement of existing treaties, agreements, and other constructive arrangements concluded with states or their successors, according to their original spirit and intent and to have states honor and respect these. Conflicts and disputes that cannot otherwise be settled should be submitted to competent international bodies agreed to by all parties concerned.

These and many other elements of the U.N. declaration are a good starting point in our efforts to protect our cultures and lands. This draft declaration was adopted by the U.N. Subcommission on Prevention of Discrimination and Protection of Minorities in 1994. Until now, however, the U.N. Commission on Human Rights has not adopted it because of opposition from governments. The most obstructive government is that of the United States. Even though it is not being adopted by the higher U.N. bodies, we are now using it as the international standard and framework for the protection of our rights. It is becoming an international customary law on indigenous peoples. The Philippine Indigenous Peoples Rights Act, which was passed in 1997, is almost a clone of this draft declaration.

We ask the support of our friends in the global justice movement to put pressure on the U.N. member states to adopt this draft declaration. We also ask you to help push for national legislation to protect our rights and to use this as the overall framework. Our greatest contribution to the struggle against globalization and homogenization will be for us to protect and develop further the diversities in our cultural and biological heritage as well as the diverse worldviews and economic and political systems that we have nurtured and sustained.

BOX J: CULTURAL DIVERSITY
The Right of Nations to Resist Cultural Homogenization

By Maude Barlow, Council of Canadians

I do not want my house to be walled in on all sides and my windows to be stuffed. I want the culture of all lands to be blown about my house as freely as possible. But I refuse to be blown off my feet by any.
— Mahatma Gandhi

In Latin America, Asia and the Pacific, Africa, and the industrialized world, the power of corporate-led globalization results in young people demanding Nike sneakers, Gap clothes, the latest CDs, Michael Jordan T-shirts, baseball caps, and other consumer goods popular in the world's most dominant economic power. Hollywood movies, the global music industry, television, and mass-market books spread a homogeneous culture. Around the world, North American corporate culture is destroying local traditions, knowledge, skills, artisans, and values. When combined with the destruction of the habitat of aboriginal peoples in many parts of the world, this assault on local cultures is having a profound impact.

Technology is also advancing one culture and one language. The United States has more computers than the rest of the world combined. English is used on 80 percent of Web sites, yet fewer than one in ten people worldwide speak the language. Everywhere, Internet access divides educated from illiterate, men from women, rich from poor, young from old, and urban from rural.

For many countries feeling the deadening and homogenizing impacts of economic globalization, cultural diversity and the right to protect it from the forces of globalization have become as important a fight as preserving biodiversity. Governments and people around the world are increasingly concerned about a global cultural homogenization dominated by the American and Western values and lifestyles carried through the massive U.S. entertainment-industrial complex.

Many societies, particularly indigenous peoples, view culture as their richest heritage without which they have no roots, history, or soul. Its value is other than monetary; to commodify it is to destroy it. There is a growing sentiment in many parts of the world that culture is not just another product like steel or computer parts. Through funding programs, content regulations, and other public policy mechanisms, many countries have encouraged their own artists and cultures and tried to maintain some space for their own intellectual creations. Still others are looking to these models in order to promote local cultural expression.

In contrast, the entertainment-industrial complex sees culture as a business—a very big business—that should

CONTINUED

of resilient, stable, energy-efficient, self-reliant local economies that serve the needs of people, communities, and nature. *Biological diversity* is essential to the complex, self-regulating, self-regenerating processes of the ecosystem from which all life and wealth ultimately flow.

Global corporations abhor diversity because for them it is a source of inefficiency, uncertainty, and most of all, a drain on profits. They seek to reduce costs and increase market control through cultural homogenization, economic specialization, and elimination of unprofitable species. These corporations profit from economies of scale, reduced management costs, and the

---

BOX J: CONTINUED

be fiercely advanced through international trade agreements like the World Trade Organization. This industry combines giant telecommunications companies, movie studios, television networks, cable companies, and the Internet working together in a complex web that includes publishing, films, broadcasting, video, television, cable and satellite systems, megatheater productions, music recording and distribution, and theme parks.

Mass-produced products of American popular culture are the biggest U.S. export, according to the United Nations' 1999 *Human Development Report*. A huge, well-organized coalition has formed that links the U.S. entertainment, media, and information-technology sectors together in a kind of common front to oppose cultural protections in other nations. Companies like Time-Warner and Disney have powerful friends on Capitol Hill and in the White House, and they work closely with the U.S. government, which, in turn, has taken a very aggressive stand in protecting their interests.

For many years, the U.S. State Department has used a variety of trade remedies to consistently strike down nation-state and local rules aimed at protecting local and national culture. In recent years, the battle has heated up as more and more countries adopt measures to support their own artists and cultural producers.

Speaking before a House committee in early 2000, then–U.S. trade representative Charlene Barshefsky was as determined as ever to use trade agreements to promote American corporate-entertainment interests. "We are developing proposals for a wide range of sectors where our companies have strong commercial interests, including audiovisual services and telecommunications. Our companies are poised to be among the primary beneficiaries from stronger commitments at the WTO," she said. This quote clearly expresses the dilemma in culture: How can you maintain the free flow of intellectual creations and art while promoting diversity?

The debate is not only about the right of states to maintain existing poliincreased dependence of individuals and communities on the products and services they find it profitable to sell. Corporate logos replace authentic local cultures as the primary source of personal identity. Communities that once created their means of livelihood through local enterprises, using local labor and resources to meet local needs, now must depend on the sale of their labor and resources for whatever the market will bear to distant corporations over which they have no control. Biological vitality is sapped by the loss of biological diversity, which creates an ever growing, unsustainable dependence on the input of expensive and often toxic fertilizers and pesticides. People

---

cies and programs. More fundamentally, it is about the right to develop new ones and to adapt or amend others as our society evolves. The measures adopted worldwide are generally not about protectionism because most of the markets remain open to the cultural products of others. It is about finding ways to provide choice so that in the deluge of cultural products available, citizens can choose to watch, listen to, or read a book, magazine, film, or sound recording that reflects their own local reality. Overall, the debate is exactly about cultural diversity.

As civil society movements form all over the world, so too is the cultural community developing international links to fight for its survival. In September 2000, a global network of NGOs concerned about cultural issues met in Santorini, Greece, and formed the International Network for Cultural Diversity. More than 160 organizations in more than thirty countries initiated this network and are committed to becoming a powerful voice in the coming decades. Many in the cultural community be-

lieve it is now time for a new international instrument to deal with this emerging issue. In this spirit, in March 2002 the International Network for Cultural Diversity put forward a draft "Convention on Cultural Diversity." The network believes that to succeed this instrument must have an equivalent status to trade agreements; it cannot be subservient. It would recognize the importance to all nations and peoples of maintaining cultural diversity, contain only those commitments that are appropriate to culture, and set out rules on what kinds of measures countries can use to promote diversity. Challenges and disputes under the new charter would need to be judged by cultural experts, not trade bureaucrats.

The instrument would have to be self-defining: what constitutes a matter of cultural significance to one nation may not be to another. These definitions must be allowed to change over time because we cannot know today what form cultural expression will take in the future.

NOTE: With special thanks to Garry Neil.

and communities pay the price for loss of the services that nature once provided for free; corporations and their distant absentee owners reap the profits.

Diversity may be bad for corporate profits, but it is essential for healthy, sustainable, vital communities.

6. HUMAN RIGHTS

In 1948, governments of the world came together to adopt the United Nations Universal Declaration of Human Rights, which established certain core rights such as "a standard of living adequate for . . . health and well-being . . . , including food, clothing, housing and medical care, and necessary social services, and the right to security in the event of unemployment." Building on this declaration, governments negotiated two covenants in subsequent decades, one on political and civil rights and the other on economic, social, and cultural rights.

Over much of the past half-century, people have struggled to press their governments to advance these rights, which remain as central to human development today as they were in the beginning. The goal of trade and investment should be to enhance the quality of life and respect core labor, social, and other rights.

Traditionally, most of the human rights debate in the United States and other rich nations has focused on civil and political rights. Although we agree that it is the duty of governments to ensure these rights, we believe they also need to guarantee economic, social, and cultural rights. This assertion has some important implications. For example, as chapter 3 explains, we believe that every person has the right to clean and safe water. That leads us to conclude that water should not be commodified or privatized for sale at market prices and that it is the obligation of government to guarantee safe water supplies. We recognize that many governments are corrupt and unaccountable, but this does not lead us to the conclusion that the private sector is a better guarantor of rights. Rather, it reinforces our resolve to press accountability on governments at every level.

Some suggest that this principle of human rights can conflict with the second principle: subsidiarity. Their reasoning is that some local societies follow practices that violate human rights, such as female genital mutilation and other violations of the right against gender discrimination. We believe that when these two principles clash, then universal human rights should trump local assertion of authority that violates those rights.

7. JOBS, LIVELIHOOD, EMPLOYMENT

The United Nations Universal Declaration of Human Rights affirms every person's "right to work, to free choice of employment, to just and favorable conditions of work, and to protection against unemployment." Most of the people in the world ensure the livelihood of their families through work outside the formal sector. In indigenous societies, the majority participate in activities that offer sustenance but are often not integrated in the national or global market. In rural areas, most make a living off the land, often engaged in subsistence agriculture or small-scale entrepreneurial activities that do not offer regular incomes. In urban areas, most people in poorer nations make ends meet without regular jobs or incomes. In each of these cases, corporate globalization is displacing greater numbers of them from dignified livelihoods than it is helping. The reversal of globalization policies that displace farmers from their land and fisherfolk from their coastal ecosystems is central to the goal of a sustainable world.

The U.N. Universal Declaration of Human Rights also affirms that everyone "has the right to form and to join trade unions." Over the past eight decades, the U.N. International Labor Organization has elaborated over one hundred conventions that further specify basic labor rights. Yet this same organization points out that today some 30 percent of workers are unemployed or seriously underemployed. Many of those who work do so under brutal, exploitative, and dangerous conditions. One of the most dynamic social movements confronting corporate-led globalization is organized labor, which has gathered over one hundred million workers around the world into trade unions. Millions more join together in associations of informal sector workers. These movements, rooted in a struggle for these core rights, are a cornerstone of the social movements that are creating economic alternatives.

Hence, sustainable societies must both protect the rights of workers in the formal sector and address the livelihood needs of the greater numbers of people who subsist in what has become known as the informal sector, as well as those who have no work or are seriously underemployed.

8. FOOD SECURITY AND SAFETY

Communities and nations are stable and secure when their people have enough food, particularly when these nations can provide their own food. People also need safe food, a commodity that is becoming increasingly scarce.

Some of the strongest citizen movements around the world today are fighting the juggernaut of globalized industrial agriculture. Monopoly control of food and seeds by a small number of corporations threatens millions of farmers and the food security and safety of tens of millions of people. Global rules of trade now favor the industrial agriculture model, rapidly destroying small-scale farmers who produce staple foods for local consumption. Globalized industrial agriculture is driving small farmers off the land and replacing them with pesticide and machine-intensive monocultures producing luxury items for export at great environmental and social cost. Meanwhile, biotechnology brings a host of new ecological and health risks.

New rules of trade must recognize that food production for local communities should be at the top of a hierarchy of values in agriculture. Local self-reliance in food production and the assurance of healthful, safe foods should be considered basic human rights. Shorter trade distances and reduced reliance on expensive inputs that need to be shipped over long distances are key to a new food system paradigm. (See also chapter 6.)

9. EQUITY

Under the current rules, economic globalization has widened the gap between rich and poor countries, between the rich and poor in most countries, and between women and men. The social dislocations and tensions that result have become among the greatest threats to peace and security the world over. Greater equity both among nations and inside them would reinforce both democracy and sustainable communities.

Reducing the growing gap between rich and poor nations requires first the cancellation of the illegitimate debts of poor countries. It also requires the replacement of the current institutions of global governance with new ones that include global fairness among their operating principles.

As for inequities within nations, a key flaw of the current dominant system is that markets respond to the wants of those with money and disregard even the most basic needs of those who do not have the means to pay. Extreme inequality in income and ownership distorts the allocation of economic resources, excludes all but the very rich from meaningful democratic participation, undermines institutional legitimacy, and creates social instability.

Economic globalization disproportionately hurts women too. Women make up the majority of the small-scale food producers who still provide most of the planet's nutritional needs. Hence, they suffer the most from a globalized agricultural system. Likewise, most of the workers on the global assembly lines of Nike, Dell, and other global corporations are women, so they suffer most from the sweatshop conditions in many of these workplaces. Whether farm or factory workers, women are the primary household workers and caregivers, and the majority of this work is unpaid. And just as the lowest rungs of the global assembly lines are made up primarily of women, corporate CEOs and global bureaucrats are overwhelmingly male, reinforcing the unequal-gender pay scale.

The claim of economic globalization advocates that those who accumulate great wealth take nothing away from those less fortunate is at best disingenuous. When those who have the money to enjoy meat-rich diets cause the market to redirect available supplies of grain away from the tables of people who cannot pay in order to feed livestock to provide meat to those who can, they contribute to the dynamics of hunger. When banks foreclose mortgages on family farms and put them up for sale to corporations to grow crops for export, they are depriving the displaced families of their means of livelihood and often condemning them to a marginal, dependent existence as landless laborers or sweatshop workers producing products for export that they cannot afford themselves. When the rich buy opulent second, third, and fourth homes, they drive up the price of land and housing and force the less fortunate onto the street. Those who profit from clear-cutting hillsides contribute to the floods that sweep away the homes and crops of those living below. Those with the wealth to engage in profligate energy consumption contribute to the storms that kill and displace hundreds of thousands of people living on coastal lowlands in Bangladesh and elsewhere. The idea that the good fortune of the rich has no consequences for the plight of the poor may comfort the consciences of the rich, but it is not true.

In an increasingly crowded world with finite environmental limits, the human species confronts an increasingly painful trade-off between expanding the profligate material consumption of the wealthy and meeting the basic needs of everyone.

Because equity is essential to social health, healthy societies set a floor on the bottom and a cap on the top, while striving to maintain true equality of opportunity and balance between incentive and equity. A century ago, the celebrated financier J. P. Morgan, himself no paragon of virtue, asserted that a company's top executive should not make more than twenty times the income of the lowest-paid worker. As we have mentioned elsewhere, in the year 2000 in the United States, the average CEO made 458 times the income of the average worker. There are a plethora of policy options to improve the incomes of both industrial and rural workers. And there are sensible proposals to remove incentives that encourage excessive executive pay.

Social justice and greater equality—among nations, within nations, between ethnic groups, between classes, and between women and men—are cornerstones of sustainable societies.

10. THE PRECAUTIONARY PRINCIPLE

All activity should abide by the precautionary principle. That is, when a practice or product raises potentially significant threats of harm to human health or the environment, precautionary action should be taken to restrict or ban it, even if there is scientific uncertainty about whether or how it is actually causing that harm. Because it can take years for scientific proof of harm to be established—during which time undesirable or irreversible effects may continue to be inflicted—the proponents of a practice or product should bear the burden of proving that it is safe. Although this proposal is considered controversial by some, it is little more than common sense. Germany and Sweden have been the first countries to make it a matter of law. Others are poised to follow.

Currently, the opposite is frequently true. Under WTO rules, regulatory systems must be based on the policy of risk assessment, which requires governments to present categorical proof of harm of new technologies and techniques in order to prevent their release or usage. Without such proof, the WTO can brand preventive measures as illegal barriers to trade and order them to be overturned. (This was the case with the European Union's ban on the sale and import of beef from cattle treated with artificial growth hormones, which are suspected of increasing the risk of certain cancers.)

Such a policy is antithetical to governments' duty to protect their citizens. Had this policy been in place in the 1950s, the U.S. Food & Drug Administration would not have been able to ban the use of the drug thalidomide, which caused severe deformities among thousands of babies born in countries (including Europe) where it had been approved and whose culpability was not fully established until the 1980s.

Adoption of the precautionary principle is thus essential if citizens, through their democratically elected representatives, are to have the right to decide what risks they or the natural environment should be exposed to.

Applying the Principles to Globalization

These ten principles seem to be mirror opposites of the principles that drive the institutions of the corporate global economy. The imperatives of this powerful system create a self-reinforcing drive toward the privatization and monopolization of common heritage resources; the centralization of power and authority for the few who are shielded from legal accountability for the impact of their decisions on the well-being of people and planet; a life-and-death competition that divides the world into big winners and even bigger losers; the unaccountable externalization of costs; the destruction of cultural, biological, and economic diversity; and the disregard of deadly risks to human and environmental health. It is time to reclaim the power taken by the institutions of corporate globalization and replace them with institutions and rules that better serve the needs of people and planet.

We offer the ten organizing principles as a basis for determining which rules, incentives, policies, and institutions can support sustainable societies. Because much of the globalization debate has centered on international trade and investment, it is appropriate to examine how these principles for sustainable societies translate into principles for international trade and investment. The following paragraphs, adapted from a statement of the Interfaith Working Group on Trade and Investment, convened by a number of U.S. faith-based organizations, offers some ideas on this subject.

- *International trade and investment systems should respect the legitimate role of democratic governments at all levels.* In collaboration with civil society, governments should be allowed to set policies on the development and welfare of their people. This means respecting the right of every community and nation to democratic self-determination, including the right to determine the terms—in cooperation with other communities and nations—under which they wish to enter into trade with others or invite others to invest in their economies. Because such decisions have far-reaching consequences for the well-being of every member of society, they should be worked out through transparent democratic processes involving the participation of all levels of government and civil society. Participation of the most vulnerable stakeholders is especially important.
- *International trade and investment systems should safeguard the global commons and respect and promote human rights, the rights of workers, women, indigenous peoples, and children.* The rights of local communities to protect and use their natural resources to secure the needs of their people in a sustainable manner need to be respected. Societies need rules to protect the public interest. As in any area of human activity, international trade and investment are properly regulated to that end—preferably by the democratically chosen governments of the nations and communities involved. Any international agreement on trade and investment should properly support such local and national regulation.
- *Finally, all international agreements should support the goal of creating sustainable societies.* This will require changes in past practice that will be addressed more fully in subsequent chapters.

Surely, it is time for a new approach.

CHAPTER THREE

The Commons
What Should Be Off-Limits to Globalization?

AS RECENTLY AS TWO DECADES AGO, large parts of the world were not part of economic globalization. The majority of people in the world still lived off the land, many with little dependence on outside markets. In many rural areas, seeds were exchanged as the collective property of the community, not the private property of Monsanto or Cargill. Many of the three hundred million indigenous people in the world lived in complete isolation from global trade activity. Most municipal water systems were under local government or community control. Much of the economic activity in the Soviet Union, Eastern Europe, and China was not linked to global markets. Most developing countries restricted foreign investment in their banking, insurance, and other critical economic sectors. Most stock markets were national, closed to global investors. Even though global corporations clamored to enter each of these domains, national and local governments and communities maintained strong barriers.

All of that has changed. Under two decades of market fundamentalism, introduced by Ronald Reagan, Margaret Thatcher, Helmut Kohl, and their counterparts elsewhere, the boundaries came crashing down. Some of this was seen in dramatic fashion on CNN in living rooms around the world, such as the destruction of the Berlin Wall. Some happened in the face of remarkable citizen opposition, such as the passage of NAFTA in 1993 and the WTO in 1994. Other battles over the global spread of corporate control occurred on the local stage, such as the determined fight by Bolivian workers and peasants to keep the municipal water system in Cochabamba out of the hands of Bechtel and the struggles of Indian peasants against the Cargill and Monsanto assertions of property rights over their seeds. During these two decades, global corporations—with the strong support of many national governments—forcefully asserted their right to any market anywhere. And today their reach has extended into virtually every domain of even remote rural communities around the world.

One of the most critical points of unity among the authors of this document is that this encroachment of corporate globalization into every aspect of life and the environment must stop. We seek to shift the framework of the overall debate on globalization in this sense: we believe that many aspects of social and economic life around the world should be off-limits to the processes of economic globalization. In this chapter, we offer the beginnings of a framework for choosing which arenas should be off-limits to which aspects of economic globalization.

On one level, there is already agreement across the spectrum of the globalization debate that certain goods and services should be kept out of trade. For example, governments around the world have created a global convention to ban trade in hazardous wastes. Likewise, there is a global convention against the trafficking of endangered species. And there is growing global action against the trafficking across borders of women sold into sexual bondage.

Now, the International Forum on Globalization would like to expand the debate beyond the "pernicious" goods mentioned above to include the rights of peoples and obligations of nations concerning what has traditionally been called *the commons*.

In this chapter, we offer an overview of the many notions of the commons around the world and spell out the current threats of economic globalization to commons such as freshwater, the genetic commons, communal lands, and others. We then introduce the concept of the modern commons—that is, the role of governments in carrying out a sacred public trust to perform certain key services that were once the province of communities and families but have been captured by and subsumed into the nation-state. We argue that selling off these services to global corporations—which operate on an entirely different set of priorities than the public interest—is a grave violation of these modern commons, many of which should never be commodified. We argue that they are also obligations of governments as trustees of the common rights and services of people. Finally, we offer a few ideas on how the commons might be protected from the worst aspects of economic globalization.

We offer these suggestions in the spirit of opening up a complex discussion. We do not pretend to present the final answers.

Understanding the Commons

Much of the thrust of economic globalization over these decades has been driven by global corporations pushing to develop and market every type of natural resource. In a world where natural resources were already seriously overexploited, corporations have attempted to convert every remaining nook and cranny of the natural world and human experience into commodified form.

Now, areas of life traditionally considered out of bounds are being considered for monetized activity, private ownership, or global trade. These are aspects of life that had been accepted since time immemorial as collective property, or the common heritage of all peoples and communities, existing for everyone to share as they have for millennia. These are what have been known as the commons.

Obvious among them are the air we breath, the freshwater we drink, the oceans and the diverse wildlife and plant biodiversity of the world, the genes all creatures pass to following generations, the stores of human knowledge and wisdom, the informal support systems of the community, the seeds that communities use for replanting, the public square, shared languages and culture, and among indigenous peoples, communal lands that have been worked cooperatively for thousands of years.

Some commons are gifts from the bounty of nature and are crucial to the survival of people and the earth. Most cultures have innumerable rituals to celebrate these gifts and rules or taboos against harming them. Other commons are new, including, for example, the broadcast spectrum or the Internet. Still others are ancient, such as the common grazing meadows of Africa, Europe, and Asia, folklore, and cultural artifacts.

Some commons may be thought of as global, such as the atmosphere, the oceans, outer space, and because they have no territorial claimants, Antarctica and the moon. Others may be thought of as community commons: public spaces, common lands, forests, the gene pool, local innovative knowledge with respect to medicinal plants, and seeds that communities have developed over centuries.

Author Jonathan Rowe of California's Tomales Bay Institute points out that the key characteristic of all aspects of the commons is that they belong to everyone. No one has traditionally had exclusive rights to them. We have inherited them jointly; they are our common heritage. They "are more basic to our lives than the state or the market," says Rowe. He goes on to say, "One cannot imagine a life without air fit to breathe, oceans rich with life, free clean water, a vibrant biodiversity. These are things we have always taken for granted. The commons have the quality of always having been there, one generation after another, available forever to all."

Later in this chapter, we will advocate for yet another category—the "modern commons" of public services like health, water purification and distribution, education, information, each of which was once achieved informally within small local and indigenous communities that have since been absorbed by the state and are also now on tap for privatization.

The modern nation-state has also taken onto itself the collective security of its citizens, which in a less technologically oriented and mobile world was once the province of communities. In that context, we need to discuss the varieties of security protection that a modern state is obliged to offer in addition to its obvious military roles. Since adopting the Universal Declaration of Human Rights in 1948, the United Nations has helped governments define basic human rights. Governments are obligated to protect human rights, as well as food security, as fundamental to life. Protection of cultural diversity is also a basic duty and right. Nothing in the global trading system should ever be permitted to reduce these fundamental priorities. (At present, many elements of the WTO and other trade agreements work directly against countries that try to protect these fundamental rights, which we now propose as part of the modern commons.)

Precise categorization of each type of commons is difficult to achieve because many cross several categories—for example, river water (which may pass through several regions and countries), biodiversity (which may be local or national), the broadcast spectrum (which may be local, national, or international), and the genetic structures of life. Similarly, protections against trade that destroys the commons—toxins, armaments, and so on— must be national and international.

Nonetheless, the purpose of this discussion is to lay on the table one central principle:

Any global trading system needs to recognize and yield to the primary notion that not every aspect of experience should be subject to its centralized rules, and many aspects should never be included in global trade or investment of any kind or in the rules that govern trade and investment.

Such complex questions are usually omitted from discussions about global trading systems, which usually keep their focus on new resources, expansion, and profit. But these questions must be addressed if any kind of social or environmental sustainability is to be obtained. How can communal spaces be effectively protected? Do any effective instruments now exist? What new ones can be proposed? How do we define the areas of the commons, common heritage, or government services that should *never* be subject to trade— or at least never be subject to the authority of global agreements that impinge on local or national sovereignty? What are the obligations of nation-states in the modern world? What goods are too dangerous—toxins, weapons, and drugs, for example—to be allowed into the global trade system at all? Should we establish taboos for certain kinds of trade?

Current Threats to the Commons

The conversion of the commons into commodified, privatized, "enclosed" form has been under way for centuries. (See the next section, "The Tradition of the Commons," for more on the history of this subject.) In the current context, the main engines of this conversion are the global corporations and the global bureaucracies that increasingly have served these corporations. With the help of the new global trade and finance bureaucracies, corporations are finding opportunities in some virgin territory that most humans never thought could possibly be fodder for corporate enterprise. Here are a few examples.

THREATS TO THE FRESHWATER COMMONS

Unthinkable as it may seem, freshwater—a common heritage basic to the survival of all human beings—is being opened up to private ownership, commodification, export, and trade. It's as if water were an ordinary commodity, like new computer parts or car tires, rather than a shared, irreplaceable, and limited resource needed by all creatures of the earth.

In many parts of the world, the rights to freshwater in rivers, streams, and lakes are being sold to giant transnational corporations like Bechtel, Vivendi, and others. (Before its collapse, Enron was also a main player in water deals.) These firms have started charging users for every drink of water or liter of irrigation. For people who cannot pay the fees—and many cannot—they, their families, and their fields go thirsty.

Private corporations around the world have identified freshwater as the last great untapped natural resource to be exploited for profit. They are quickly taking control of water and water services to kick-start trade in what authors Maude Barlow and Tony Clarke have labeled *blue gold.* Indeed, water is becoming just as important as a prior era's black gold—oil.

Companies have been able to proceed aggressively because water has been defined as a tradable commodity by both NAFTA and the WTO. Once the tap is turned on—that is, once any deals are made by *any* state or municipality in a country to privatize water or water services—the tap cannot be turned back off without violating corporate rights. The WTO contains specific provisions prohibiting the use of export controls to prevent the export of water, and NAFTA contains a clause (chapter 11 of NAFTA) that gives companies the right to sue governments for lost *future* profits. This applies, for example, in cases where governments try to stop water export. Water services are also among those slated to be labeled as a commodity in the new General Agreement on Trade in Services (GATS), under a new category called "Environmental Services." (For more on this, see the later section "Threats to the Modern Commons.")

Once water is privatized, commodified, and put on the open market, it is not available to everyone who needs it but only to those who pay. Right now, contrary to popular understanding, most of the world's freshwater is used by corporate industrial agriculture and in manufacturing, such as in the computer industry for manufacture of computer chips. Relatively little is left for drinking or small-scale farming.

Already, the privatization of water has been the subject of enormous angry protests in many countries, notably Bolivia, South Africa, Canada, and elsewhere. In Cochabamba, Bolivia, for example, hundreds of thousands of people rose up against the fees being charged by Bechtel Corporation after it gained control of the municipality's water distribution system and immediately raised prices. On the brink of a revolution, the Bolivian government finally cancelled its agreement with Bechtel, which responded by suing the government under investment rules of a Bolivia-Netherlands trade agreement that mirror the NAFTA rules. As we go to press, the case is still pending.

THREATS TO THE GENETIC COMMONS

Another commons that few people ever thought could be subject to privatization and development is the genetic commons—the vast building blocks of all life on earth. Yet this too is now subject to reinvention through genetic engineering and transformed into patentable commodities.

The late David Brower of Earth Island Institute once called the genetic commons "the last untapped wilderness on earth," but that is no longer true. Like our great forests, the genetic commons are on the verge of rampant commercial intervention. In some areas, like agriculture, the process is well under way. Third World agriculture activists call it *biopiracy*. (See Box K.)

According to Andrew Kimbrell of the International Center for Technology Assessment, "Corporations are now scouring the globe seeking valuable plant, animal, and human genes that they can claim as their own private property, as if they invented them. Thousands of gene patents have already been given to corporations, which are now able to patent whole life forms and own them."

Most of this activity falls within the life science industries. Corporations like Monsanto, Novartis, DuPont, Pioneer, and others have benefited enormously from the WTO's TRIPs agreement, which confirms their ability to patent plant and seed varieties according to their genetic makeup. Even though these varieties were developed over centuries by indigenous farming communities that shared them with one another freely in a process that is at the core of these cultures, now fees must be paid to use them.

Global corporations insist that this valuable genetic material should not be locked up by small communities but that the whole world should have access to it. Indeed, corporations use the language of the global commons until such time as they confirm their monopoly patents on the material. At that point, all arguments in defense of the commons are abandoned. Instead, the corporations then argue that *they* should be permitted to lock up these genetic materials through patents in order to have a chance of recouping their research investment—for the benefit of all humanity.

Pharmaceutical corporations are especially eager for access and the rights to patent genetic materials. Their representatives travel the globe, exploring traditional native remedies in jungles and fields. They also extract blood and scrape "buccal mucosa" from the skin of native peoples wherever they can, hoping to find genes that contain natural resistance to certain maladies. Usually they accomplish this without disclosing why they are doing it or how much profit they stand to make from their findings and their patents. Among indigenous peoples, the right of "free and prior informed consent" has now become a major international demand before governments can bring in development projects and before companies are permitted to enter.

The cynicism of such practices became especially clear when global pharmaceutical corporations refused to set aside the rules of the WTO's TRIPs agreement in South Africa to permit low-cost, locally developed AIDS drugs to be substituted for the expensive patented varieties they controlled. Only after intense global protest did the patent holders agree to lower prices for AIDS victims there. But the TRIPs rules remain in force for all other instances.

The authors of this document believe that seeds, medicines, and other genetic materials that have been developed in communities for centuries or millennia should always be subject to community control. Any agreement with outsiders to use these materials must be on the basis of fair and equal negotiations on a case-by-case basis, after full discussion of all the relevant facts.

THREATS TO COMMUNAL LANDS

In hundreds of cultures around the world, the notion of private, individual land ownership is anathema. Communal land ownership—or no land ownership—is traditional practice and belief among indigenous and farming communities on every continent. This worldview is fundamental to these millions of people, their cultures, their agriculture, and their economic, political, and spiritual practices. In peasant farming communities of South

BOX K: FROM COMMONS
TO CORPORATE PATENTS ON LIFE

By Vandana Shiva, Research Foundation for Science, Technology, and Ecology

During the Uruguay Round negotiations of the GATT, the United States succeeded in forcing its own patent system onto the world through the WTO. U.S. corporations had a major role, having drafted and lobbied on behalf of the Trade-Related Intellectual Property Rights agreement (TRIPs). As a Monsanto spokesman said about the lobbying effort, "The industries and traders of world commerce have played simultaneously the role of patients, diagnosticians, and prescribing physicians."

TRIPs not only made U.S.-style IPR laws global, but also removed critical ethical and moral boundaries by including life forms and biodiversity into patentable subject matter. Living organisms and life forms that are self-creating were thus redefined as if they were machines and artifacts made and invented by the patentee, despite the fact that the corporations made only minor modifications in their labs—just enough to be redefined as "inventions." Intellectual property rights laws and patents then give the patent holder a monopolistic right to prevent others from making, using, or selling these "inventions" even if the seeds were originally developed by local farmers. Seed saving by farmers had thus been redefined from a sacred duty to a criminal offence: stealing corporate "property." And all practices of sui generis ownership of seeds and other forms of local biodiversity were directly undermined. Article 27.3(b) of the TRIPs agreement, which relates to patents on living resources, was basically established by the life sciences companies to confirm themselves as "lords of life."

Life science corporations now claim patents on genes, plants, animals, and seeds. Ciba Geigy and Sandoz have combined to form Novartis; Hoechst has joined with Rhone Poulenc to form Aventis; Zeneca has merged with Astia; DuPont has bought up Pioneer HiBred; and Monsanto now owns Cargill seeds, DeKalb, Calgene, Agracetus, Delta and Pine Land, Holden, and Asgrow. Eighty percent of all genetically engineered seeds planted are Monsanto's intellectual property. Monsanto also owns broad species patents on cotton, mustard, and soybeans—crops that were not invented or created by Monsanto but that have evolved over centuries of innovation by farmers of India and East Asia working in close partnership with the biodiversity of nature.

This process of patenting life forms is truly perverse, in many ways:

Ethical Perversion   Current IPR laws permit the claim that seeds, plants, sheep, cows, or human cell lines can be classified as "products of the mind" created by Monsanto, Novartis, Ian Wilmut, or PPL. This ignores that living organisms have their intrinsic self-

CONTINUED

America and Asia and in indigenous communities everywhere, the notion that an individual or corporation could legally gather under its own authority large fruitful tracts of land—thus depriving the people who shared it for millennia—is outrageous beyond all understanding.

Native American activist Winona La Duke has described the land own-

---

BOX K: CONTINUED

organization; they make themselves, and hence cannot logically be reduced to the status of inventions and creations of patent holders. They cannot be owned as private property because they are our ecological kin, not just genetic mines.

Criminalization of Saving and Sharing Seeds
Recognizing corporations as owners of seed through intellectual property rights converts farmers into thieves when they save seeds or share with neighbors. Monsanto actually hires detectives to chase farmers who might be engaging in such theft and brings them to court.

Encouragement of Biopiracy Biopiracy is the term the South now uses for the theft of biodiversity and indigenous knowledge through these patents. It deprives the South in three ways:

- It creates a false claim to novelty and invention, even when the knowledge has actually evolved since ancient times. Biopiracy is intellectual theft, robbing Third World people of their creativity and their intellectual resources.
- It diverts scarce biological resources to monopoly control of corporations, depriving local communities

and indigenous practitioners. Biopiracy is resource theft from the poorest two-thirds of humanity who depend on biodiversity for their livelihoods and basic needs.

- It creates market monopolies, excluding the *original* innovators from their rightful share of local, national, and international markets. Instead of preventing this organized economic theft, WTO rules under TRIPs protect the powerful and punish the victims. In a dispute initiated by the United States against India, the WTO forced India to change its patent laws and grant exclusive marketing rights to foreign corporations on the basis of foreign patents. Since many of these patents are based on biopiracy, the WTO is in fact promoting piracy through patents.

Over time, the consequences of TRIPs for the South's biodiversity and the Southern people's rights to their diversity will be severe. No one will be able to produce or reproduce patented agricultural, medicinal, or animal products freely; the livelihoods of small producers will be eroded and the poor will be prevented from using their own resources and knowledge to meet basic ership issue among indigenous peoples by pointing out that in her own Ojibway culture, the term *nishnabe akin* means "the land to which the people belong." It is a notion that is the exact opposite of Western ideas about land ownership. It is also at the heart of many teachings about humans and land being in *relationship* with each other, with reciprocal obligations.

---

needs of health and nutrition. Royalties for the use of these patented items will have to be paid to the patentees and unauthorized production will be penalized, thus further increasing the debt burden.

Indian farmers, traditional practitioners, and traders will lose their market share in local, national, and global markets. For example, the U.S. government recently granted a patent for the antidiabetic properties of *karela, jamun,* and *brinjal* to two nonresident Indians, Onkar S. Tomer and Kripanath Borah, and their colleague Peter Gloniski. The use of these substances for control of diabetes has been everyday knowledge and practice in India for ages. Their medical use was documented long ago in authoritative treatises like "The Wealth of India," "The Compendium of Indian Medicinal Plants," and "The Treatise on Indian Medicinal Plants."

If there were only one or two cases of such false claims to corporate invention on the basis of biopiracy, they could be called an error. However, biopiracy is an epidemic. Plant species like *neem, haldi, pepper, harar, bahera, amla, mustard, basmati, ginger, castor, jaramla, amaltas,* and *new karela* and *jamun* have now all been patented. The problem is deep and systemic; it calls for a systemic change, not case-by-case challenges.

Some have suggested that biopiracy happens because Indian knowledge is not documented. That is far from true. Indigenous knowledge in India has been systematically documented, and this in fact has made piracy easier. Even the folk knowledge, spread orally in local communities, deserves to be recognized as collective, cumulative innovation. The ignorance of such knowledge in the United States should not be allowed to convert corporate biopiracy into invention.

The potential costs of biopiracy to the Third World poor are very high because two-thirds of the people in the South depend on free access to biodiversity for their livelihoods and needs. In India, 70 percent of seeds are saved or shared farmers' seed; 70 percent of healing is based on indigenous medicine using local plants. When corporations steal and control those genetic resources through patents, the poor are directly deprived.

SOURCE: Vandana Shiva, "War Against Nature and the People of the South." In Sarah Anderson, ed., *Views from the South: The Effects of Globalization and the WTO on Third World Countries.* San Francisco: International Forum on Globalization, 2000.

In contrast, the new trade agreements and policies of international banks and corporations are designed to delegitimize the authority of any such reciprocal arrangements and to solidify private ownership so that land can be more easily bought and exploited. For example, one of the United States' specific demands in NAFTA negotiations with Mexico was that Mexico break up the traditional *ejidos* of the Mayan corn farmers, the system of communal land ownership that began with the successful Zapatista revolution of the early 1900s.

The history of the "enclosure" of the commons is largely devoted to the privatization of communal lands throughout the planet. In most places, the process is so far along that it is rarely publicly argued. However, this has begun to change as mass movements like Brazil's landless peasant movement (Movement of Landless Rural Workers) and other such movements around the world have demanded dramatic land reforms and redistribution under the principle that land, like water, is basic for sustenance.

APPROPRIATION OF THE GLOBAL COMMONS FOR WASTE SINKS

Ownership and privatization are not the only threats to the commons. There is also the effective appropriation of particular global commons as free dumping grounds and waste sinks for the activity of global corporations.

The atmosphere, oceans, and even outer space have become dangerously polluted, freely appropriated by oil, energy, shipping, and toxic industries as convenient sites to dump effluents and wastes. In the case of automobiles, ships, and the fossil fuel industry, it is an intrinsic result of the technologies that effluents rise to the atmosphere.

When similar pollution takes place in a local commons or inside national borders—say, local smokestack emissions or runoff into rivers—government agencies exist specifically to try to do something about it. This is not to say these agencies do a good job of regulating such activity—often they do not—but at least they offer an authority to address the matter and a place where citizens may focus their complaints.

When it comes to the global commons, however, few such agencies exist. There have been some efforts over the last half-century to apply some pollution regulations. The Kyoto Protocol on Global Warming, the Montreal Protocol on Substances That Deplete the Ozone Layer, the United Nations

Convention on the Law of the Sea, the Stockholm Convention on Persistent Organic Pollutants agreement, among other multilateral environment agreements (MEAs), are efforts to control impacts on global commons. But all have suffered from tremendous political resistance, weak regulatory regimes, and poor enforcement ability. Still, MEAs remain one hope for rational international recognition, on a case-by-case basis, of the collective rights to maintain the commons in a condition that serves all people and the planet's other species.

An important problem, however, is that when such agreements do begin to make progress in limiting corporate activity, the World Trade Organization can threaten to negate them by asserting its own superior authority on behalf of the primacy of global trade activity. For example, at the November 2001 WTO ministerial meeting in Doha, Qatar, the WTO made explicit its intentions to codify its superiority to MEAs, potentially wiping out generations of effort.

Other solutions to the problem have also been proposed. They include a variety of trust agreements where certain commons would be held as the explicit property of all people in trust for the future. Any encroachments would have to go through very complex permission procedures, thus at least slowing and making visible the problems before they occur.

~

Sadly, there are hundreds of examples of threats to the commons of the kind we have given here. All reflect increased global pressure on remaining pristine areas. Fortunately, however, there is also increased popular resistance to these encroachments. New methods and instruments must be found or created to prevent continued destruction.

The Tradition of the Commons

In most parts of the world, the tradition of the commons is ages old, though it varies from place to place and culture to culture. These are a few examples.

EUROPE

In Europe, the concept of the commons dates back at least fifteen hundred years. It referred to commonly shared areas of land and resources enjoyed by all members of village communities, including pasture for the grazing of animals, water from streams and lakes, and all the products of field and forest that people used to sustain their lives. The notion that any of these could be enclosed or turned into the private property of individuals or institutions like corporations was, at first, unthinkable.

The commons deteriorated over time in feudal Europe. There were struggles over definitions of the commons, and large parts of them were appropriated through military force by feudal lords and kings. Still, vast areas remained available for village use as traditional common areas.

As trade developed between regions, and especially with the rise of a large European-wide market for wool, lords and merchants increasingly sought to ensure and expand their own supply by privatizing more and more of the common areas, most importantly land. As they succeeded in enclosing ever larger areas, peasant communities began to lose access to resources they had previously taken for granted. Self-sustainability became more difficult. Rather than remaining as subsistence farmers who also traded in local markets, peasants increasingly became "cottagers"—small artisanal producers—or sought day-labor jobs with the large landowners on lands they had formerly shared. With the coming of the Industrial Revolution, cottage industries declined, and people were entirely removed from their land and sources of sustenance. They became factory workers with no connection to the land. The peasants thus evolved into the proletariat.

Some mainstream economists have justified and praised this conversion of the commons to private property as a way of establishing clear ownership and therefore the ability to protect resources from exploitation. But this justification for what was essentially robbery of shared common resources ignores two important facts. First, the people whose lives depended on the commons were almost always excellent caretakers of it and remained so over many centuries. In fact, it was basic to the survival and success of the commons that the entire community shared its values as well as its sustaining virtues and helped protect and preserve it. Second, the people who enclosed the commons, appropriating it for private use, were nearly always outsiders, absentee owners with little personal dedication to nurturing, conserving, or taking care of these resources for the future. The reason they sought private ownership was to exploit the resources as fast as possible.

They did not try to own it in order to save it, the assertion of mainstream economists notwithstanding. Rather, they usually pillaged and polluted it.

With the advent of corporate ownership and rights of private property, ownership was made still more abstract or removed from resources, which were increasingly understood only in quantifiable, objective terms. Forests, for example, were no longer appreciated for their community sustainability, the biodiversity they fostered, or their spiritual contexts. Instead, they became "board-feet," ripe for exploitation. That is certainly the situation we face today, in its most amplified form.

INDIGENOUS COMMUNITIES

In other parts of the world, terms like *commons* were not well-known, but the concepts of shared community use and protection of common resources were basic, endemic, understood and respected by entire societies.

Among indigenous peoples around the world, virtually all political, social, and spiritual values have traditionally been so deeply intertwined with the values and teachings of the natural world that these societies say they are inseparable. It is not really a question of a community commons, as understood by the Europeans. It is more that all creatures—human as well as plant and animal—are directly related, equal, and with equal rights to exist in a fulfilling manner. All economic, political, and spiritual teachings are rooted in that primary relationship.

It is little wonder, therefore, that invading societies—at least those that did not actually slaughter the native populations—made enormous efforts to undermine and destroy their commitment to their traditional relationships to land and nature. That was the only way they could succeed in getting their hands on the resources they desired. (See also box I, page 65.)

Native peoples were pushed to separate from their lands in hundreds of different ways. Primary among these efforts was the aggressive attempt to undermine traditional religious values and cosmologies as well as traditional native stories and teachings about the need to live in harmony with, and as part of, nature. The actions of missionaries throughout the Americas, the Pacific Islands, and Africa are well-known in this context. They actively helped shift the traditional value system toward a new and more hierarchical view of humans and nature and toward the individualistic notion of private property. In the United States, Australia, and elsewhere, "reeducation" also played an important role—that is, young people were forcibly removed from their traditional communities and placed into boarding schools that did not allow native languages or teachings. The result was a kind of self-loathing that undermined native cultures and their traditional collective economic values.

Equally important were legal maneuvers, such as requiring adjudicatory land title. Since native societies did not traditionally conceive of themselves as "owners" of land but as part of it as a community, "title" and "ownership" of land were an absurdity, but one which they were required to address. The histories of the relationships between invading and native societies are replete with stories of how legalistic maneuvering succeeded in separating Indians from millions of acres of land they formerly enjoyed in a collective manner. These acts of removal and separation continue to this day, notably in the United States.

One particularly appalling recent example is the U.S. Congress's creation of the Alaska Native Claims Settlement Act (ANCSA), purported to be a guarantor of native land rights in Alaska, where these rights had never been abrogated. In fact, ANCSA was the final step in extinguishing the native relationship and rights to enjoy the lands in the traditional manner. Rather than native Alaskans being granted title, or simply granted recognition of "aboriginal rights of ownership" as requested, the Alaskan lands were divided and made into native corporations, managed by native boards of directors, who were given ownership of the lands. But in order to survive, these corporations needed to cut down their forests or exploit their minerals just as any corporation would. These corporate acts, albeit carried out by natives, were contrary to their prior indigenous values. So for the larger society, the desired outcome was achieved: the communal relationship to nature was removed and replaced by an exploitative one, thus providing new fodder for global corporations.

The global invasion of communally held native lands—which has happened on every continent and continues today—has had terrible outcomes, from destruction of the traditional reciprocal relationship between humans and nature to major social breakdowns.

The conflict of values endemic to these pressures over ownership of common lands and resources was very well described in the book *A Basic*

Call to Consciousness, published in 1977 by the Iroquois Nation, in a submission to the United Nations Conference on Indigenous Peoples. Here are some short excerpts:

> The majority of the world does not find its roots in Western culture or tradition. The majority of the world finds its roots in the natural world, and it is the natural world, and the tradition of the natural world, which must prevail.
>
> . . .
>
> The original instructions direct that we are to express a great respect, an affection, and gratitude toward all the spirits which create and support life. When people cease to respect and express gratitude for these many things, then all life will be destroyed.
>
> . . .
>
> To this day the territories we still hold are filled with trees, animals, and the other gifts from the Creation. In these places we still receive our nourishment from our Mother Earth. Many thousands of years ago, all the people of the world believed in the same way of life, that of harmony with the universe. [But] the way of life known as Western Civilization is on a death path on which their own culture has no viable answers.
>
> . . .
>
> The Indo-European people who have colonized our lands have shown very little respect for the things that create and support life. We believe that these people ceased their respect for the world a long time ago. The air is foul, the waters poisoned, the trees dying, the animals disappearing. Even the systems of weather are changing. Our ancient teachings warned us that if Man interfered with the natural laws, these things would come to be.
>
> . . .
>
> The traditional native people hold the key to the reversal of the processes in Western Civilization. Our culture is among the most ancient continuously existing cultures in the world. We are the spiritual guardians of this place. We are here to impart this message.

ASIA

Traditional societies everywhere on the planet share values similar to the ones expressed by the North American Iroquois leadership. Concepts like Mother Earth combined with belief in nonhierarchical, nonownership-based, communal relationships to field and forest can be found among all peoples who still live in a direct relationship with the earth.

Most people in India today still derive their livelihoods and meet their survival needs from the biological resources of the country, as forest dwellers, farmers, fisherfolk, healers, and livestock owners. Indigenous knowledge systems in medicine, agriculture, and fisheries are the primary basis for meeting their food, health, and cultural needs. In these traditional communities, the biodiversity of the forests and fields and the historic innovations of plant life for food and medicinal purposes have never been seen as the individual property of any person or family but as community resources available to all people. None can be excluded, and neither the state nor any other economically powerful entity can monopolize use of any aspect of the commons, biologically or intellectually.

There is a vibrant struggle in India today over the commons—not only the biological commons (land, forests, water) that have been the basis of sustainability for a great majority of India's population to the present time but also the *intellectual commons.* This refers to the cumulative knowledge that agricultural communities have collected and freely shared for centuries, as well as the innovations they have achieved in developing plant varieties for food and medicine. Global biotech and pharmaceutical companies have been aggressively patenting these examples of the intellectual commons, preventing their common use, and privatizing them for their own purposes. This invasion has led to a level of outrage on the part of India's farmers, indigenous people, and peasant communities that has brought literally millions of people onto the streets in protest against the World Trade Organization's TRIPs agreement, which protects the rights of corporations to engage in these practices.

Community rights to control the biological and intellectual commons are recognized in law as sui generis rights—equivalent to a patent, but recognizing roots in a community rather than an individual. This system is based in part on usufruct rights, which entitle farmers and laborers access to resources needed for their own sustenance, such as common pastures, water, and biodiversity. Sustainability and justice are inherent in such a system of usufruct rights because there are physical limits on how much any one person can labor; hence there are limited returns for labor, unlike capital and private property.

The battle over the biological and intellectual rights of farmers in India, and against the WTO's TRIPs agreement, comes at the end of a long and painful history of prior enclosures of the commons in India. The policy of deforestation and enclosure of the commons in India began in 1865, when the Indian Forest Act authorized the government to declare forests as "unmeasured" lands or "reserves" for state use. This began what was called the scientific management of forests, but it was really the first step in a long series of moves to remove forests from people and convert them to commodities available for private ownership. Peasant communities that had formerly sustained themselves based on the forests' resources were forced to produce indigo instead of food and pay taxes for salt. They experienced the rapid erosion of their usufruct rights to food, fuel, and livestock pastures, as well as forests and sacred sites. This was a primary cause of their later impoverishment, which led directly to their resistance to further erosion of their common rights by global biotech corporations.

Threats to the "Modern Commons"

In most developed countries, it is hard to remember the time when the central political and economic unit was the local community or when resources were commonly shared. Over the past several centuries, political, economic, and technological evolution in much of the world has conspired to bring far more specialization and industrialization of economic activity, far less economic and social self-reliance, and far greater dependence on dominant centralized political units—cities, states, provinces, and national governments—to provide for the common fundamental needs and services that people require, such as education, transportation, health care, environmental protection, security, and the certainty that there will be sufficient food, housing, and work.

All governments now acknowledge their responsibility in these matters, though they perform them with varying levels of success. Canadians and Danes tend to believe their governments have performed well, at least until recently, whereas Russians and Burmese may not feel this way. Most governments get mixed grades on these matters—good in some ways, bad in others. The United States, for example, has kept its economic and sanitation performance generally high but has been very poor in matters of health care and transportation, and its delivery of these services is marked by extreme inequality. Maude Barlow's forthcoming book, *Profit Is Not the Cure*, details the impact of the World Bank, the IMF, the WTO, and their market-opening policies on the erosion of health care services all over the world, and she chronicles the private sector firms that have benefited. Two decades of these policies have left a legacy of unequal access and health crises for the poor worldwide.

The United Nations Universal Declaration of Human Rights asserts that in addition to the services that nations are expected to perform, governments are also expected to ensure certain basic human rights, religious and political freedoms, and the right to *meaningful* work at fair wages with human dignity. In fact, the U.N. declaration asserts that every person on the planet has an "inherited right to citizenship," which includes health care, education, and work. Moreover, every government has the duty to *defend* the fundamental human rights of every one of its citizens, even beyond its borders. Such assertions also imply that governments have the duty to protect their own ability to perform these services and ensure these fundamental rights against attempts to weaken them.

The authors of this report believe that these services and protections qualify as a kind of "modern commons," in which the state has assumed the responsibility for the common good that once resided in local communities. Even as more power devolves back toward the local—an outcome most of us support—we believe that states have a vital role to play in protecting the community stewardship of both traditional and modern commons. The performance of these responsibilities, however, is now under tremendous threat from global economic institutions.

Great pressure is being applied to national governments by corporations and global bureaucracies to privatize and commodify most public services. Global corporations seek to put them in the same category of commercial activity as toothpaste, cars, real estate services, or movies, provided by private industry at market rates.

Yet there are profound differences between the sacred trust arrangement of governments to provide for basic needs and rights and the private, contracted provision of products, entertainment, and commercial services. Corporations operate from a hierarchy of values that requires profit and growth. Yet as corporations make inroads as providers of health, education, water, or food security, the delivery of these services will go only to people who can pay the market rate. The many who cannot will essentially fall out of the system. *Hence, we would argue that any acts that separate governments from their obligation to provide for all people regardless of economic status are to be prevented.*

Similarly, any efforts by global bureaucracies to *require* that governments privatize such services should be resisted by governments and activists alike—and ultimately banned. At this moment, the current WTO negotiations in Geneva over the expansion of the General Agreement on Trade in Services (GATS) are a case in point.

If the GATS agreement is finalized, then most of the services we have listed here as fundamental rights of citizens and obligations of governments will be subsumed under the new rules of GATS. In other words, corporations will have the right to establish a commercial presence and operate what have until now been domestic services inside countries. These include health care, elder care, child care, water purification and delivery, education, prisons, domestic rail and air transportation, public broadcasting, parks, museums and cultural institutions, social security and welfare programs, and public works of all kinds. As mentioned in Chapter 1, the United States or Canada might find ExxonMobil running public broadcasting while Mitsubishi runs social security; France might have Disney operating the Louvre; Enron or WorldCom could be running the German health care system; and Shell Oil could be in charge of the Japanese railroads and perhaps child rearing as well. Such outcomes are not unrealistic: as we already mentioned, U.S. giant Bechtel was on the verge of running a significant piece of Bolivia's water delivery system until recently, nearly causing a revolution because of its prices to the poor.

The U.N. Covenant on Economic, Social, and Cultural Rights includes the right to education and health. Of all services, these are shaping up as the most potentially lucrative for the global corporations pushing the GATS agreement. Global expenditures on education now exceed $2 trillion, and global expenditures on health care exceed $3.5 trillion. Global corporations are aiming at nothing less than the dismantling of public education and health care systems. Already they have succeeded in lobbying over forty countries, including all of Europe, to be listed in the GATS.

The obligation of governments to provide services for their citizens may soon be reduced to whether some distant corporation will or will not charge an affordable rate for people to send their children to school or to a doctor.

In our view, no global agreement should have the power to forcibly intervene in the trust agreement between governments and citizens.

~

Of course, there are many other threats to basic social programs and services and basic rights to food and health, aside from the upcoming GATS agreement. In chapter 1, we discussed the structural adjustment programs of the World Bank and the International Monetary Fund. To be eligible for development loans or debt relief, dozens of developing countries were forced to abandon a multitude of social programs and allow for-profit foreign corporations to enter, commercialize, and privatize these operations to the detriment of local people.

We have also discussed the WTO's TRIPs agreement, which enables global corporations to claim intellectual property rights over the genetic heritage of people and communities and to redefine the role and form of agriculture. Farming and the community way of life it has sustained are becoming dominated by global corporations who have rendered farmers dependent on them for seeds, fertilizers, pesticides, and herbicides. Structural adjustment programs have also played a big role in this shift in agriculture, requiring nations to convert their farms to export-oriented, specialized production and permit entry of global corporations that accelerate the process. This has driven farmers off lands where they formerly grew food for their communities and has increased hunger and migration.

Because food security is one of the most fundamental human rights, every government has an interest in ensuring it as an essential foundation for social stability and public health. We believe this means that no development banks or trade agreements should be given the right to *require* that any country revamp its agricultural production systems, allow foreign entry and investment, or open itself to cheaper food from abroad to its own detriment. Of course, any country may choose to allow such entry if conditions warrant, but it should not to be *forced* to do so.

Cultural diversity and integrity is another area that can be seen as part of the commons and is arguably a fundamental right that should be protected by nations. It too is now threatened in many ways by global trade agreements. The right of social, religious, cultural, and indigenous groups to preserve their practices, beliefs, artifacts, and artistic expressions is crucial to maintaining diversity within and among nations and in the world.

This also applies to the efforts of nation-states to prevent foreign domination of their own national cultural expressions, through media and artistic creations. Many countries, notably Canada and France—both deeply concerned about retaining film and television industries in domestic hands—have been fighting strenuously to retain their rights to protect their own cultures.

Current WTO trade law subjects culture to the disciplines of the agreement, including "national treatment," "most favored nation," and the prohibition against quantitative restrictions. (All of these WTO rules open up countries to foreign media and other cultural products, often to the detriment of local cultural expressions, which can be overpowered.) There have been several complaints over culture at the WTO since its inception. All have had the effect of limiting the right of a state to protect its cultural industries. The most significant was a 1997 ruling in which the United States successfully forced Canada to abandon protections of its magazine industry, even though American magazines already made up 85 percent of all of those available at Canadian newsstands. Then–U.S. trade representative Charlene Barshefsky said the decision would serve as a useful weapon against Canada's and other countries' protection of their film, books, and broadcasting industries. (See Box J in chapter 2.)

The United States is taking such a hard line because any exemption for Canada would set a negative precedent for other countries, especially in the developing world, where cultural protection is an emerging issue. The fact that the effort to undermine these protections failed at the Seattle WTO ministerial meetings does not mean the problems are over. Both the GATS and the TRIPs agreement will have a direct impact on the telecommunications sector, including the Internet, digital and e-commerce spheres, public broadcasting, patents, trademarks, and copyright law. All are now on the table. They should be taken off.

In sum, we argue that in all of the preceding issues, nation-states and communities should not be subjected to the rules of global trade agreements or multilateral institutions like the WTO or the IMF. Trade in these areas should be subject to national and local decision-making processes alone. Only in this way will it be possible for nations to act on behalf of the common interests of their citizens and to fulfill their own obligations to them.

Proposals

At the start of this chapter, we said that the issues raised here—the preservation outside of the global trading system of the remaining nonmonetized, nonprivatized commons and the governmental trust in preserving fundamental services and rights (the modern commons)—would be nuanced and complex. We proceeded from the principle that not every aspect of human experience or nature should be commodified or subjected to the rules of global trade regimes that require adherence to the global free trade model. However, defining exactly which aspects to exclude, and precisely when, is not simple and needs to be the subject of continuing discussion and debate. Stimulating that discussion has been our main purpose in this chapter.

To further the process, we end the chapter with a short list of broad policies consistent with the ten principles for sustainable societies.

The Authority of Trade Agreements Must Be Narrowly Defined   Global trade bureaucracies and international financial agencies should not have authority over state or national decision making when it comes to the commons, natural heritage resources, the preservation of national choice in domestic services, or fundamental human rights. Trade and investment agreements should not be allowed to require a national or state government to privatize or commercialize remaining areas of the commons or public services, or to force countries to open up these areas to foreign investment and competition, either by imposing rules requiring governments to conform or penalizing them for not doing so.

Decisions on Common Property Resources and Public Services Should Be Local or National
Decisions about common property resources and public services should be reserved to the localities and nations involved, consistent with the principle of subsidiarity. (See chapter 4.) Local commons are the province of local communities. National commons should be subject to national democratic decision-making processes. Global commons should be addressed by multilateral agreements on issues of sustainability and equitable access. No commons—whether local, national, or global—are the proper subject of a multilateral trade agreement. Decisions about the ownership, control, and operation of fundamental public services—including health care and hospitals, water management and delivery, natural resource use, education,

transportation, public broadcasting, agriculture and food security, culture, social security, welfare, military, police, and jails—should be specifically excluded from multilateral trade and investment agreements.

Some nations and communities may determine that it is in their public interest to contract for private operation of some of these resources and public services. Indeed, there is sometimes a role for private ownership and markets to play in the management, allocation, and delivery of certain common heritage resources—including land, seeds, and water—but only in a framework of effective, democratically accountable public regulation that guarantees fair pricing, equitable access, quality, and public stewardship. However, decisions in these matters are properly local or national and have no place being prescribed by global trade and investment regimes concerned only with advancing private commercial interests. Nor is it acceptable for any international agreement to dictate actions by local or national jurisdictions that would result in excluding individuals or communities from equitable access to services and resources, such as clean water, that are essential to life and health.

Things Fundamental to Life and Human Survival Should Not Be Privatized or Monopolized   Certain aspects of the commons that are basic to survival should not be privatized or subject to trade agreements. These include the atmosphere, bulk freshwater, and the genetic and molecular building blocks of life (including the human genome). It may be permissible to patent truly distinctive seed varieties created by privately funded research, for a limited period of time, but the patenting of naturally occurring seeds or seed varieties developed by farming communities or by publicly funded research should not be allowed.

Some Aspects of Life Should Not Be Patented or Otherwise Monopolized   Here we include some areas of life that *are* now partly privatized and traded but should never be subject to corporate *patent* rights or monopoly ownership as offered by TRIPs. At present, these include genes, seeds, plant varieties, and animal breeds—with the possible exception of temporary rights to the exclusive production and sale of distinctive plant and animal varieties created through privately funded breeding programs. The general principle is this: No patents on life. There is also a need to rethink patent rules on life-sustaining pharmaceuticals—for example, AIDS drugs—to ensure fair pricing and access by all who need them, without regard to financial means.

The Right of Countries to Choose Not to Import or Export Goods They Deem Harmful and Pernicious Should Be Protected; Trade in Certain Pernicious Goods May Properly Be Prohibited by International Agreement   A country properly has the right to ban the import or export of certain goods that it considers to present a threat to health and safety, including GMOs, toxins, weapons, and addictive drugs, as well as tobacco and alcohol, for which existing trade agreements now prohibit exclusions. Some currently traded goods are so harmful to the environment, public health, safety, peace, and the global commons that it may be appropriate to create an international agreement to ban them entirely. Candidates would include toxic and nuclear wastes, endangered species, land mines, and sex workers. Such issues, however, are appropriately addressed by international forums and agreements devoted specifically to these topics, not by specialized trade bodies or trade and investment agreements.

International Agreements Are Needed to Protect Global and Transnational Commons Because certain activities in one country can have serious consequences for common resources in other countries, a system is needed to regulate them. For conditions like acid rain, air pollution, ozone depletion, ocean pollution or overexploitation, climate change, and so on, or where common resources such as rivers serve multiple jurisdictions, negotiations are needed on a bilateral or multilateral basis to protect the threatened commons and secure a just and equitable allocation of benefits. These negotiations should take place in forums dedicated to dealing with such issues and should be placed outside the jurisdiction and authority of trade bodies.

CHAPTER FOUR

The Case for Subsidiarity
Bias Away from the Global Toward the Local

IT IS THE MAJOR CONCEIT, or gamble, of the proponents of economic globalization that by removing economic control from the places where it has traditionally resided—in nations, states, subregions, communities, or indigenous societies—and placing that control into absentee authorities that operate globally via giant corporations and bureaucracies, all levels of society will benefit. But as we have seen in earlier chapters, this is not true, and it is a principal reason why so many millions of people are angrily protesting.

The captains of globalization are driven by what is still essentially an economic ideology. They operate on a macroscale removed from the everyday realities of local conditions or awareness. They lobby for their ideas and theories as though they were viable and cogent, as if they themselves were expert visionaries and managers of their new centralized global architecture. They continue to praise their formulas despite the numerous spectacular breakdowns they have caused: the Asian financial crisis, the Russian financial crisis, the near economic meltdown of Brazil, and the collapse of the Argentine economy, along with the global increase in poverty, hunger, inequity, dependency, and powerlessness. These theories do not work and cannot work; the main beneficiaries, unsurprisingly, remain the global corporations and economic elites that have instituted these processes.

As we have seen, the central modus operandi of the globalization model is to delocalize controls over economic *and* political activity in a systematic appropriation of the powers, decisions, options, and functions that through history have been fulfilled by the community, region, or state. Another modus operandi of globalization is to anonymize. On the other hand, it is a principal virtue of localization that it restores face-to-face, knowing relationships of trust to economic transactions.

When sovereign powers are removed from the local and put into distant bureaucracies, local politics must also be redesigned to conform to the rules and practices of distant bureaucracies. Communities and nations that formerly operated in a relatively self-reliant manner, in the interests of their own people, are converted into unwilling subjects of these larger, undemocratic, unaccountable global structures.

Meanwhile, millions of people all over the world continue to go to work every day, trying to maintain their traditional small-scale, artisanal, or indigenous livelihoods. In fact, the local economy is the foundation for most communities, whether North or South, rich or poor. Even traditional economists like Paul Krugman acknowledge that most U.S. cities are locally rooted because of the expanding service economy. Yet these local economic activities are under constant attack. They are increasingly subject to, and dependent on, mysterious eruptions and gyrations in the larger system. These may include the vagaries of distant export markets, fluctuations in prices and exchange rates, abilities of national governments to service interest payments on loans, and centralized decisions about international capital flows, commodity specializations, and the like—decisions made by authorities in Washington, Geneva, Brussels, Rome, and Tokyo without the slightest nod to democratic processes. At the local level, such mundane issues as the price of coffee, tomatoes, oil, wheat, or rice depend on these unfathomable distant factors. Financial assets such as stocks and bonds, as well as prevailing wage rates for labor, are also governed less and less frequently by local conditions and instead fluctuate according to the manipulations of economic networks by financiers and corporations.

But most affected of all, tragically, is democracy itself and all its institutions.

If democracy is based on the idea that people must participate in the great decisions affecting their lives, then the movement of basic life decisions to distant venues—particularly venues that abhor democratic participation, openness, accountability, and transparency—brings the death of democracy. If local economic activity is something that people have been able to do for themselves, globalization is something done *to* people rather than *by* them.

We have reached the end of the road for that process. It's time to change direction.

Understanding Subsidiarity

Because globalization is the problem, then logically a return to the local is inevitable—a reinvigoration of the conditions by which local communities regain the power to determine and control their preferred economic and political paths. Instead of shaping all systems to conform to a global model that emphasizes specialization of production, comparative advantage, export-oriented growth, monoculture, and homogenization of economic, cultural, and political forms under the direction of transnational corporate institutions, we must reshape our institutions to favor exactly the opposite.

The operating principle for this turnaround is the concept of *subsidiarity*—that is, favoring the local whenever a choice exists. In practice, subsidiarity means that all decisions should be made at the lowest level of governing authority competent to deal with them. Global health crises and global pollution issues often require cooperative international decisions. But most economic, cultural, and political decisions are not international and can be made at the national, regional, or local levels, depending on the issue. Power should be encouraged to evolve downward, not upward. Decisions should constantly move closer to the people most affected by them. Wherever economic production, labor, and markets can be local, they should be, and rules should help achieve that. International, regional, and subregional trade will continue to exist, of course, but it should serve as a final resort, not as the purpose of the system.

All systems should emphasize local production and consumption rather than be deliberately designed to serve long-distance trade. This means *shortening* the length of lines for economic activity: fewer food miles, fewer oil supply miles, fewer travel-to-work miles. Technologies should also be chosen that best serve local control, rather than megatechnologies that operate globally. (The authors of this volume prefer solar, wind, mini-hydro, micropower, and conservation over nuclear and oil; we prefer small-scale local agriculture and local markets over globalized industrial agriculture for export markets.) Firms should continue to operate, but only within the confines of a "site-here-to-sell-here" policy, and investment and capital should remain rooted in the community, constantly recycled, and locally controlled.

We want to clarify that such self-reliance does not mean autarky. Indeed, there is a compelling argument that many healthy local economies will continue to have exports and imports, but spread among hundreds of items, none of them critical to the survival of the community. North Dakota's electricity sector can provide a good example. Some are now urging that if North Dakotans want to become energy independent, they should build large-scale wind farms. Then, if they found themselves dependent on imports of wind machines, they might develop a local wind-machine industry. If they did this, they would likely depend on imports of metals and parts. Thus, the process never ends, but a process of import substitution steadily leads toward a more diverse, healthy, and self-reliant economy.

Where commons are found to exist—water, land, biodiversity, local knowledge—these should remain the property of the community as a whole. Wherever indigenous activities or effective nonmonetized activities continue to occur, these should be respected and encouraged as legitimate economic forms, providing real services to people and communities if not to global corporations and the market. The goal can no longer be individual or corporate wealth; rather it must be community self-reliance, public health, equity, accountability, and democracy. (See chapter 2 for more on this issue.)

Clearly, a reversal of this kind—consciously favoring the local over the global—will not sit comfortably with the largest and most powerful institutions in the world, all of which depend on the larger global system, long supply lines, expanding trade, and centralized absentee control. Those are the forms that were made in their image, as it were, and that offer maximum profit opportunity. But citizen groups and general populations around the world are making their own preference clear, and that is to move in the direction of reempowerment of local communities. Farmers, workers, unions, small businesses, consumer groups, peasant organizations, environmentalists, human rights advocates, and all groups seeking functional democracies are already working to reverse course. They will not be denied, but they need help in doing more faster.

One important reason why these people will not be denied has to do with the economics of local, small-scale alternatives. As we have noted, small-scale alternatives are already generating most of the goods and services people need in a cost-effective manner, and many trends suggest that their role will expand. Among others, the most salient trends are these:

- Distribution costs are getting proportionately larger than production costs (suggesting opportunities, as in food, for creating cheaper products through direct marketing).
- Global transportation costs will rise as oil prices rise, to begin to reflect real costs that have until now been externalized (see chapter 6) and as green taxes are enacted.
- Niche marketing increasingly favors local producers who best know local consumers.
- The shift from goods to services inherently favors local business.
- The growth of computers and the Internet makes it easier to run complex businesses from anywhere, including the home basement.
- Large corporations are generally worse places to work than smaller ones.
- Terrorist threats increase the importance of unhooking from the corporate-global juggernaut and returning to local self-reliance.

Elsewhere in this volume, we describe changes in key global institutions consistent with the kinds of shifts we speak about here. For example, we describe desirable changes that are occurring in the dominant Bretton Woods institutions, in corporate structures, and in the essential operating systems of society like energy, transport, and agriculture. Here we get down to issues of the *scale of governance* and processes to bring economic and political power back toward the communities and nations from which it has been lifted.

The Road to the Local

Localization attempts to reverse the trend toward the global by discriminating actively in favor of the local in all policies. Depending on the context, the *local* is defined as a subgroup within a nation-state; it may also be the nation-state itself or, occasionally, a regional grouping of nation-states. In all cases, the idea is for power to devolve to the lowest unit appropriate for a particular goal.

Policies that bring about localization are ones that increase democratic control of the economy by communities or nation-states, taking it back from the global institutions that have appropriated it. These policies may enable nations, local governments, and communities to reclaim their economies, make them as diverse as possible, and rebuild stability into community life—to achieve maximum self-reliance nationally and regionally in a way that ensures more sustainable forms of development.

(One disclaimer: We are aware that localization is not a panacea. Localization does not *guarantee* democracy or equality or human rights; it just makes them far more likely. Smaller communities offer people greater access to the sources of power and greater opportunity for positive outcomes. However, history offers many examples of ruthless opportunism even on the local level, and advocates like the National Front in France and Joerg Haider in Austria offer a current warning. What is sure, however, is that globalization offers *no opportunity* at all for democratic empowerment. We have a better chance with smaller-scale systems. We will return to this later.)

To move in the direction of localization will require a complete change in society's assumptions and will also require a long time and many steps. But to get our thinking started, we mention here a few points that have been spelled out by Colin Hines in his book *Localization: A Global Manifesto,* Michael Shuman in *Going Local,* and Helena Norberg-Hodge in her chapter on localization in *The Case Against the Global Economy.*

Reintroduce Safeguards That Were Traditionally Used to Protect Domestic (Local) Economies   Traditional safeguards include tariffs, import quotas, investment restrictions and rules, and nontariff barriers concerning health, worker and environmental, and investment standards. All of these protections instituted by national governments have been the direct target of global trade rules established by the WTO and other bureaucracies intent on undermining local authority and its ability to maintain self-reliance.

Change Subsidy Policy   Presently, countries offer huge subsidies for infrastructure development, especially for large-scale energy, transport and communications, and other megadevelopment schemes, as well as for the externalized costs of pollution-creating activity. Such policies should be wholly reversed to favor vital local enterprises such as small-scale organic agriculture for local markets, small-scale energy and transportation infrastructures (solar, wind, small-scale hydro, and so on, dedicated bus lanes, and pedestrian and bicycle accommodations), as well as community banking and development and loan funds. Municipal governments should screen local subsidies to test for local ownership and local import replacement. These subsidies include loans, loan guarantees, bonds, capital improvements, and so on. Subsidy programs of this nature would benefit from two further requirements, that they be duly noticed and bid upon (to prevent backroom dealing and to encourage transparency) and that they be performance-based (you get the tax break after you produce the promised jobs).

Put New Controls on Corporate Activity   Such new controls would include site-here-to-sell-here policies for manufacturing, banking, and other services, whether domestic or regional. Localities should have the right to require any of the following: changed composition of corporate boards to include labor or environmental or other local stakeholders; limits on corporate freedoms to buy other businesses, especially in other locales; strict limits on mobility and capital movement; loss of corporate personhood laws, which give corporations the rights of ordinary citizens without the responsibilities; abandonment of limited liability rules that protect corporate shareholders from liability for crimes; requirements for public transparency; and so on. (See chapter 5 for more on corporate personhood and limited liability laws.)

Ground Capital and Investment in the Community   Profits made locally should remain primarily local. Outside direct investment is permissible and desirable only when geared toward local conditions and requirements. The Canadian labor-sponsored investment funds (LSIFs) offer a good example of how to ground capital. LSIFs invest pension funds exclusively in businesses that are labor and environmentally friendly and are locally owned in the provinces. The key to their success is that the government must be able to provide tax breaks to those who put money into these funds. There is also a great potential role for the selective investment of public pension funds and surplus revenue funds of public entities. Also desirable are the new local money systems designed for community use. Later in the chapter, we return to the issue of capital and investment.

Make Major Changes in Taxation Policies   Increases in resource taxes as well as the introduction of pollution taxes are needed for extraction and depletion of natural capital like forests, water, and minerals. These will more accurately reflect the true costs of corporate development activities and put the onus on corporations to cover currently externalized costs subsidized by governments. Other taxes would include the introduction of "Tobin taxes" on speculative financial transactions. (The fact that they are now untaxed has increased their volume and the great harms they cause.) There should also be a reassessment of current policies that tend toward greater tax breaks for large-scale enterprises than for smaller, local ones (including elimination of investment tax credits and accelerated depreciation allowances now enjoyed by big businesses to the detriment of smaller ones). Much of the income from such changes in tax policy could help finance the shift to localization.

Increase Direct Public Participation in Policymaking   Increased participation helps ensure equity and diverse viewpoints. This is a primary feature of localization: it makes possible a greater level of direct democracy.

Reorient International Aid and Trade Rules   The domestic policies that influence those changes should also be revised so that they contribute to the rebuilding of local rather than global economies, particularly through enhanced global transfer of information and technology. Self-reliant communities may turn out to be the best actors for spreading the capital, technology, policies, and experience necessary to help partner communities in other countries become self-reliant. This is a fundamentally different paradigm for development and development assistance.

Institute New Competition Policies   At present, global competition policy as reflected in the rules of the WTO and other bureaucracies enhances competitive opportunities for global corporations forcing their way into local and domestic domains. Under localization policies, global corporations that continue to exist will no longer have such access unless they conform to all local investment rules, including the requirement to keep capital local. Competition among local firms, however, will be strongly encouraged in order to stimulate innovation. Localities should have the right to encourage (not force) citizens to buy local. Local labeling should be permitted, as well as selective government purchasing of local goods and services.

Encourage Social Cohesion and Local Economic Renewal   The push toward the global has left most local communities bereft of viable local instruments that encourage local environmental and social values. It is crucial that attention be paid to the quality and vitality of local culture and community programs on housing, livelihood, sustainable lifestyle, and a safe and healthy environment. Attention must focus on everything from land use and zoning considerations to microlending, development trusts, credit unions, community transport activity, community recycling, community self-building schemes, and myriad conservation activities that are all required aspects of the overall shift in approach. Not least important is a reformed educational system that grasps and can convey the values of this alternative system.

Investment and Finance Issues

An equally important issue in the viability of local economic systems is how and whether sufficient capital can be found to keep them operative and innovative. Clearly, in a local economy, the operating costs are entirely different from a globalized economy. Measurements of successful performance are not based on traditional economic growth figures like GDP and GNP, but rather on more subjective social and environmental characteristics that also include the value of not cutting down the forests and not putting vast dollars into security and military expenditures (which count as GDP). Conversely, they give *positive* value to unpaid and nonmonetized aspects of a local economy that are reflected in personal care, household labor, self-sufficient livelihoods (sometimes based on barter), and the general goal of community self-reliance rather than individual or corporate wealth.

At least for a long while, however, capital and investment factors will continue to play major roles, so it is necessary to address them. Here are some of the ideas that are being studied to help such a system work.

CAPITAL

We mentioned in the previous section of this chapter that localization advocates seek to keep capital local. Capital flight has been the death of more than one otherwise viable community, and it must be prevented. Among the measures that may be considered are these: reintroduction of exchange controls; reregulation of banks and finance institutions so that greater advantages are achieved through local investment than flight; introduction of very high "speed bumps" that penalize investors who move money in and out of investment opportunities rapidly and prevent them from exporting more than a small percentage of their funds; 100 percent reserve requirements for banks seeking to create money through loan policies; introduction of Tobin-type taxes to hold down speculative investment and instabilities caused by frequent movement of money; higher margins for purchasing bonds; and restrictions on the use of derivatives to require that banks have cash or liquid assets in reserve to back up such contracts.

Governments also can and should put deposits in community-friendly banks to support their expansion. They can and should create new kinds of secondary markets for financing the new, local economy. Also, because a great deal of savings in most economies go into equities, incentives and subsidies that encourage local reinvestment are critical. Michael Shuman suggests that some of the most intriguing opportunities for these types of local initiatives are through consortiums of like-minded municipalities. Community reinvestment is a good example. By definition, a community that reinvests 100 percent locally cannot achieve geographic diversification in its portfolio, which increases risk. One solution is for several communities to aim for 90 percent local reinvestment, with the remaining 10 percent invested in the others' funds. All the funds would therefore support local business. A similar case can be made for intermunicipal cooperation to promote fair trade, serve as a clearinghouse for local currency exchanges, and to put together flexible manufacturing networks for goods that require larger economies of scale for production or distribution.

TAXATION

We have already discussed several tax changes intended to reduce capital flight and speculation and to recover formerly externalized costs that the public sector has had to pay. We have also mentioned elimination of special tax breaks for large-scale enterprises and the need to *increase* taxes on energy use and natural capital.

Other important changes include less taxation on labor, which has had the undesirable effect of encouraging corporations to eliminate workers as a way of reducing taxes. Such taxes now include payroll or income taxes, social welfare taxes, and value-added taxes, among others.

Capital gains taxes should be *increased*, especially for short-term holdings. Far more preferential treatment should be offered for taxes on income that is based on productive work compared with passive earnings based on moving money between investments.

Governments can severely limit tax evasion by forcing public disclosure of corporate finances, especially global taxes paid or avoided; closing national and global tax loopholes; penalizing and eventually eliminating tax havens; monitoring and halting intracorporate financial transfers used to avoid paying national taxes (for example, transfer pricing); and imposing tax penalties for downsizing or relocation.

NEW RULES OF INVESTMENT

The present rules of globalized finance and investment encourage moving control away from the communities that need to have it. Capital has been made almost completely mobile so it can always move wherever profit opportunity is greatest. Mobility of capital—which, as we mentioned in chapter 2, was opposed by the original gurus of free trade David Ricardo and Adam Smith—has required that local communities change their economies and their priorities to appeal to foreign capital investment and then follow their negative strictures from structural adjustment programs to draconian loan conditions.

Subsidiarity and localization require a reversal of that formula to emphasize and favor local direct investment over foreign investment. Where foreign investment continues to be sought, local communities should control its conditions. The goal is to redirect all benefits to the local community, including jobs, local livelihoods, services, local urban community development, small-scale energy, manufacturing for domestic and local markets rather than export, and the like. For example, governments could impose capital penalties on firms that depart a community, rather than the current policy in many municipalities of allowing the firm to write off the moving expenses.

Favoring Local Direct Investment

Colin Hines has proposed an alternative investment code for foreign investors, with some of the following new directives. Preferential treatment should always be given to local direct investment; this reverses such WTO rulings as most favored nation status, which outlawed local preferences and smoothed the way for massive dependency on investors. Investments may continue to be encouraged, but only if they have the effect of increasing local employment with decent wages and otherwise serve to improve the quality of local life. All investors should respect basic human rights and protect the environment as top priorities.

Existing laws that give preferential treatment to foreign or absentee owners of community enterprises must be rolled back over a few years time span.

Under the provisions of an alternative investment code, states and communities would be explicitly *permitted* to impose a code of performance requirements (again in direct opposition to current WTO rules) as follows: require a certain percentage of domestic content or local content in all manufactured products; require a given level of local personnel and respect for labor and environmental standards; protect enterprises that serve community needs from any unfair foreign competition; give preference to locally produced goods.

Other reversals of current policies now imposed by trade agreements and the Bretton Woods institutions would include these:

- Communities need some leeway in setting rules on investors that can result in expropriation if the investor breaks its promises. To prevent abuse of such rules, a community should have the right to impose a wide range of potential expropriation rules only before an investment is made; existing firms could be given a few years' notice.
- Governments should also be able to set limits on the amount of capital and profit that may be expatriated to source countries by foreign investors. Citizen groups and community institutions should be granted rights to sue investors for violations of this investment code. All judicial proceedings on these matters should be open and transparent.

Encouraging Long-Term Local Investment

With conditions made more difficult for capital movement and a new set of requirements for responsible performance, the opportunities and advantages formerly enjoyed by foreign direct investors will be reduced, and there will be a desirable swing toward local direct investment and the goal of keeping money recycling productively within a community.

To encourage the shift to local long-term investment, the following measures would be helpful:

- Offer higher tax breaks for long-term local investment and create severe tax penalties for rapid capital movement (especially among foreign investors).
- At the local level (including the national level), give central banks authority to directly influence the structure and profitability of local banks, favoring those that support local investment for local development. National policy should encourage increased market regulation, establish small banks designed for microlending, and increase the emphasis on credit unions, Local Exchange Trading Systems (LETS), and tax breaks for the breakdown of large-scale enterprise into smaller, decentralized, locally owned operating units. Central banks could also set lower discount rates for community-friendly banks.
- Close down all offshore banking centers where capital hides from banking and securities laws or from national or state income taxes. National banking systems would be prohibited from honoring the transfers of offshore capital.
- Encourage long-term savings in local banks by offering higher interest rates there, thus providing local banks with additional development funds for local projects.

Response to Critics of Subsidiarity

In the face of the globalization juggernaut and its widely propagated utopian visions, advocates of more decentralized, localized alternative paths tend to meet fierce criticism and disbelief about the viability of such solutions.

We have already mentioned how advocates of globalization assert that local systems are less democratic than the advancing global political constructs. We have already agreed that local governance does not guarantee democracy, human rights, equity, or good governance. We join others in citing examples where local governance has been authoritarian, oppressive, even brutal. Nevertheless, bringing governance and economies down to smaller-scale systems—where people are closer to the sources of power—offers far greater opportunity and promise for democratic participation than the present model. There are many examples of this throughout the world, some among indigenous populations, some in smaller communities, and some in large cities such as Brazil's Porto Alegre and Curitiba (for more on this, see chapter 6). Globalization, on the other hand, offers no democratic promise. Globalization actually *guarantees* absentee rule by giant corporations that are designed to act solely in their own economic interests and have no real concern about conditions faced in the daily lives of most people. The real choice, therefore, is between allowing corporate-led systems controlled from faraway cities, or attempting to strengthen forms that may bring power back to the local, where opportunity for democracy, equity, and attention to local social and environmental conditions still exists. The better choice seems obvious to the authors of this report, though vigilance is mandatory.

As for defining and upholding human rights, that is the preserve of appropriate international agreements among nations, which have sufficient powers to institute sanctions of the kind that helped bring down the white racist regime in South Africa a few decades ago. Keep in mind that subsidiarity envisions a role for higher-order rules, whether national or global. It just insists that these rules be few and truly consensual, especially if they are going to restrict local action. It is worth noting that such sanctions as were applied in South Africa would now be far more difficult to introduce because they are nearly outlawed by the rules of the WTO. In fact, such sanctions would be explicitly banned by the new FTAA agreement or any reiterations of the proposed multilateral agreement on investment (MAI) that was fought off by activists a few years ago. Many of the elements of the MAI continue to resurface in other agreements, including the WTO's proposed new investment agreement. (If such rules had been in place twenty years ago, Nelson Mandela would likely still be in jail. So much for the globalizers as protectors of human rights.)

Other critiques of localization are essentially restatements of the many theoretical benefits of global free trade: that wealth will "trickle down" to the poor, that prices will be lower, and that greater diversity (of products) will exist in the marketplace. On the first point, that globalization lifts people from poverty, this is manifestly, tragically false. As chapter 1 of this volume explained, the benefits of globalization actually trickle up to the very wealthy. It accelerates gaps between rich and poor within countries and among countries. (A special report by the IFG, *Does Globalization Help the Poor?* provides more data on this phenomenon.) As for globalization bringing a greater diversity of products, that may be the case for some product categories and some segments of society that can take advantage of expanded choices in foreign cars, designer clothing, and exotic cheeses and meats, for example. But in many cases, localization increases the diversity of products: we think it is better to have one thousand microbreweries than one Coors, and many varieties of tomato and potato rather than the industrial, single-crop variety. In any case, for most people who are simply trying to feed their families, product diversity is an abstraction. Meanwhile, cultural diversity and biodiversity—which affect everyone—are actively suppressed by the globalization model.

It is true that the global marketplace does sometimes bring cheaper products in sectors where competition still exists. This is because the rules of free trade encourage free entry of foreign agricultural and manufactured goods, sometimes with lower prices. However, these lower prices do not signify a new efficiency brought by globalization. Often they signify export dumping (when domestic overproduction threatens high domestic prices and profits). They are also the result of high levels of direct subsidies, of subsidies through infrastructure development, or of the outlandish subsidies caused by the externalization of environmental or social costs of industrial monocultures, as explained earlier. If these subsidized costs—which ultimately are paid for by taxpayers and ordinary people—were actually included in the price of commodity imports, they would not be cheaper. Even if they *were* cheaper, however, is it better social policy for a country or community to sacrifice the vitality and cohesion of its economic system—especially the production of food staples, which also has important environmental and cultural benefits—on the chance that consumers can save pennies at the supermarket? We think not. Indeed, today local companies may offer lower prices, and local banks may offer lower rates, yet these entities fare poorly because of the superior marketing clout of giant firms and banks.

In any case, all of this activity is based on the tenuous theory of comparative advantage. Under comparative advantage concepts, the viability of economic systems depends entirely upon whether the importing community can pay for its imports with the earned income from export items in which it has this so-called comparative advantage in production. In practice, this neat formula rarely works. Export markets are variable, volatile, and unreliable. More than one nation is now facing a hunger crisis caused by the failure of comparative advantage theories, as export prices crash.

Others argue against localization by positing that small businesses usually pay lower wages and offer fewer benefits, and few are unionized. In fact, this is often untrue. Over time, as small companies grow, early employees usually get big salary boosts and increased benefits. Another argument is that it is harder to regulate one hundred mini-mills than one giant smokestack. Perhaps this is true, but weigh against this the political clout of the giant, which eliminates regulation, and the fact that local residents are usually the best judges of local smokestacks. Finally there is the argument is that some communities are better endowed than others. This is certainly true. Hence, redistribution mechanisms are needed.

Conclusion

Obviously, any nation or community's security would be better enhanced if its own people could grow their own foods—at least ensuring thereby their survival free of market idiosyncrasies—and also manufacture as many of their other needs as possible before entering global markets. The goal of societies should not be to find cheaper prices for products but to find the means to ensure that all the needs of all people are met and that a satisfactory and stable life is perpetuated within a system that does not collapse from being part of the volatile global market. If people grow their own food, produce their own necessities, and control the conditions of their lives, the issue of price becomes irrelevant.

CHAPTER FIVE

Corporate Structure and Power

IN DECEMBER 2001, shock waves rippled first through the business world and then through all segments of society. The front-page story of almost every newspaper in every country shifted from the war on terror to another: one of the most dominant and successful energy companies in the world had suddenly filed for bankruptcy. Enron Corp., once celebrated as the leader of a new wave of innovative enterprise, had managed to spearhead the conversion of electricity provision in much of the United States into a privatized speculative commodity, contributing to big energy problems in California while avoiding government oversight. It had also brilliantly contributed toward and then exploited the global deregulation juggernaut that accompanied the new rules of the WTO, the GATS, and other agreements in order to gain entry into foreign countries and gather up tens of billions of dollars in overseas assets, while causing grave social and environmental problems in such countries as India, Bolivia, the Dominican Republic, and over two dozen others.

Enron had also enjoyed windfall benefits from the structural adjustment loan programs of the World Bank and the IMF by steering—with the help of the banks—development loan funds given to foreign governments back to itself through fat contracts built into the loans. It used corporate-friendly U.S. tax laws to hide negative performance and appear profitable despite dangerously overextending itself.

Finally, on the brink of ultimate failure, the company abandoned the interests and loyalty of its own workers by knowingly allowing their stock investments in the company to collapse. At the same time, top executives sold their own stocks at huge profits, even receiving bonuses as they departed.

Once it was exposed, Enron's performance was seen as so shocking, and the public outrage was so great, that even company backers in the White House found themselves too politically vulnerable to assist their former friends and colleagues. They tried to treat Enron as if it were the rare exception to otherwise responsible corporate behavior in the United States—the proverbial "one rotten apple in the barrel."

Unfortunately, the Enron experience actually teaches very different lessons. First, the emerging evidence shows that although its activities were unconscionable, many were within the bounds of the law—the fruits of corporate cohabitation with government and a deregulated system.

Second, this kind of reprehensible behavior was entirely predictable, considering the nature of corporate structure today and the prevailing rules that guide corporate priorities and institutional investors—short-term profit and hypergrowth with little place for community concerns.

Finally, as has been exquisitely revealed by subsequent examples, from WorldCom to Halliburton, Xerox, Tyco, and other corporate giants, the problems are far from unique to Enron. In fact, they are *systemic*. Enron was only a case in point. The way to fix Enron, like other corporations, is to fundamentally change the system.

~

At the dawn of the twenty-first century, the global corporation stands as the dominant institutional force at the center of human activity and the planet itself. Indeed, according to a report by Sarah Anderson and John Cavanagh of the Institute for Policy Studies, by the year 2000 the combined sales of the world's top two hundred corporations exceeded a quarter of all countries' measured economic activity. If one listed the top one hundred economic units on the planet, fifty-one would be corporations, and only forty-nine would be countries.

These globe-girdling firms have become both the prime beneficiaries of and the driving forces behind the new architecture for global governance and the trade, finance, and investment regimes that now rule people and life on earth.

The immense scale and extreme concentration of the powers of global corporations stifle both democratic expression and market competition. In six key industries, for example—consumer durables, automotive manufacturing, aircraft manufacture, aerospace, electronic components, and steel—five firms control more than 50 percent of the global market. So, rather than contributing to healthy market competition as envisioned by globalization and capitalist theories, globalization has instead led directly to global oligopolies. In many cases, as in agriculture, the dominant few global corporations (Archer Daniels Midland, Monsanto, Novartis, and others like them) exercise control over multiple aspects of the production cycle—the raw material inputs and distribution, the seeds and chemicals, the farmers, the processors, the distributors, and the retailers—amounting to extensive vertical integration. Global prices and the food supply—and its quality—are thus subject to corporate control. Such staggering corporate concentration utterly overpowers and defies traditional market theories that envision a multitude of healthy small and medium-size enterprises competing with each other over quality, price, and innovation. It also impedes all conditions favorable to democracy, economic justice, and environmental values.

Corporations have become the primary organizing instrument for economic, political, and social activity on the planet. Through their market power, billions of dollars in campaign contributions, public relations, advertising, and sheer scale, corporations create the visions we live by and exert great influence over the political power structures that rule us. It is fair to conclude, as David Korten has written, that corporations have already achieved "corporate rule" to the detriment of democracies, social equity, and nature. It is exactly for such reasons that fierce global protests have brought millions of people onto the streets to demand massive structural change in corporations, the rules they operate by, and their very existence.

In any just and sustainable society, it is unlikely that global corporations would operate as the primary organizing force they are in our world today. Indeed, if we are to achieve such a society, corporate structure will need to be altered—away from the current model that brings with it an intrinsic set of values that have to do only with the narrow successes of the corporation itself and are diametrically opposed to the ten principles for sustainable societies outlined in chapter 2. We must dramatically change the publicly traded, limited liability global corporation, just as previous generations set out to eliminate or control the monarchy. Any citizens' agenda for transforming the global economy must be rooted in plans to solve this problem.

This chapter focuses on the possibilities for such change. It begins with a brief review of certain key features of corporate structure today because much of the problem of corporate behavior is rooted in the institutional forms and structures themselves.

Next, the chapter reports on the variety of activities already being undertaken by citizen groups around the world, covering a spectrum from reform of corporations to their decommissioning. Finally, it presents some ideas about alternative business structures that are far more consistent with our ten principles.

Corporate Structure Today

Corporations are generally divided into two categories, those that are *privately owned* by a small number of individuals or families and those that are *publicly owned and traded*. There are important and consequential distinctions between them.

PUBLIC AND PRIVATE CORPORATIONS

Some privately owned corporations have grown very large, even global (for example, Bechtel, Cargill, and the other highly secretive grain-trading companies). These large private companies have gained many of the benefits that publicly held corporations have: efficiencies of scale, domination of markets and resources, political influence, attractiveness to lending institutions. But large private corporations are relatively few in number, and their overall impact is less than the greater number of large publicly held, limited liability global corporations.

When corporations are said to be *publicly traded*, it means that their ownership shares are freely exchanged in public share markets by large numbers of people who have little involvement with the operations of the firm, other than hoping for a passive financial return. Trading in such public shares is called *investing*, but it also may be likened to a sophisticated form of gambling, rather like betting on a horse race. Most shares of public corporations are not actually held directly by individuals but by professionally managed mutual funds, insurance companies, pension plans, and other investment institutions. When people buy shares in these managed funds, they usually have little knowledge about precisely which companies the funds own, let alone what kinds of activities those companies engage in with their invested money.

To attract investments from the public, there is heavy pressure on most public corporations to make their stocks seem as appealing as possible in terms of growth and profitability, leading many to make decisions based on short-term appearances of health (as with Enron, WorldCom, Halliburton) or to engage in rapid depletion of natural resources, like forests or fisheries, to create short-term profits at the expense of long-term environmental health and a permanent resource base. The intrinsic need of public corporations to drive optimistic impressions of investment opportunity is at the root of considerable social and ecological harm. Publicly held companies must seek continual growth and expansion—ever more markets, labor, and resources—because they must show positive balance sheets, even in their quarterly reports, to impress investors, bankers, and the financial communities on which they depend. The homily "grow or die" is especially apt for public companies as growth and profit become obsessive goals, far outweighing any moral, ethical, or environmental considerations.

On the other hand, although privately held companies often behave exactly as public companies do, they do not have the same built-in systemic imperative to impress the financial community or investment markets because they are partly outside that system. A family or individuals running a private corporation have, at least theoretically, greater freedom to make decisions that are not solely in the interest of maximizing profits but might be thoughtful of the community, workers, and nature. There is room in a private company for a mix of values, and we have seen examples of privately held, usually smaller companies—Patagonia, Ben & Jerry's, and The Body Shop are a few—that were willing to sacrifice some profits to support greater community or environmental goals. Of course, the private corporation sometimes "goes public" through stock offerings or is bought out by a much larger public company. Once that happens, altruism may decline or disappear. None of this is meant to ignore the performance of those private corporations that seem never to have noticed that they have a greater opportunity for responsible behavior. Indeed, some companies remain private for secrecy reasons, because private companies are not required to file financial reports with the SEC and other government agencies. And some private firms, particularly in the textile sector, have abysmal labor records.

As for the term *limited liability*, it refers to the fact that though corporate management is technically accountable to shareholder-owners and acts in their behalf, shareholder-owners have no personal liability besides their investment in the firm for any consequences of corporate management acts. This built-in distance between the technical owners of the corporation and the people who actually operate it insulates them from liability for (and even knowledge of) any harms eventually done by the corporation. It also removes a level of engagement, accountability, and transparency that would more likely exist if investor liability was maintained. (In practice, most CEOs are now paid overwhelmingly through stock options and have become large owners of the companies they also run; in this ownership capacity, they too enjoy limited liability.)

CORPORATE CHARTERS

Corporations dominate societies and help create the power structures that rule us, yet they remain paradoxically ephemeral entities. Although such names as ExxonMobil, McDonald's, Shell, Microsoft, Disney, Sony, and Monsanto are emblazoned in our brains, as familiar to us as old friends, in fact these institutions have no real physical existence. They own buildings and stadiums and wield stupendous powers, but corporations themselves have no concrete form. They have people who work in them, but corporations are themselves not alive, so they cannot inherently embody the same range of values and emotions that we expect of responsible people: altruism, shame, community concern, loyalty to one another, and so on. This distinction between corporate structure and the people who work within corporations becomes crucially important in explaining, as former American University professor Ralph Estes puts it, "why corporations make good people do bad things" (from his book *Tyranny of the Bottom Line*).

In the United States, corporations gain their existence through the laws of state governments, augmented by federal regulation. Corporations are direct legal creations of state corporate charters, so theoretically they are expressions of popular sovereignty. State corporate charter rules *could* theoretically set any conditions that popular will might dictate—from who should be on the boards to the values corporations must operate by, to whether they may buy up other enterprises, move to other cities and countries, or anything else that affects the public interest.

Hundreds of years ago, state charters contained significant restrictions and much higher standards of accountability and responsibility than they do today. But as the landmark research of Richard Grossman and Frank Adams of the Program on Corporations, Law and Democracy (POCLAD) has revealed, corporations have managed over the centuries to wear down the kind and quality of state charter rules as well as the state and federal laws that govern their existence. By now, these directives contain relatively few restrictions, and even when corporations violate these restrictions their permanent existence is rarely threatened. Governing bodies today, beholden to corporations for campaign finance support, are loath to enforce any sanctions except in cases of extreme political embarrassment, such as has occurred with Enron, Arthur Andersen, and others. Even then, effective sanctions may be few and small.

These virtual entities that we call corporations have now advanced to where they enjoy a great many rights similar to those granted human beings. As we explain later in this chapter, U.S. courts have ruled that corporations are "fictitious persons," with the right to buy and sell property as if they were people, to sue in court for injuries, and to express "corporate speech." Advertising, public relations, and campaign funding have all been ruled legitimate, *protected* forms of corporate speech—under the First Amendment of the U.S. Constitution.

Although corporations enjoy legal "personhood rights," they have not been required, for the most part, to abide by normal human responsibilities. They are strongly protected by limited liability rules, so shareholder-owners of a corporation cannot be prosecuted for acts of the institution. Nor, in any meaningful sense, is the corporation itself vulnerable to prosecution. Corporations are sometimes fined for their acts or ordered to alter their practices, but the life of the corporation, its (virtual) existence, is very rarely threatened—even for great crimes that, if carried out by people in many states of the United States, might invoke the death penalty.

In fact, corporations are likely to outlive the human beings who have been part of their operation, even those who own them, the private or public shareholders. Unlike humans, corporations have the possibility of immortality, at least until some future generation of owners files papers that put them to death.

The central point is this: lacking the sort of physical, organic reality that characterizes the existence of human beings—including the feelings of altruism or, on the other hand, shame—the corporate entity, this concept, this collection of paperwork that has been granted such enormous power, is literally incapable of the social, environmental, or community ideals that we keep hoping it will pursue. Its entire design is to advance only its own self-interest.

Under the distorted system by which corporations are chartered today, it is not in their structure or nature to operate with altruism, idealism, or community or environmental values. When corporations do trumpet such values—as they sometimes do in public relations and advertising or in response to scandal or political pleadings—it is usually precisely because public outrage about a lack of morality has forced them to do so.

Of course, most people will argue that corporations could be more responsible or moral and less self-interested if only the individuals working in them would steer the machine in a more positive direction. (A section following this will make that point.) But the possibilities of that kind of change are ultimately small, at least for publicly held corporations. We have the terrible experiences of the *Exxon Valdez* oil spill off Alaska, for example, and the Union Carbide chemical releases in India. In both cases, when the accidents became known, the heads of each corporation expressed great personal grief and issued apologies for the actions of the corporation. And yet, within a few weeks, they had completely reversed themselves. Where they had first reacted as human beings, they soon had to withdraw from personal feelings that were inapplicable to corporate structure. They began battling mightily against all legal efforts to force them to admit blame or agree to pay damages. This too is built into the corporate form. If corporations officially admit guilt, then stock prices fall, shareholders revolt, bankers withdraw support, lawsuits develop, and investigations and prosecutions sometimes ensue. As for the executives making such admissions, they would certainly be fired for violating the limits of the corporate form, and the next person would be strapped onto the wheel. *When it comes to corporate behavior, form determines function.*

In addition to these unfortunate characteristics, the corporation is also one of the most authoritarian of human institutions. Management authority resides in a chief executive officer, who is accountable to a board of directors charged with assuring that the CEO represents shareholder financial interests. Although the size of a large corporation demands substantial decentralization of actual decision making, formal power resides primarily with the CEO, who has virtually unlimited authority to hire and fire employees, open and close plants, and buy and sell companies. Those whose lives are harmed—even devastated—by these decisions have little recourse.

These limitations of publicly held corporations are particularly evident in U.S. firms. Some Asian and European countries have created checks that allow more space for corporate actions that reflect the broader public good. In Germany, for example, firms larger than a certain size must place worker representatives on their boards of directors. This introduces the direct concerns of a vital segment of society into the corporate boardroom.

Similar rules could, of course, be made in any country about board structure, involvement of stakeholders from the community, restrictions on corporate mobility, worker rights, environmental values, or reinvestment of profits. In the United States, an appropriate mechanism would be to build such new rules into state charters, giving the citizenry a much higher degree of control over corporate behavior and options than at present and confirming citizen sovereignty over the institutions that run society. The Program on Corporations, Law and Democracy is currently attempting to institute initiatives to realize this strategy; we will come back to those later in this chapter. And some years ago, consumer advocate Ralph Nader promoted the idea of a federal charter for corporations, with many new rules to assure responsible behavior by corporations and a shift away from the value system by which corporations currently operate. Shifting the locus from the state to the federal level eliminates the option that corporations might relocate out of any state that adapts tougher chartering language. With the Enron and WorldCom scandals still fresh in our minds, this might be a good time to reintroduce the concept of a federal corporate charter in the United States.

Meanwhile, such possible innovations notwithstanding, corporations as currently structured remain free of any ultimate responsibility to act in moral, altruistic, or any other ways that are beneficial to the community, workers, or the environment. For corporations today, the only principles that have meaning are these:

- The absolute imperative to make a profit
- The imperative to continuously grow and expand territorially and functionally
- The need to control the regulatory, investment, and political climates—locally and globally—to remain as unrestricted as possible in behavior, geographical reach, and access to markets, resources, and labor

Citizen Actions Against Corporate Power

There is a rich history of citizen and worker movements attempting to resist corporate power around the world. The issues gained a new urgency during the 1990s as corporations accelerated their global consolidation.

Citizen activists have pursued a variety of campaign strategies to resist the corporate advance, ranging from reformist to transformative approaches. Reformist strategies—which include attempts to increase corporate responsibility and accountability and to exclude or remove corporations—assume that although there is a need to fine-tune the existing system to somehow strengthen the role of social and environmental values in corporate decision making, the system is basically sound and corporations are, on balance, playing essential and positive roles. *Reformists* implicitly believe that global corporations are here to stay, have a right to exist in their current form, and have the potential to function as responsible citizens—even to chart humanity's collective course to a just and sustainable world.

Some activists, however, reject the idea that corporations have a natural right to exist. Following the Battle of Seattle, Kalle Lasn, and Tom Liacas of *Adbusters* magazine called attention to what they term the *corporate crackdown.*

> The corporation won't come out of this intact. The new activists—and this is what . . . all the keepers of the old order don't get—are no longer protesting against the harms that corporations do, they are protesting against *the corporation itself.* These new activists want to go back to the beginning, back to the laws and legal precedents that gave birth to the corporate "I." They want to tinker with the corporate genetic code, to change the laws under which

charters are granted and revoked, the laws that protect investors from even the foulest taint of their investments, and the rules and regulations under which corporations operate from the local to the international level.

We can call this group the *corporate abolitionists* because they believe it is no longer sufficient to single out those corporations that cause harm to people and the environment and try to make them become more socially responsible. They seek the death penalty for corporations with a habitual record of criminal activity. They call for a comprehensive rethinking and redesign of the corporate charter and corporate law to eliminate those characteristics that make public corporations a threat to the well-being of people and planet, with their concentration of power, absentee ownership, and limited liability.

The underlying premise of the corporate abolitionists is that to end corporate rule, it is necessary not only to eliminate persistent corporate recidivists but also to eliminate those features of the corporation that make corporate rule possible. It will take decades to achieve this end.

In the meantime, there is a place for all of the varied strategies that the different activist groups currently employ. We lay out six options here, starting with the more reformist and going through to the more transformational.

PROMOTE CORPORATE RESPONSIBILITY

One of the long-standing strategies of corporate activists is to call for corporate responsibility. More than the other reformists, those calling for corporate responsibility accept the existence of corporations but ask them to act in a more socially responsible manner, often in relation to specific environmental, labor, and human rights issues. This call is often backed by consumers and shareholders. Religious organizations that have investments in a corporation, for example, may file a shareholder resolution calling for changes in its operations concerning a concrete case of social or ecological harm and organize other shareholders to support the resolution. This strategy was effectively used during the 1970s and 1980s to press commercial banks and other financial institutions in North America and Europe to withdraw loans from the apartheid regime in South Africa. Eventually, this shareholder call for divestment proved to be an effective tool in weakening the apartheid regime.

New York–based Corporate Campaign, Inc. carries out what it calls a *power analysis* of the main stakeholders of offending corporations in order to develop strategies targeted to those corporations' critical vulnerabilities. The strength of this approach was demonstrated by environmental activists in British Columbia in the mid-1990s, in their successful campaign to stop clear-cut logging in old growth forests. By targeting the customers and suppliers of the big forest corporations, they were able to exert sufficient counterpressures to compel the companies to change their destructive practices.

In recent years, corporate responsibility strategies have taken other forms as well. Litigation continues to be used as a tactic to promote socially responsible behavior on the part of corporations. In the United Kingdom, for example, cases have been brought before the British courts against Rio Tinto for uranium dust exposure, and against Thor Chemicals for mercury exposure affecting workers in other countries. In addition, voluntary codes of conduct have been negotiated with big clothing manufacturers, like The Gap and Levi Strauss, to encourage them to adopt more socially responsible employment practices for workers in the Central American and other factories where they have subcontracting relationships. Yet there is no guarantee of compliance, and lack of enforcement invariably arises as a problem because even the most committed corporation faces constant market pressures to cut corners on social and environmental responsibility.

Many corporate responsibility initiatives center on voluntary codes of conduct. This is the case with the United Nations Global Compact, which was launched in 2000. A number of transnational corporations in various sectors of the global economy were invited to sign nine guidelines for responsible corporate action. Those that joined the compact agreed to send case study reports once a year, showcasing their best practices advancing labor, environmental, and human rights standards, to be posted on a United Nations website. For many of the participating corporations—like Nike or Rio Tinto, which have poor track records on human and environmental rights and have been the targets of activist campaigns—the Global Compact turned into little more than a calculated public relations exercise.

Indeed, its sponsorship of the Global Compact dealt a blow to the credibility of the United Nations. By appearing to certify the actions of socially and environmentally destructive corporations, the U.N. became tainted by their actions. The Global Compact delivered an even more direct blow to

U.N. credibility when business leader Goran Lindahl, whom Secretary-General Kofi Annan had appointed as a high-level adviser and recruiter for the compact, was forced out of his position in the wake of a pension fund scandal at Asea Brown and Boveri Corporation, where he was CEO until 2001. Lindahl left with a retirement package of some U.S. $53 million in a year when the company lost $691 million, and its stock price plummeted on the announcement of previously undisclosed asbestos liabilities. The Swedish prime minister called on Lindahl to resign; Kofi Annan decided not to renew his contract; and the company he once headed demanded that he return some of the money.

Despite all this, global corporations argue vigorously that they should not be subject to public oversight or regulation. They maintain that voluntary codes of conduct allowing individual corporations to determine the standards to which they will subscribe, monitor their own performance, and choose which results, if any, they will make public are adequate to deal with issues of corporate responsibility.

Former corporate executive, staunch Republican conservative, investment fund manager, and corporate turnaround specialist Robert Monks makes this observation in his book *The Emperor's Nightingale:*

> From the perspective of company management today the decision whether to obey the law is simply a cost-benefit calculation. The corporation in effect asks whether the costs of disobedience—discounted by the probability of being discovered, prosecuted, and fined (there is almost no risk of jail)—equal the costs of compliance. In many cases, the costs of disobedience are lower than the costs of compliance, and so many corporations find it to their economic advantage to break the law . . . . Corporations are not people; they have no conscience. Although corporate acts are carried out by individuals, even individuals with high moral standards often find themselves caught up in a corporate action that is beyond their control—or even, in some cases, their knowledge.

Monks's conclusion is confirmed in the daily reports of criminal corporate conduct in the *Wall Street Journal.* Such disregard of the law poses severe challenges for the effectiveness of voluntary, self-monitored, self-enforced codes of corporate conduct. Besides breaking the law, lying is another logical manifestation of current corporate structures. The Enron scandal is only a more visible example of the practice of corporate lying not only to the public and the government but also to their own shareholders—and with the complicity of their auditors, whose professional function is to certify to shareholders, the government, and the public that the corporations' financial statements accurately present their financial condition. There was much discussion in the business press after the Enron story broke, about how lying has become virtually a way of life in the corporate world. It is widely acknowledged that the dot-com stock bonanza of the late 1990s was built largely on marketing hype. As a practical matter, it must be assumed that institutions that habitually lie to their shareholders and treat obeying the law as a cost-benefit calculation may also lie about their compliance to voluntary corporate codes, with the complicity of their auditors.

Although promoting corporate social responsibility may not ultimately solve the problem, such efforts as consumer boycotts and shareholder actions do serve two important functions: they temporarily reduce some of the damage, and they engage citizens in the practice of democracy and raise public consciousness of the realities of corporate wrongdoing.

ESTABLISH CORPORATE ACCOUNTABILITY

Corporate accountability campaigns seek to establish legally enforceable standards for corporate conduct. These strategies are pursued through legislative initiatives on wages and working conditions, public health and safety, the environment, financial institutions and transactions, political campaign contributions, and lobbying practices. Often such regulations are voted into place only in the wake of serious scandal and public outcry.

Some local communities are leading the way in passing legislation aimed at making corporations more publicly accountable. A referendum passed by local voters in 1994 gave the town council of Arcata, California, a clear directive to ensure democratic control of all corporations conducting business in the city.

At the national and global levels there have been initiatives aimed at making the overseas operations of home-based corporations more publicly accountable. For example, representative Cynthia McKinney (D-GA) introduced a bill before Congress that would require U.S. corporations to act in a more publicly accountable manner domestically and internationally. The standards include paying a living wage to workers; banning pregnancy testing, retaliation against whistle-blowers, and mandatory overtime for workers under age eighteen; respecting basic ILO standards, such as the right to unionize and health and safety protections; and adhering to both international and U.S. environmental laws and regulations. The code would be enforced first by giving preference to compliant corporations in granting U.S. government contracts and export assistance, and second by empowering the victims, including non–U.S. citizens, to sue the corporations in U.S. courts. Similarly, there is a U.K. case designed to set a precedent for making the head offices of global corporations accountable for the actions of their overseas subsidiaries through the British courts. At a global level, Friends of the Earth has led a coalition effort calling for a corporate accountability convention that would require firms to disclose information to the public about their environmental, labor, and human rights policies.

Such efforts go far beyond voluntary codes of corporate conduct and reduce the organizing burden on consumers and stockholders. However, they do not change the nature of the corporation itself, and they leave governments saddled with the burden of attempting to enforce the law against institutions that are able to spend millions of dollars on lawyers, lobbyists, and politicians to weaken the rules and thwart enforcement action.

EXCLUDE OR EXPEL PREDATORY CORPORATIONS

Some activists have acted to bar unwanted transnational corporations from their communities. For example, when the chemical giant DuPont attempted to relocate a hazardous nylon manufacturing plant from the United States to the Indian state of Goa during the early 1990s, the U.S. trade representative was dispatched to apply pressure at high levels of the Indian government to facilitate the process. As a result, the central government of India not only approved the application but also provided DuPont with land in a village of Tamil Nadu, without consulting the local government. The villagers rose up and refused to accept the plant, forming an anti-DuPont committee to lead the resistance. When the villagers organized a blockade, corporate representatives and the local police attacked; one youth was shot while dozens more were injured in the clashes. After the land was repossessed by village squatters, the local government decided to overturn the planning permit, an act later upheld by a ruling of the high court of India. It was a stunning demonstration of the ability of an organized community to block the entry of a powerful corporation backed by the U.S. government.

The DuPont case is only one of several examples of corporate exclusion campaigns in India. Ever since the Union Carbide plant explosion in Bhopal that resulted in the deaths of thousands of innocent people, there has been a strong resolve on the part of that country's citizens to resist and expel unwanted corporate intruders. In recent years, Coca-Cola, Kentucky Fried Chicken, Monsanto, Cargill, and Enron have all been the targets of popular resistance. For instance, a "Monsanto: Quit India" campaign was launched in 1999 by farmer and consumer organizations after hundreds of suicides in small farm families due to the failure of genetically engineered cotton crops.

Many U.S. communities too have successfully mobilized to exclude Wal-Mart, Rite Aid, and other large retailers. Applying the "three strikes, you're out" principle, Pennsylvania's Wayne Township passed a law stating that any corporation with three or more regulatory violations over seven years is forbidden to establish operations in its jurisdiction.

Although these are basically "not-in-my-backyard" initiatives, they raise public consciousness of the destructive impact of global corporations on people, communities, and the environment. They also prove that corporate domination is not inevitable if citizens organize to take a stand.

REVOKE OR REVISE CORPORATE CHARTERS

In some countries, notably the United States, citizens are reclaiming their right to participate in government decisions about whether specific corporations should be granted a license to operate. As we already noted, a corporation comes into being only when a government grants it a corporate charter. Without that, the corporation does not exist as a legal entity and therefore cannot own property, borrow money, sign contracts, hire and fire, or accumulate assets or debts. In the early days of the United States, corporations were created to serve the public good and existed at the pleasure of the legislature, which could withdraw a charter at will. Citizens could thus keep corporations on a short leash, spelling out the rules they had to follow and holding their owners liable for harm or injuries caused. This situation began to change after an 1886 Supreme Court ruling recognized corporations as "natural persons" under the U.S. Constitution. Hundreds of state laws were struck down, and new laws were passed granting corporations ever greater rights and protections, including limitations on the liability of their shareholders.

Today, the Program on Corporations, Law and Democracy in the United States is leading the way in assisting citizens in reclaiming their sovereign rights over the chartering and rechartering of corporations. According to POCLAD, citizens have the historic right to insist that state-sanctioned corporate charters be periodically reviewed, renewed, and if necessary, revoked. In Pennsylvania, for example, citizen groups have initiated an amendment to the state's corporation code, calling for corporate charters to be limited to thirty years. A charter can be renewed, but only after successful completion of a review process during which it must prove it is operating in the public interest. In California, a coalition of citizen organizations (including the National Organization for Women, Rainforest Action Network, and National Lawyers Guild) petitioned the attorney general to revoke the charter for Union Oil Corporation. Citing California's own corporation code, which authorizes revocation procedures, the coalition fortified the petition with a battery of evidence documenting Union Oil's responsibility for environmental devastation, exploitation of workers, and gross violation of human rights.

Rewriting corporate charters is a step toward changing the nature of the corporate institution. Revoking a charter—the corporate equivalent of a death sentence—begins to put some teeth into the idea of accountability. Eliot Spitzer, attorney general of New York State, declared in 1998: "When a corporation has been convicted of repeated felonies that harm or endanger the lives of human beings or destroy the environment, the corporation should be put to death, its corporate existence ended, and its assets taken and sold at a public auction." Although Spitzer has not won a death sentence against a habitual corporate criminal, he has taken up battle with several giants, including General Electric.

In 1998 in Alabama, Judge William Wynn went so far as to personally file a legal petition to dissolve six tobacco companies on the grounds that they had broken state child abuse laws. Wynn referred to his actions as a "citizen's arrest," but the ruling judge, after meeting with the tobacco companies' legal team, dismissed the case on a technicality.

Although dechartering a major corporation and selling off its assets at a public auction (discussed in the next section) would not solve the larger structural problem, it would certainly send a strong signal to corporate managers and shareholders that obeying the law may be a financially prudent choice.

ELIMINATE LIMITED LIABILITY
AND CORPORATE PERSONHOOD

As already noted, corporations have acquired special rights and exemptions that place them beyond the reach of many laws and liabilities to which ordinary mortals are subject. Shareholders enjoy virtual immunity when it comes to legal responsibility for harms committed against the environment, workers, or communities. So, for example, when Union Carbide caused the deaths of thousands of people in Bhopal because of a plant explosion, or when Exxon destroyed a coastline as a result of the *Valdez* oil leak, the shareholders who invested in these corporate giants were not held liable. Changing the rules to make investors liable for harms done to others in their name would make investing a more serious affair and would greatly change financial calculations made by corporations when deciding what actions to take to protect people and nature. Investors would be compelled to evaluate the environmental, labor, and human rights track record of a corporation before becoming shareholders. Similarly, the CEO and management would give such concerns a higher priority. Some activists are developing legal strategies to challenge and change the laws that grant limited liability to corporate shareholders. Changed laws would truly transform corporate accountability.

As amazing as it seems, the 1886 decision that established the legal doctrine of corporate personhood was based on a simple pronouncement by a single judge. According to the official case record, U.S. Supreme Court Justice Morrison Remick Waite made this pronouncement before the beginning of argument in the case of *Santa Clara County v. Southern Pacific Railroad:*

> The court does not wish to hear argument on the question of whether the provision in the Fourteenth Amendment to the Constitution, which forbids a State to deny any person within its jurisdiction the equal protection of the laws, applies to these corporations. We are all of the opinion that it does.

Few judicial pronouncements have dealt democracy and human rights a more bitter blow. This one established a legal doctrine of corporate personhood that has been used ever since, by corporate lawyers in country after country, to place corporations ever further beyond public accountability for their actions. The authors of this volume strongly endorse citizen action working toward legal and legislative action to eliminate the legal fiction of corporate personhood.

DISMANTLE CORPORATIONS
AND BUY OUT ABSENTEE OWNERS

Finally, some civil society activists are also calling for breaking up large corporations and spinning off their component businesses for sale to workers, customers, suppliers, and community members. This would at once eliminate harmful concentrations of power that distort markets and political processes and greatly reduce the public scourge of absentee ownership—not to mention making markets more efficient.

The challenge is to put in place regulatory regimes and tax policies that mandate or support the breakup of large corporations into human-scale enterprises owned by local stakeholders. Where appropriate, such firms could join cooperative associations or networks to carry out larger projects or achieve economies of scale. When such associations are entered into by local stakeholder-owned enterprises, activities of virtually any scale can be undertaken while remaining locally rooted and accountable. Fast food and beverage franchises might be reorganized as individually owned units that operate under the umbrella of a branding and marketing cooperative. Specifics would vary by industry and corporation, but society should always work from the principle that smaller and locally owned is preferable, in the absence of a compelling argument to the contrary, with the burden of proof resting with those who argue in favor of concentration.

Antitrust reform can tighten the standards for what constitutes excessive concentration. Graduated taxes on assets and total sales—with larger corporations paying a sharply graduated marginal rate—would make size increasingly costly, thus forcing larger enterprises to be more efficient or break themselves up voluntarily. Banking rules might prohibit a single bank from having more than three branches, for example, forcing the breakup of banking conglomerates to spin off clusters of independent community banks. Or there might be a rule that a single enterprise could not own more than one radio or television station using the public airwaves and that its ownership must be limited to people who live in its service area, thus forcing the breakup of media conglomerates and the sell-off of individual stations to people in their own communities. (For detailed recommendations on policy measures to encourage employee ownership, see Jeff Gates, *The Ownership Solution*.)

Ending Corporate-State Collusion

A belief that sovereignty resides in people and gives them an inalienable right to self-governance is the sacred foundation of democracy. Governments are the voluntary creation of the people and therefore subject to their will. Corporations are in turn created when governments issue corporate charters. They are therefore properly subject to the will of the people through their governments. Yet people the world over find corporations corrupting the political system and the courts, in order to co-opt governmental powers and rewrite the laws to advance their own interests.

This process has been carried out by corporate elites who forge common agendas outside the formal institutions of democracy. They use forums such as the Trilateral Commission, the International Chamber of Commerce, the World Economic Forum, trade associations, and the many national and international business and industrial roundtables. The IMF, the World Bank, and the World Trade Organization have all been used by these elites to replace democratic decision making in economic affairs with processes dominated by corporate interests. Although they pay lip service to democracy, the truth of their politics was well stated in a 1974 report of the Trilateral Commission, titled "The Crisis of Democracy," which set forth the argument that "an excess of democracy" had created "a deficit in governability."

By the 1990s, governmental and corporate elites in most countries had largely recast the state from protector of human rights and interests to protector of corporate rights and property. Public resources directed to securing human welfare were redirected to securing corporate welfare. The underlying principle of democracy was turned on its head.

Governmental bodies at both global and national levels now function as if sovereignty resided in global corporations. Their function is to serve the corporate interest, using their coercive powers to protect corporate property, guarantee corporate profits, break up unions, sell off public assets at give-away prices, stifle dissent, and make sure that people fulfill their roles as obedient workers and compliant consumers.

Efforts to transform the corporate institution to eliminate its capacity to rule society must be supported by parallel efforts to restore the integrity of democratic institutions and reclaim the resources that corporations have co-opted. This will require a five-pronged program of action.

GET CORPORATIONS OUT OF POLITICS

It is the place of corporations to observe the rules and restrictions that people democratically choose to impose through their elected representatives. A corporation has no rightful role in making those rules; its role is to provide the information that governments or citizens request of it. Except in the case of criminal proceedings, such requests and the information provided should be public.

Shareholders, managers, employees, consumers, and others have every right as private citizens to express their political views for or against the corporate interest. They also have the right to form and fund not-for-profit organizations to advance any cause they wish to support privately, using their personal funds. Corporations have no such natural right. Nor do corporations have the right to use shareholder monies for political purposes that may be contrary to individual shareholders' preferences. Appropriate legislation would establish the following:

- *A prohibition on any for-profit corporation providing political funds or in-kind support or services.* This includes giving to a political candidate, public official, political action committee, political party, lobbyist, ballot initiative, political convention, meeting of public officials, issue ad, policy group or institute, or any organization that engages in public education or advocacy on matters of public policy. Corporate officers responsible for the violation of this prohibition would be subject to criminal penalties, including imprisonment.
- *Criminal penalties, including imprisonment, for any person who acts in the capacity of corporate officer to solicit political contributions.* Such penalties would

also cover those who request or contract with others to support a political party or candidate, or otherwise seek to influence public policies, regulations, or appointments to positions of public trust.

END CORPORATE WELFARE

Contrary to their claims of efficiency, most large corporations are massively inefficient, spending an inordinate portion of society's resources on advertising, executive perks and salaries, transportation and communications to far-flung corporate empires, and lobbying expenses. Most depend for their profits and survival on a complex regime of public subsidies, exemptions, and externalized costs, including the indirect subsidies they gain when allowed to pay less than a living wage, maintain substandard working conditions, market hazardous products, dump untreated wastes into the environment, and extract natural resources from public lands at below-market prices. Ralph Estes, CPA and professor-turned-corporate-critic, estimates that in 1994 corporations extracted more than $2.6 trillion a year in such subsidies in the United States alone—roughly five times their reported profits. By extrapolation, this suggests that the global public costs of corporate welfare may exceed $10.7 trillion annually. It is one of the basic principles of efficient market function that the full costs of a product or service be borne by the seller and passed on to the buyer. Yet many corporations would be forced to close their doors or restructure if they had to bear the true full costs of their operations. It is time to test the corporate claim of market efficiency by taking legislative action to eliminate all direct cash and in-kind subsidies to corporations, establish and enforce appropriate regulatory standards to compel the full internalization of social and environmental costs, and eliminate special corporate tax exemptions.

GIVE PREFERENCE TO INDEPENDENT ENTERPRISES

To build sustainable communities, it is imperative that local citizens exercise substantial control over the means of production and distribution on which their livelihoods depend. This requires reforming industrial and tax policies—from the global to the local levels—to favor ownership of enterprises and productive resources by local, nonfinancial stakeholders such as workers, community members, customers, and suppliers. Educational programs should inform citizens about the powers and responsibilities of ownership participation and the dysfunctions of absentee ownership.

As chapter 4 detailed, much can be done to encourage local communities to assume responsibility for their own economic and environmental revitalization. Steps can be taken to strengthen community capacity to understand the issues; set clear local economic priorities favoring local ownership and self-reliance; deal with industrial pollution, housing shortages, land use, and transportation issues; hold corporations with operations in a jurisdiction accountable to local social and environmental priorities; and use industrial, environmental, and tax policy measures to encourage the responsible use and maintenance of local natural resources, including forests, fisheries, and water.

Community boards composed of elected citizen representatives might be established to review, approve, and monitor the local operations and investment plans of domestic and foreign-based corporations. These boards might help to establish community accountability rules and obligations for enterprises in their jurisdiction, including banks and other financial institutions.

REREGULATE CORPORATE INVESTMENT

As we have seen, governments have been largely stripped of the powers and tools they once had to regulate the investments of global corporations. Yet regulating corporate investment is essential if people are going to take democratic control of the operations of global corporations and banks. A series of new measures needs to be designed for legislative action, such as "site-here-to-sell-here" policies, the chartering of corporations, restrictions on plant closures, and rules against the patenting of life forms. Governments should be challenged to establish new investment requirements for job content, food safety, and environmental standards, as well as to put more emphasis on worker control, community ownership, and related social responsibilities as conditions for investment. Similarly, governments need to be pressed to reassert control over fiscal policies by reregulating financial instruments (such as derivatives) and banking. To move in this direction, steps need to be taken to identify the obstacles to government control that are built into the new free trade agreements and find strategies to repeal them.

RENEGOTIATE OR ABROGATE TRADE DEALS

As we have seen, the new globalization regimes—for example, the WTO, NAFTA, and the proposed Free Trade Area of the Americas—are, in effect, the constitutions of the new world order, designed primarily to protect the rights and freedoms of global corporations. A program to dismantle this corporate rule, therefore, would have to include strategies either to terminate altogether or to renegotiate specific components of these agreements, keeping in mind that they themselves contain specific clauses and procedures for abrogation that can be exercised by one or more of the partners. The main power tools of NAFTA, such as the investor-state mechanism that allows corporations to sue governments, should be eliminated. Chapter 7 of this volume calls for the decommissioning of the WTO and its replacement with a smaller international trade authority that advances the ten principles for sustainable societies. A variety of social movements actively engaged in campaigns against NAFTA and the FTAA have already shifted their attention to identifying the economic, social, and environmental priorities that need to be addressed as well as other provisions that need to be included in alternative systems based on fair trade. Common platforms can be developed around such campaigns to repeal or renegotiate specific components of free market regimes. Steps could also be taken to organize communities into WTO- and NAFTA-free zones.

Toward Alternative Business Structures

Modern life is now so dominated by global corporations that it is difficult for many people to imagine how the world might go on without them. But businesses may assume many other forms. Transition to more economically democratic structures becomes easier to visualize once we recognize that many human-scale, locally owned enterprises already exist. They include virtually all of the millions of local, independent businesses now organized as sole proprietorships, partnerships, cooperatives of all types, and worker-owned businesses. They include family-owned businesses, small farms, artisanal producers, independent retail stores, small factories, farmers' markets, community banks, and so on. In fact, though these kinds of businesses get very little government support, they are the primary sources of livelihood for most of the world's people.

There are very few of our daily needs that cannot be met by small and medium-size enterprises operating within a market economy of a kind—but one that is characterized by a multitude of small players rather than a handful of giant, absentee owners. And all of them would operate without the benefits of stock market investing, limited liability, or corporate personhood, so crucial to large corporations.

From the point of view of sustainability and democracy, there is no reason why giant transnational corporations are needed to run hamburger stands, produce clothing and toys, publish books and magazines, grow and process and distribute food, make the goods we need, or provide most of the things that contribute to a satisfying existence. In truth, the largest corporations often contract out many of their actual production processes to networks of smaller, independent producers. The dominant global corporations, however, maintain control of market access to be sure of their own ability to dictate terms and prices—in violation of basic market principles—capturing profits for themselves and shifting risks to smaller producers. This is a gross misuse of power, not a sign of superior efficiency. Change is mandatory.

In this chapter, we have described in detail the spectrum of actions now being taken to attempt to control corporate behavior and change many structural elements. In summary, however, from a macro perspective, there are three key ingredients that will characterize any overall shift away from the domination of global corporations and toward more democratic and socially and ecologically sustainable enterprises:

- *Where globalization has encouraged globe-spanning corporate concentration, the course must be reversed.* This can be done by giving priority to smaller businesses capable of functioning as human-scale communities of interest in which people know each other, are dedicated to a common purpose, and share rewards more equitably. The era of CEOs being compensated at five hundred times the level of office workers or line workers must end.
- *Where global corporations now enjoy complete mobility, businesses must be required to be rooted in a place.* They must be owned by people who have direct involvement in the operation—workers, community representatives, suppliers—rather than by distant investors who buy and sell without personal engagement other than profit, growth, and balance sheet figures.

- *All businesses must be transparent and accountable to all stakeholders in the community.* These people bear the ultimate impact of decisions taken. They may include workers, environmentalists, public health officials, human rights advocates, and the like. All have suffered from local activities controlled by distant owners.

And so we see that size, ownership, and accountability are the main issues. Smaller enterprises, with local roots and equitable ownership of productive assets, combined with democratic regulation are essential for socially just, efficient, and sustainable enterprises.

~

By their nature, *human-scale* enterprises—of small and medium size—will distribute power and ownership far more equitably and democratically than global corporations could possibly do. Lacking a global corporation's ability (or desire) to "buy" politicians, dictate consumer choice, or manipulate the symbols of personal identity through mass advertising, smaller enterprises are intrinsically more likely to be responsive to community interests.

The European Commission has defined small and medium businesses as those with less than 250 employees, annual sales under $35 million, and total assets under $24 million. Even this may seem too large for some, but not by the standards of megacorporations: total sales of the Forbes Global 500 list of companies for 2002 ranges from a low of $4.9 billion to $217.8 billion—Wal-Mart—to Citigroup's $1,051 billion in assets. Still, the category of small and medium can include substantial enough enterprises to be able to produce most essential goods and services efficiently.

Where necessary to help deal with new technologies and sophisticated markets, smaller-scale enterprises have shown they can collaborate and network with one another to achieve some efficiencies of scale. Chapter 6 offers some examples of these, but we mention here the case of Denmark, where the entire industrial sector has traditionally been made up of small firms that have sometimes formed consortiums to deal with larger projects. For example, a group of apparel firms jointly employ a designer who has turned once-uncoordinated product lines of clothing into a tailored collection aimed at the larger German market. A consortium of small furniture makers, woodworkers, and interior designers have undertaken joint bidding on the furnishings of convention centers and other projects that are larger in scale than any one company can handle. Similarly, Northern Italy's furniture industry is built on networks of small firms supported by a producers' association that helps provide common services such as warehousing, purchasing, and inventory management.

Although the authors of this report favor *local* procurement and marketing wherever possible, such arrangements as these demonstrate the possibilities of achieving advantages of scale in a system that remains predominantly local.

Of course, the role of *ownership* is also crucial. As discussed earlier, there is an obvious and important distinction between an *engaged stakeholder-owner*—a person who lives within a community and is deeply concerned about its future—and the presently dominant global system of largely *absentee owners*, who have no direct relationship to any community. Global corporate management may be thousands of miles away, across oceans; investors may be anywhere at all, completely unaware of a firm's local activities or impact. This kind of absentee ownership is a perfect precursor for the production of out-of-control harms to the community, just as absentee owners of a house or a building can make life impossible for a local tenant, who has no recourse.

People who live in a place—whether they operate a business or own a home or live on the land—are far more likely to invest well in its maintenance and nurture relationships with their social and environmental context. Ownership adds to their commitment. When businesses are similarly owned by their workers, customers, suppliers, and community members, the owners bear the actual outcomes of their decisions. *Accountability* is built into the fabric of the economic system; *transparency* and openness are impossible to avoid.

In addition to all this, every society also needs enforceable rules, and the marketplace is no exception. The present trend toward deregulation of corporate enterprises, as if they were the one social element that can be counted on to behave responsibly, has been producing disaster after disaster. Enron provides a case in point.

Without comprehensive and firm regulatory mechanisms, even optimum conditions for social and economic efficiency will quickly erode. Size must be regulated, costs internalized (including the environmental and social damages now absorbed by taxpayers), contracts enforced, and health, safety, and environmental standards observed and enforced with great dedication. The previous chapter on subsidiarity suggests many other rules for optimizing social and environmental benefits by businesses, from site-here-to-sell-here rules, to encouragement of local investors rather than outside sources, to corporate finance and mobility regulations. When ownership and rule making are predominantly rooted in local realities, with community welfare as the primary value, then everything else may fall naturally into place, fairly and effectively balancing the interests of local business enterprises with other community values for the mutual benefit of all.

⌒

What we have presented here is only a blueprint, and many practical questions remain. Skeptics may fairly ask if such localized, small arrangements would satisfy people's need to earn a living. Who would provide the food? Who would finance research into new medicines? And if publicly traded corporations were eliminated—and with them the stock market—who would finance retirements? These and other giant issues need to be exhaustively discussed; we hope this chapter serves as a beginning point of such discussions. But we must also begin the discussion with full recognition that the system we have now has utterly failed to solve any of these problems satisfactorily, equitably, and without great harms.

Take the question of jobs. For all their economic power, the number of jobs that global corporations provide relative to the world's workforce is trivial. According to the *Top 200,* a report by Sarah Anderson and John Cavanagh of IPS, although sales of the world's two hundred largest corporations are equivalent to 27.5 percent of world GDP, they employ only 0.78 percent of the world's workers. As we have said, the majority of the world's jobs are provided even today by small and medium-size enterprises—the same enterprises that are also responsible for creating nearly all new jobs. As corporations get ever larger and consolidate, merge, and consume other companies, they convert to production systems and technologies that *reduce* jobs rather than increase them.

Next, food. Before a combination of intentional public policy and corporate monopolization of marketing and distribution forced most independent farmers into bankruptcy, small farms were the backbone of most communities and the primary suppliers of food, even in the Northern industrial countries. Even now they retain central roles in most Southern countries. Smaller, independently managed farms using environmentally sound organic agricultural practices are far more efficient in their use of scarce land than are corporate factory farms, and they provide more jobs. Localizing production to reduce the distance between farm and market means fresher, more nutritional food and big energy savings—a subject that will be addressed in more detail in chapter 6.

As for drug research, if development of copycat drugs is excluded, most basic research on new drug treatments is publicly funded and much of it carried out in universities. For all their claims that monopoly pricing is necessary to recover research costs, drug companies spend far more on marketing than on research. These costs are a larger factor in the exorbitant drug prices than research costs. The greatest barrier to the deconcentration of drug production and distribution is not technology but the granting of monopoly patent rights to giant pharmaceutical companies for essential drugs developed with public research money. A reduction in patent protection to allow entry to smaller, more local competitors would be a step toward freeing the market to gain the benefits of greater competition.

Financing retirement? Those who are presently fortunate enough to have the money to participate in the stock market, and lucky enough to pick the right stocks at the right time, can use it to finance an affluent retirement. However, we must not be misled by the fact that although some retirement accounts profited handsomely from the giant stock bubble of the 1990s, many others were decimated. It would be a stretch to assume that society can feed, house, clothe, and provide medical care for an aging population based on stock bubbles. Meeting the needs of the retired necessarily depends on the willingness of those of working age to lend their labor and assets to the task of providing for them as part of an intergenerational social contract. The corporate global economy is actually decapitalizing the human and physical infrastructure needed to support the young and old alike in favor of short-term financial gains, eroding the social contract between generations. To rebuild the social contract—the social and physical infrastructure needed to meet the needs of children, working people, and the elderly—it is essential to restore the concept of community, in part by rebuilding prosperous community economies.

When the full costs are taken into account, most of the real needs of people can be more efficiently met by a local market system, which also has the potential to improve the quality of life of nearly everyone. With proper care and a just distribution of the planet's sustainable bounty, the world's six billion–plus inhabitants can live full and dignified lives. Hardship and material deprivation can be eliminated. This necessarily means less material consumption for the world's favored few. It may, however, prove that "less is more" in terms of achieving sustainable societies.

CHAPTER SIX

Alternative Operating Systems

IN CHAPTER 2, we listed ten principles that should set the standards for all economic activity: democracy, subsidiarity, ecological sustainability, common heritage, diversity, human rights, sustainable livelihoods and employment, food security and safety, equity, and the precautionary principle. These principles guide our recommended changes in the institutions that form the basic architecture of the global economy. No longer should bureaucracies and global corporations operate on *their* set of values, placing economic growth and corporate profits at the top of a hierarchy that does not take crucial social and ecological norms into consideration.

But our discussion would be incomplete if we did not recognize that the problems reside not only in the bureaucracies and corporations that presently deprive citizens and nation-states of the ability to act on their own behalf. They are part of the fabric of the practical operations of society, especially in its most important economic systems: energy, agriculture and food, transportation, and manufacturing.

It should not come as a surprise that each of these sectors has adopted standards, or forms of production and distribution, that are anathema to the core values that we propose should govern society. In fact, they are entirely compatible with—indeed they exude the same fundamental values as—the larger globalizing forces. They are all part of a single integrated megastructure that *is* the global economy, which extends right down into our nations and communities. It will not be possible to build more sustainable international structures without also redesigning many of the world's key operating systems.

~

It is not the purpose of this report to issue a full analysis of every economic operating system in our society; we save that for another day. But this chapter will examine five key elements: the four systems we have mentioned—energy, agriculture, transportation, and manufacturing, which are the primary structures of day-to-day economic life in modern society—and fifth, the measurements and indicators that society now uses to evaluate its overall performance. All of these systems, like the entire global bureaucratic architecture, must be changed to reflect a new hierarchy of values that we hope will eventually dominate all economic activity.

Over the next few years of this exploratory process, we will be directly involving grassroots organizations throughout the world in a multiyear program to amplify and complete the directions we are now beginning to set forth.

I. Energy Systems

No domain of global economic activity does greater social, environmental, and political harm than today's dominant energy systems, from source to waste. Yet ironically, there is no area so susceptible to satisfactory, short-run conversion and excellent available alternatives.

New energy production in most parts of the world today, but especially in the Western industrial nations, is based on fossil fuels: oil, coal, and natural gas, augmented in some places by large-scale hydroelectric and nuclear power. Production is highly concentrated on a global basis. In petroleum, for example, a handful of gigantic oil companies and a small number of global production cartels among the oil-producing nations control much of the world's supply and pricing.

Global trade and finance bureaucracies have consistently made rules and policies that strongly favor fossil fuel production above all other options, to the detriment of the many viable alternative systems that would be far more appropriate and efficient and far less environmentally, socially, and politically damaging.

The only alternatives to the fossil fuel–based production that the Bretton Woods institutions now find acceptable are either large hydroelectric dams or nuclear energy. Both of those share with fossil fuel systems the inherent large-scale centralized attributes that make them appropriate processes for global enterprises alone to control. They both also share the same strong potential for environmental and social catastrophes. So they offer little in the way of alternative possibilities.

Each of the energy systems named has environmental problems that are well enough known that it is probably not necessary to repeat them here, except to mention what is specifically looming as the major crisis of our time and is a direct result of fossil fuel production—rapid and devastating climate change. No world problem demands more immediate attention than this because it will otherwise overwhelm any efforts to achieve sustainable future societies, and it threatens the survival of human and other species. Nonetheless, fossil fuel production continues to be subsidized by nation-states at a phenomenal rate, amounting to $300 billion globally. The United States alone directly subsidizes these energy systems at more than $20 billion annually. Even this figure, however, does not begin to cover the *full* costs of fossil fuel systems, including staggering environmental damage and the immense investment in military programs to protect vulnerable supply lines as well as the often corrupt oil-producing nations.

Despite the many environmental, social, and political dangers of fossil fuel systems, major international financial institutions have consistently rewarded enthusiastic financiers and promoters of fossil fuel and other large-scale energy systems, especially in the developing world.

According to a report by the Institute for Policy Studies (IPS) authored by Jim Vallette and Daphne Wysham, the World Bank has financed $13.6 billion worth of energy products since the Rio Earth Summit in 1992, including fifty-one coal, oil, and gas-fired power plants and twenty-six coal mines. These projects will emit thirty-eight billion tons of carbon dioxide over their lifetimes, nearly double the emissions of all countries combined in 1996. Meanwhile, less than 3 percent of the World Bank's energy budget is devoted to alternative, renewable energy systems. Between 1992 and 1998, it spent over twenty-five times more on fossil fuel projects than on renewable energy. As for conservation programs, the bank spent nothing at all despite the many simple programs (like switching a country from incandescent to fluorescent lightbulbs) that would have eliminated a high percent of large-scale fossil fuel developments and would have been faster and cheaper. But the immediate beneficiaries of the World Bank's projects are global corporations, which have been granted 95 percent of the contracts; they would gain nothing from conservation.

Meanwhile, the Overseas Private Investment Corporation (OPIC) and the Export-Import Bank (Ex-Im)—U.S. export credit agencies (ECAs) that use taxpayers' monies to subsidize U.S. commercial interests in developing nations—have also devoted billions of dollars to fossil fuel–based energy projects. According to IPS, the cumulative support for coal, oil, and gas projects by Ex-Im and OPIC between 1992 and 1998 totaled $23.2 billion. These projects will ultimately release 29.3 billion tons of carbon dioxide over their lifetimes. There is a similar story for the British Export Credit Guarantee Department, which has backed coal-fired plants in China as well as enormous plants in India, Indonesia, and elsewhere, thus effectively subsidizing such companies as Shell, Amoco, Mitsubishi, Enron, and Texaco.

In most cases, multilateral development banks ignore renewable energy projects and undermine localized systems of production and consumption that could reduce overall energy consumption. Thus, by emphasizing fossil fuel development to meet the demands of globalization, the World Bank and the other development agencies are playing a lead role in accelerating climate change.

~

Besides these global development and lending bureaucracies, as well as the oil-producing cartels and the oil companies themselves, the most important actors in this crisis are the most developed nations. The United States has been the leading consumer and promoter of fossil fuel usage and the main opponent of meaningful reforms. It even declined to sign the very modest reforms outlined in the Kyoto Protocol on Global Warming, which was endorsed by most other countries.

The United States now uses about 25 percent of the world's oil production, even though its population represents only about 4 percent of the global total. The oil is used largely to service U.S. automobile and other fuel-intensive transportation systems. So dependent has this country become on oil shipments from faraway places—notably Saudi Arabia, which has 25 percent of the world's known oil reserves—that it spends an estimated $25 to $35 billion a year to militarily protect a corrupt Saudi regime and other Middle Eastern sources. Meanwhile, domestic opportunities in the United

States for easing the dependency on foreign oil by converting to alternative renewable energy forms have been resisted by the government, and particularly by the oil-friendly George W. Bush administration, as too impractical or expensive (as if wars were not).

Some scholars and critics—notably the London-based New Economics Foundation (NEF) in its report *The Environmental War Economy*—argue that Western industrial nations have already so overused their proportional share of the global fossil fuel supply and have caused so much more than their proportional share of pollution within the "global atmospheric commons" that they owe a major "ecological debt" (as well as a financial one) to the less developed countries of the world. Many Southern countries agree, and they go so far as to argue that such agreements as the Kyoto protocol must drastically reduce energy use in Northern countries, whereas less developed Southern countries should be granted some time to make up for prior exploitation that has hindered their development. (Southern countries also put forward the argument that in addition to the oil-based ecological debt, Northern countries owe them a major debt based on their ravaging of the biodiversity of the South for some five hundred years. (See Box K in chapter 3 for more on this.)

The concept of a global atmospheric commons is amplified by Peter Barnes, founder of Working Assets. In his book *Who Owns the Sky*, Barnes proposes a system by which all citizens of the world are given recognized "property rights" over the atmosphere. They would have rights to determine whether "use" may be made of the atmosphere by any commercial players, or whether alternative energy forms are a better choice. If permission is granted for some level of atmospheric pollution—presumably an amount that is tiny by today's standards—high fees would be paid by the commercial parties for this right, and those fees would ultimately go back to individual citizens on an equal basis, per capita by country. Barnes argues that this would reverse present subsidies and unaccountability for energy development and create a disincentive for this form of energy.

⌒

Perhaps the most problematic systemic aspect of the global oil-based economy is the inherently long and highly vulnerable "supply line" between producers and consumers.

The oil must be moved by some combination of supertankers crossing oceans and truckers crossing countries on public highways, or else through vulnerable oil pipelines that traverse thousands of miles of terrain, often in fragile wilderness regions and indigenous lands. These pipelines also span several nation-states with varying political and military climates and varying degrees of protection.

Each of these modes of transport can (and has) brought enormous geopolitical and ecological problems, including recent oil wars. Worst of all, the very length of these supply lines combined with the extreme volatility of oil make them spectacularly vulnerable to deliberate disruption. For example, one oil pipeline running through Colombia's jungles has been bombed more than four hundred times by varying sides of a three-way war that is presently waging there, causing ecological havoc. In Alaska, a lone gunman recently fired rifle shots into the Alaskan pipeline, spilling thirty-five hundred barrels of oil over the fragile tundra. As for the other methods of transport, readers know the many examples of oil tankers spilling their cargo into the ocean and onto beaches, killing wildlife and destroying delicate aquatic ecosystems. The sheer length of these supply lines have made it necessary to spend enormous sums to try to protect them militarily as well as to subsidize cleanup costs. These subsidized costs do not show up in the price of oil at the pump.

Finally, of course, who could possibly forget that its volatility made jet fuel the perfect choice of terrorists on September 11, 2001, when it was delivered by hijacked airplanes with horrifying results? Those attacks on New York and Washington, D.C., have in turn led to a war costing tens of billions of dollars. Tens of billions more will be spent to rebuild Afghanistan and protect Saudi Arabia, and to cover the *annual* costs of U.S. homeland defense. It is surely fair to include some of these expenses when reckoning the whole bargain that is involved in oil dependency.

THE PROMISE OF ALTERNATIVE ENERGY SYSTEMS

There is no longer any reason for this unsustainable situation to persist—that is, none other than the immense pressures by the oil companies themselves as they seek to maintain state and global institutional interventions on their behalf. Considering the social, environmental, and security problems intrinsic to fossil fuel–based economies, it is a wonder that this form of energy production has survived to the present at all.

A number of countries have already shown that it is possible to eliminate dependency on electricity generated from nuclear power, which also poses an unnecessary threat to the health and security of millions of people around the world.

- Italy shut down all five of its nuclear reactors between 1987 and 1990, after the accident at Chernobyl and a vote by the Italian people in a referendum against nuclear power.
- Following a referendum in 1980, Sweden announced that it would phase out its twelve nuclear reactors, which generated half of the country's electricity. The first has already been closed as this volume goes to print. A second will close by 2003. New capacity will come largely from energy conservation and wind power.
- Belgium announced in 1999 that it would phase out its seven nuclear reactors, which generate nearly 60 percent of the country's electricity, between 2015 and 2025.
- The Netherlands is closing down its two nuclear reactors by 2003.
- Germany pledged in 2000 to close down all of its nineteen nuclear reactors, which generate 30 percent of its electricity, by 2021. Wind power will replace them.

Right now, most of the technology needed for a complete transformation of our energy infrastructure is already available. We can increase energy efficiency many times over and meet all our remaining needs with a mix of renewable resources: solar, biomass, geothermal, minihydro, micropower turbines, and most imminent and important, wind energy and hydrogen fuel systems; the latter is directly applicable to cars, trucks, airplanes ships, and all other modes of transit.

None of these alternative technologies are difficult to develop or esoteric; in fact, all are already in use in many places. For example, Denmark already gets 15 percent of its total electricity from wind turbines. Hydrogen and solar energy systems are already powering the U.S. space program and many other military programs. In Germany, BMW is already operating and selling hydrogen-powered cars with conventional engines that are far more efficient than gasoline-powered cars. In Japan, Mazda is converting its rotary engine to hydrogen; it will be ready in 2004. DaimlerChrysler, Ford, Honda, Toyota, and GM are also developing hydrogen fuel cell cars. And the Rocky Mountain Institute—an important technology think tank and research institute directed by Amory Lovins—has completed design and construction of a prototype hydrogen fuel cell "hypercar" that will be inexpensive, has most of the safety and performance features of standard cars, and is claimed to achieve the equivalent of ninety-nine miles per gallon using hydrogen. (See Lovins's book *Hypercars: Materials, Manufacturing, and Policy Implications.*)

Hydrogen has none of the geopolitical problems of oil, and it is *not* scarce. It is, in fact, the most plentiful element in the universe and can be converted directly from water. It can be unlocked from water by electrolysis, using electrical energy from wind turbines, or it can be reformed from natural gas. The process is relatively simple; it does not pollute—its only tailpipe emission is water—and *no global cartel can control it.*

Iceland has begun work to achieve its goal of becoming the first country in the world to use hydrogen-fuel cell technology to displace all of its remaining fossil fuel use by 2030. And the state of North Dakota is gearing toward the introduction of ten thousand megawatts from wind generation on farmlands there. Denmark plans to build a new series of large-scale offshore wind farms in the North Sea and the Baltic that will generate half of the country's power by 2030.

Clearly, change is already under way.

Lester Brown, founder of the Worldwatch Institute, predicts that in many countries wind turbines will supply both electricity and, through electrolysis of water, hydrogen. Together, says Brown, "electricity and hydrogen can meet all the energy needs of a modern society."

In another report from Worldwatch, "Hydrogen Futures," Seth Dunn predicts a nearly complete transition from fossil fuels to hydrogen within a century, although it could be argued that we should move much faster than that if we are to save the global climate. Dr. Ty Cashman, former secretary of energy of California, says that "an informed global public may be all that is required to bring an end to the climate-destabilizing fossil fuel era." And U.S. Windpower Corporation founder Alvin Duskin, now head of the new Committee for the Conversion of the Oil-Based Economy, an NGO in San Francisco, says, "The only thing limiting the immediate conversion is the assumption that hydrogen is more expensive to produce than oil, but only if you ignore the repeating military costs from protecting oil suppliers and fighting wars, and the environmental costs from cleanups of oil spills and the like. If you delivered those costs to the pumping station, hydrogen would already be far cheaper. In any case, within a few years the unit price will be lower than gasoline, no matter how the costs are calculated."

⁓

In a recent comprehensive report, "Energy Innovations: A Prosperous Path to a Clean Environment," the Cambridge, Massachusetts–based Union of Concerned Scientists (UCS), founded by the late Nobel laureate Dr. Henry Kendall, undertook a thorough analysis of steps needed to make a transition from fossil fuels to an energy future without the myriad political, economic, environmental, and social harms that are inherent in the present model. In addition to endorsing most of the alternative systems already mentioned, UCS cites recent advances in membrane technologies, advanced gas turbines, and integrated green building designs that would further reduce dependency on either fossil fuels or nuclear sources. UCS also suggests a highly innovative set of new tax strategies that could reallocate costs to motivate higher energy efficiency and lower emissions while avoiding any overall increase of taxes and fees.

Other well-circulated tax ideas include a so-called carbon tax on fossil fuels and a Tobin tax on all international financial transactions. This latter tax could be earmarked directly for the conversion away from a fossil fuel economy. It should be remembered that thirty years ago, production tax credits helped kick-start a vital new turn to solar and wind. But when oil prices plummeted and Ronald Reagan took office, all that changed. It must now be revived again.

All of the above is aside from the great contribution that could be made to this transition from even minimal efforts at direct energy conservation. The New Economics Foundation points out that energy has been conserved on a mass scale with enormous success in many countries in periods of crisis. During World War II, for example, the United Kingdom reduced its fossil fuel use by 80 percent yet still mounted a major military effort. The United States had similar results on the occasions in its history when energy conservation became a national priority—unlike the present, when additional consumption is the national goal. In recent years, countries such as Germany, Japan, and Sweden have drastically reduced their energy use without notable diminishment in lifestyle. Indeed, such changes would likely bring a far more peaceful, healthful existence within newly stabilized and localized democratic systems.

If we converted now to this kind of combination of new energy sources for all electricity and transportation, we would immediately achieve the following positive outcomes:

- Greenhouse gas emissions (global warming) would be reduced by at least 30 percent in two decades, and much more after that.
- Dependency on expensive, environmentally disastrous long-distance shipment of petroleum would be eliminated.
- The powers of corrupt, undemocratic governments and gigantic industry cartels would be undermined.
- Vulnerability to oil price and supply shocks that bring global economic crises would be reduced.
- Military expenditures for the protection of oil-producing nations and the supply lines that connect them to their customers would be reduced.
- New jobs in more labor-intensive localized alternative energy fields would be created.
- The primary contributor to air and land pollution as well as acid rain would be eliminated.
- The impact on indigenous peoples of the world, whose lands are often targeted for exploitation and invasion for their oil reserves, would be lessened.
- Vulnerability to accidents or terrorist attacks would be reduced. (Most experts believe that a hydrogen-powered jetliner striking a skyscraper would have produced no explosion at all.)

~

The reports we have cited here are only a few of dozens of recent reports and books that demonstrate why a transition from fossil fuels is practical, viable, and desirable. (See sources, at the end of this volume, for many more.) Clearly, there is no longer any reason to continue to be held hostage to an energy system that has, as part of its inherent package, such grave environmental, political, and military challenges and benefits only large corporations and political tyrants. We have the technologies and know-how to convert to energy forms that offer permanent benefits to the environment, public safety, and democracy.

To increase the political viability of this transformation, many NGOs and some government agencies are circulating draft domestic sustainable energy statutes, as well as draft international treaties, to establish independent international agencies to work with and lead governments in making these changes. Among the more comprehensive and widely circulated is an international sustainable energy fund statute prepared by the New York–based Global Resource Action Center for the Environment (GRACE). A full draft was released at the World Summit on Sustainable Development in Johannesburg in August 2002 (see www.gracelinks.org). The fund would support sustainable energy programs for the world's two billion poor and would finance them with the savings from the phaseout of government subsidies to fossil fuels. Imagine the impact if such a fund were established and the fossil fuel lending of the international financial institutions and government export credit agencies were eliminated.

And Michael Northrup of the Rockefeller Brothers Fund, a foundation in New York, argues that the people of most countries are way ahead of politicians, especially in the United States. On climate change issues, for example, he says, "Growing evidence suggests that a real movement has begun at the *subfederal* level to lower greenhouse gas emissions, often at rates equal to or better than those proposed in any international accord." He offers the following inspiring list of grassroots actions in the United States:

- Six New England states, together with five eastern Canadian provinces, agreed this past spring to reduce greenhouse gas emissions by 70 to 80 percent to help stabilize the globe's climate system.
- New York State is now in the process of formulating a climate action plan.
- Massachusetts became the first state in the nation last year to mandate reductions in carbon emissions from power plants.
- California legislators recently passed new state automobile efficiency rules to meet the Kyoto auto emissions reduction target.
- Fifteen states have developed clean energy funds with $3.5 billion in

expected assets to underwrite the development of clean energy generation in their states.

- Thirteen states have adopted policies that require some portion of the power generated to come from renewable sources.
- Nearly forty states have put in place net metering rules that allow utility customers to generate energy at home, using solar arrays, wind power, and eventually fuel cells, and to sell the excess energy back into the electric power grid. (This reduces the cost for households wishing to install renewable energy systems by allowing them to pay down purchase costs more quickly.)
- More than one hundred municipalities across the country have developed plans for greenhouse gas reductions of up to 20 percent.
- Seattle's city council formally passed a measure adopting the Kyoto protocol.
- Chicago announced that it would demand that 20 percent of all its energy come from renewable sources.
- San Francisco voters passed a referendum that will turn city rooftops into solar collectors to generate clean power.
- Six hundred hospitals recently announced that they want to purchase renewable power.
- Faith communities are also getting involved, with scores of churches, mosques, and synagogues around the country promising to reduce their emissions.
- Several universities, including Tufts, have adopted the Kyoto protocol and are analyzing their emissions footprints and adopting reduction strategies.
- Wesleyan University announced that it would seek to buy 10 percent of its power from renewable sources.
- Anecdotal evidence is emerging of increasing numbers of individual households adopting their own emissions reduction strategies.

Although these examples of grassroots action are still insignificant on the larger plane, they do signify an awakening public. And getting the United States to take real action is critical. Although the rest of the world community is willing to take action without the United States, a strengthened subfederal reductions movement connected to federal policymaking could help the transition happen faster.

II. Transportation Systems

In the previous section, we briefly mentioned some implications of an expanded global transportation infrastructure. Built to service the global economy, it brings a multitude of negative consequences. With export production as a central feature of free trade, there has been a massive increase in ocean shipping, highway transport, air cargo transport, rail, and so forth, with a tremendous corresponding increase in infrastructure development. The latter includes new highways, seaports, airports, canals, and pipelines, often built in pristine wilderness areas, on coral reefs, in indigenous lands, and in rural communities. Considerable social problems have resulted in some instances, but the environmental problems are also crucial, not the least of which is the dramatic acceleration of climate change.

THREE PRIMARY MODES

Let's look briefly at the three primary modes of transport.

Ocean Shipping

Ocean shipping has expanded more than tenfold since the 1950s, primarily because of increased commodity export activity from economic globalization. Ocean shipping accounts for more than 90 percent of commodity trade shipments, with the industry consuming more than 140 million tons of fuel annually, polluting oceans, destroying wildlife, and emitting carbon dioxide. Particularly problematic is that most ocean shipping is fueled by very low-quality oil known as "Bunker C," an extremely heavy polluter. Many experts predict a doubling of transoceanic shipping activity over the next ten years.

Air Transport

A smaller amount of cargo is shipped by air than by sea or by land; it is by far the least efficient means of transporting goods to market. Nonetheless, air cargo is the fastest growing transport sector. Boeing forecasts a tripling of air cargo activity by 2017. The results would be dire for the environment. As mentioned in Box C in chapter 1, each ton of freight that moves by air uses forty-nine times as much fuel per kilometer as the same goods carried on ships. Worse, aircraft emissions are made at high altitudes, where the impact of emissions on the greenhouse effect is maximized.

Increases in air miles and new airports are the result not only of shipments of commodities but also of an exponential increase in business and tourist air travel in the global economy. Between 1980 and 1996, the number of tourists traveling internationally increased from 260 million to 590 million, and they traveled mostly by air. This growth, in turn, increases tourist infrastructures to service the larger population of travelers: development in pristine places of new hotels, golf courses, marinas; use of high-speed boats and off-road vehicles; construction of entertainment and restaurant complexes; and so on. In some parts of the world, this invasion of tourists has been extremely unwelcome as it often pushes indigenous populations away from traditional sustainable livelihoods in agriculture and fishing. Some lose their ability to survive while others are converted into maids, waiters, and bellboys serving wealthy foreign tourists. The cultural impact is devastating. The new ecotourism trend has not improved matters much, though some native communities are attempting now to make compromises that they believe they may somehow be able to control.

Trucking

Freight movement across land has also increased sharply because of economic globalization. Europe, for example, has seen a tripling of transborder truck traffic, from four hundred billion ton-kilometers in 1970 to twelve hundred billion in 1997. The conversion of agriculture to industrial production for export has drastically increased "food miles," or the distance that food travels from source to plate, often amounting to thousands of miles in the global economy at great environmental cost. (See the following section on agriculture.) From 1986 to 1991, for example, the distance that food traveled increased by 19 percent over previous levels, even though the total volume of food shipment was up only 8 percent.

In the United States in 1994, trucks traveled 182 billion miles on U.S. interstate highways, whereas total intercity truck transport was about 900 billion miles.

To accommodate such a spectacular increase in truck travel, vast new networks of highways and railroads are being built all over the world. The European Union alone is building twelve thousand kilometers of new highways to help further market integration throughout Europe. A similar picture prevails globally.

About 60 percent of the world's use of oil goes directly toward transportation activities, and this percentage is increasing annually.

SUBSIDIES

None of this growth in transport activity could take place without the hundreds of billions of dollars that governments spend on transportation subsidies. We have already mentioned $300 billion in direct subsidies worldwide for fossil fuel production, including tax incentives for oil companies. These subsidies are an important reason why prices at the pump stay relatively low. But if we included the money that governments around the world invest in roads, rail, airports, seaports, and other transportation infrastructures, the direct subsidies to oil companies would be dwarfed. *If that kind of gigantic subsidy regime went instead to public mass transportation systems and alternative transportation schemes, many of our problems would be solved.* The reason they do not comes down to the immense power of global corporations to control governments and international bureaucracies.

Like nearly every aspect of the globalization model, the transport industry is characterized by oligopolistic conditions in every sector. Ten automobile companies account for about 65 percent of global car and truck production; nine oil companies account for about 80 percent of petroleum production. According to the U.S.–based Institute for Policy Studies, of the one hundred largest economies in the world—this includes nation-states as well as giant corporations—twelve are oil or automobile companies. These companies illustrate the advantages of global scale augmented by favorable rules and free entry interventions from global economic bureaucracies like the WTO.

It could be argued that the most important single act to improve the health of the planet and the quality of urban life would be to lessen the volume of international and long-distance transport. This goal can only be achieved by consciously reversing present priorities favoring large-scale export-oriented global economies and instead invoking the principle of *subsidiarity*: emphasizing local economies, using local resources and labor, and primarily benefitting local communities. As we have said earlier, we do not suggest eliminating international trade, only that it become the last option rather than the first. It should be saved for the times when local needs cannot be locally satisfied. The net result of this conscious reversal toward subsidiarity would be a swift downturn in export and import activity, a diminishment of the volume of transport activity, and a quick benefit for the global atmosphere and climate and global ecosystems and habitats. It could also mean a revival of local economies, especially if savings in subsidies now directed at global transport infrastructures were used for local infrastructures servicing local needs. In turn, this would mean a diminishment of the powers of global energy and oil companies and the kinds of geopolitical problems that result from this situation.

THE PRIVATE CAR

Although every means of transport has intrinsic problems, the private automobile has the greatest impact of all. By now it should be clear that one of the worst decisions ever made by modern society was to embrace the concept of the private car and the internal combustion engine, at the turn of the twentieth century, and then to glorify it, subsidize it, and design all of life around it.

Even in less developed nations, the private car has become the predominant factor in the organization of everyday life. Urban environments have been centered on accommodating it, finding ways to move it without congestion, parking it, regulating its speed, controlling its dangers. And yet its impacts are unabated. According to the World Resources Institute, in 1990 there were already 580 million four-wheeled motor vehicles on the road; by 2010, the estimate is 800 million.

Automobile companies have been exceedingly effective in creating advertising images of the joys of private car ownership as the apex of social achievement, even in poverty-stricken countries. In the United States, as elsewhere, automobile companies in the early and mid-twentieth century were able to lobby governments to destroy very workable and sustainable transportation systems—notably light rail—and to replace them with highways, new infrastructures, and auto accommodations. This happened especially in California, notably in Los Angeles and San Francisco. A wonderful light rail system that bound together the entire San Francisco Bay Area was eliminated, only to be replaced twenty years later by a new, very expensive

Bay Area Rapid Transit System (BART) that does not cover sufficient area and is far more costly to use. In the United States, urban passenger transportation systems are now more than 90 percent auto-based.

Automobiles have been the primary technology in the post–Industrial Revolution era to reorganize life on earth and bring us to the urban situation we are now in.

~

Problems with the automobile do not begin and end with the fuel it uses or with how efficiently it operates. True, it would be hard to imagine any technology less efficient than a large structure built of steel, rubber, and hundreds of other materials, weighing 2,000 pounds, to carry a single passenger weighing 150 pounds while burning enormous quantities of gasoline to do so. But the ramifications of the car are far broader than that.

Aside from a dependence on oil, the private car uses more scarce resources in its construction than any other product on earth. Highways and concrete now cover virtually every region of the developed world and much of the rest of the world too. Noise from cars is omnipresent, even in wilderness regions, comparable to a society-wide case of tinnitus. The many kinds of pollution that automobiles bring include smog, acid rain, lead poisoning, ozone depletion, and others. The problem of solid waste disposal for used automobiles, which is often toxic, is also reaching crisis proportions, especially as automobile manufacturers continue to bombard us with appeals to throw away cars we may have only recently purchased.

Some of the world's most diversely interesting cities are being rapidly homogenized in service to the car. Mexico City, London, Manila, Bangkok, Rome, Paris, Athens, Sao Paulo, Tokyo, Madrid, Jakarta: like New York, Chicago, and Los Angeles they are being rapidly ruined by the domination, congestion, smog, noise, and danger from cars. According to a report by Logan Perkins, published in *Livable Cities,* more than fifty thousand people in the United States alone are killed in automobile accidents annually, with pedestrians counting as one-fifth of those. Throughout the world, the experience of urban life is being unified but at the lowest common denominator— a new standard of unpleasantness and dysfunction. All this is to benefit a small number of gigantic automobile and oil companies who have actively, over decades, lobbied against and otherwise destroyed alternative systems.

ECOCITIES

Recently, there have been a series of important ecocity conferences as urban areas try to gain control of their transportation systems and other ecological and social problems caused by the present trend of sprawl—housing that requires longer distance transport, usually by private car, and separates life's functions. Jobs are a hundred miles from home; shopping is somewhere else altogether; and public places are largely absent.

Already, some cities have moved to the forefront of these experiments in redesigning transportation, notably Porto Alegre and Curitiba in Brazil (see Box L) as well as Copenhagen, Stockholm, and Portland, Oregon, among others. Once democratic processes are under way, solutions are not complex, and they have the advantages of being less costly than present systems and far more convivial. The goal is obviously to reduce the impacts of the noisy, dangerous, gas-guzzling, dominant global transportation technologies and replace them with more efficient (in terms of material and energy consumption per capita) public transit systems. These include a combination of high-speed rail (for long-distance travel), and for cities, light rail, buses that can run on fast dedicated lanes, and greater emphasis on bicycles for short-distance private travel. These can be augmented by taxis—over the long haul they are far cheaper to use than cars—or by flexible jitney and shuttle services. Accommodations for the private car might eventually cease.

In addition, cities around the world have already begun to experiment to varying degrees with excluding cars from parts or all of the city. Amsterdam allows no private cars at all in most of the city center, while accommodating bicycles, light rail, and very small lorries needed for business purposes, as well as canal barges. In Copenhagen, 32 percent of all trips are by bicycle. And throughout Western industrial countries, bicycle riders are undertaking demonstrations on wheels—often under the banner "Critical Mass"—demanding dedicated bike paths, access to public transportation with their bikes, and other accommodations.

Lester Brown of the Worldwatch Institute predicts that bicycle manufacture, like industries devoted to hydrogen energy and solar and wind energy, will be among the great growth industries of the near future. "Because the bicycle is nonpolluting, frugal in its use of land, and provides the exercise much needed in sedentary societies, future reliance on it is expected to grow," says Brown. "As recently as 1965, the production of cars and bikes was essentially the same, but today more than twice as many bikes as cars are manufactured each year. Among industrial countries, the urban transport model being pioneered in the Netherlands and Denmark, where bikes are featured predominantly, gives a sense of the bicycle's future role worldwide."

There are some regrettable anomalies, however. With the opening to free market activity in places like China, and especially now with China's admission to the WTO, it will soon be experiencing exactly the opposite of the positive steps that we've described. Major global automobile companies are eager to move their production facilities to low-wage China and to push hard for tax breaks and other accommodations, to convert China from a country where the bicycle has been the favored transport device to the private car. This kind of pressure is also being applied in Vietnam.

~

Of course, it will be helpful in the long run, in order to reduce dependence on the private car, to redesign urban environments altogether so they are no longer spread out across great distances, as are Los Angeles, London, and Bangkok. There are so many good new ideas for altering such arrangements. *The ultimate goal is to reduce the distance that people need to travel, just as we also try to reduce the distance, in other contexts, that goods need to travel from source to market.*

Among the emerging ideas are the reinvigoration of urban mini-cities— cities within larger cities. This effectively attempts to reestablish the smaller-scale townships that existed for centuries but later merged into metropolises. London, for example, merged dozens of smaller towns, like Richmond, Hampstead, Stratford, and Kensington. New York merged Brooklyn, Chelsea, the Bronx, and so on. Tokyo has likewise merged towns that were formerly disconnected. Now the idea is to design smaller mini-cities that are fully integrated and offer jobs, parks, communal spaces, residence, entertainment, even wildlife. This requires thinking of cities as three-dimensional rather than "flat," with taller buildings, smaller streets, many pockets of convivial spaces and markets, urban gardens, and larger open spaces surrounding them. According to Richard Register, president of Urban Ecology in Berkeley, California, "Tall buildings and dense downtowns are not a cut-and-dried negative like smog or toxic waste, abject poverty, or epidemic disease. In the right context, and built in an ecologically well-tuned manner, heights and densities of a relatively high level are part of the solution to a long list of problems. For example, they save acreage for agriculture and nature; promote energy-saving, non- or low-polluting pedestrian, bicycle, and transit access; make commerce and culture and social diversity of all kinds easily available; and can be built to provide multilevel solar green-houses, rooftop gardens, fruit trees along streets, restored creeks, and renewed biodiversity within a city."

In his book *Ecocity Berkeley*, Register writes: "Instead of thinking of going places, think in terms of being places. That is, think in terms of establishing desirable places close to one another. Transportation is what you

---

BOX L: CURITIBA, AN ECOLOGICAL CITY

By Simon Retallack, The Ecologist

Although it is nearly impossible to make large modern cities fully sustainable, there are examples of cities that have accomplished significant ecological achievements. Freiburg in Germany is one such case. Another is the city of Curitiba in Brazil. As Paul Hawken and Amory and Hunter Lovins explain in their book *Natural Capitalism: The Next Industrial Revolution*, Curitiba, a city with the population of Houston, has been revolutionized under the stewardship of its mayor, Jaime Lemer.

The downtown was made into pedestrian streets and covered with tens of thousands of flowers; low-income houses were built near jobs, shops, and recreation; schools, clinics, and shops were built in the suburbs to minimize travel; new buses were built and bus lanes created to provide a highly efficient, reliable, comfortable, rapid, and entirely self-financing public transport system that is now used by three-fourths of the city's commuters; and cyclists use one hundred miles of well-designed, traffic-separated bike paths. As a result, Curitiba now has no traffic problem, has the cleanest urban air in Brazil, and saves seven million gallons of fuel a year.

Sixteen large new parks were created and hundreds of thousands of trees planted, and regulations and tax incentives were created to protect and increase private gardens and woodlands, so that public green space in the city has expanded from 5 to 581 square feet per person in twenty-five years. The city has recruited over five hundred nonpolluting industries, which provide one-fifth of its total jobs. They are all required to dispose of their solid wastes on their own land to encourage firms to

CONTINUED

have to get to places that are inconveniently located; the less the better. The less [transport] that is necessary, the healthier your life and your environment. If diversity is designed into the city, commuting is minimized, local and long distance travel can be reserved for special occasions."

The end of flat cities sprawled over the landscape and their replacement with three-dimensional, taller, denser environments that emphasize footpaths, bike paths, public transit, urban gardens, restored creeks, universal recycling, and use of building materials and energy systems that are ecologically appropriate are subjects now under discussion in hundreds of communities around the world. Such ideas are examples of a kind of "devolution" in urban design that expresses a changed focus, away from dependence

---

BOX L: CONTINUED

reduce, reuse, and recycle. In fact, nearly everything is recycled in Curitiba, not least because of an initiative that now has 70 percent of households sort recyclables for three-times-weekly curbside collections. As a result, landfill use has been reduced significantly, together with threats to groundwater. Families can get garden plots in the suburbs to grow food for their own use and sale—the city even offers instruction in home-growing medicinal plants—and environmental education starts in early childhood and is integrated across the curriculum. Consequently, a city has been created that is both enormously pleasing to live in and probably more ecologically sustainable than any other in the world.

But people elsewhere on the planet do not have to wait for an inspirational mayor to win office and transform their cities. Groups of people have long collectively decided to pursue ways of life that are ecologically sustainable, inde-pendent of the unsustainable world that surrounds them. One such movement that has sprung up in recent times is the Movement of Landless Rural Workers (MST) in Brazil, one of the country's largest and most dynamic social movements. As Jan Rocha explains, on the land that they have occupied, many farm organically and set up cooperatives to produce milk, fruit, flour, and other products. In Sao Paulo, MST settlers are planting thousands of saplings to counteract the erosion produced by the years of deforestation by ranchers. In the Amazon, they have begun replanting mahogany and native species such as the jaborandi to counter the effects of slash-and-burn agriculture. The MST has also organized protests against genetically modified soya planted illegally by large farm operations in the south, and MST schools foster environmental awareness. (More on MST follows in the section on agriculture.)

on ecologically and socially damaging transport systems, and a furthering of the concept of subsidiarity.

Lester Brown summarizes it this way: "An economy that is in sync with the earth's ecosystems will contrast profoundly with the polluting, disruptive, and ultimately self-destructing economy of today—the fossil fuel–based, automobile-centered, throwaway economy."

III. Agriculture and Food Systems

If globalized energy systems are the primary cause of the world's environmental and geopolitical crises, then the undermining of small-scale, diversified, self-reliant, community-based agricultural systems and their replacement by corporate-run, export-oriented monocultures has been the primary cause of landlessness, hunger, and food insecurity. Furthermore, this conversion of agriculture is increasing rapidly as agriculture corporations spend billions of dollars annually in lobbying, advertising, and public relations efforts to promote trade policies that accelerate it. Such corporations argue that industrial agriculture is more efficient than traditional farming and has a better chance of feeding a hungry world. Yet all the evidence consistently shows the contrary; industrial farming's so-called efficiencies are sustained only by large government subsidies. And it causes more hunger than it solves.

We briefly described some of this problem in chapter 1, but to maintain a perspective on the scale and importance, we will review it here. Roughly half of the world's people still live directly off the land, growing their own staple foods, feeding their families and communities. They use indigenous seed varieties developed over centuries; they have perfected their own fertilizers, crop rotation, and pest management. Their communities have traditionally shared all the local commons, including water, labor, and seeds. They have been exemplary in preserving the biodiversity necessary for community survival. As one United Nations Environment Program (UNEP) report observed, "In India, peasants grow over forty different crops on localities that have been cultivated for more than two thousand years without a drop in yields, yet have remained free of pests" (quoted in Darrell Posey's *Cultural and Spiritual Values of Biodiversity*).

The same UNEP report cites many indigenous peoples for their "agroecology" approaches over millennia. Their procedures are "based on eco-logical knowledge and understanding" and are "highly efficient and pro-ductive and inherently sustainable. They have successfully adapted to difficult environments with innovative techniques for irrigation, drainage, soil fertility, frost control, and disease management." In Meso America, for example, ingenious raised-bed systems known variously as *chiampas, waru waru,* or *tablones* have overcome truly terrible environmental conditions and have been successful in feeding the population without ecological damage. Similar locally appropriate systems are found in Africa, the Andes region, South Asia, and many other places.

Indigenous and peasant systems have also preserved traditional medicinal plants still used by a majority of the world's population, though these medic-inal plants are now being fiercely hunted and patented by global corporations.

The UNEP report concludes that "modern agriculture" has become "one of the major threats to the indigenous and local communities as well as to biodiversity, healthy ecosystems, and food security." Yet no matter how suc-cessful it has been, small-scale community agriculture remains anathema to global corporations and trade bureaucracies.

As explained earlier, local systems, small owners, indigenous systems, and family farming cannot be made compatible with global corporate opera-tions, and so we face the very aggressive international campaign to under-mine small farmers, get them off their traditional lands, and make way for industrial agricultural systems, absentee owners, and the introduction of luxury monocultures for export markets. The net outcome is that once-viable, self-reliant communities are being increasingly made landless, home-less, cashless, and hungry; there are few jobs available in an industrial model that emphasizes machine- and pesticide-intensive production or biotech-nology. Meanwhile, food-growing activities that had been the economic, social, and spiritual heart of community life are decimated, the core fabric of the culture along with them. This has been true as much in the United States as everywhere else in the world. Thus, once self-reliant farmers become dependent on welfare systems for survival or flee to already over-crowded cities, searching for the rare factory job in competition with all the other new arrivals.

Those who are able to continue farming find themselves pushed to the least productive soils or submit to feudal arrangements with large export-oriented landowners who control supplies, production methods, and prices and try to squeeze the small producers as much as possible in order to keep costs low and profits high. Most important, these absentee owners do not grow diverse food crops for local families and communities to eat but rather emphasize luxury monocultures, like cut flowers, potted plants, cotton, coffee beans, shrimp, beef, luxury vegetables, soybeans, and so on, meant to be directly shipped to countries where the majority are already overfed. Land that once fed millions of poor families now feeds the overfed.

That such an export-based system can be promoted as helping to feed the world by companies like Monsanto and Archer Daniels Midland through billions of dollars in advertising is highly cynical. Victims of this free-market propaganda can be found throughout the world. As the Institute for Food and Development Policy (Food First) has reported, even during the time of the greatest acceleration of global trade in food, the past thirty years, world hunger has increased at a rate even higher than population growth. There are now nearly eight hundred million hungry people in the world.

Indeed, many countries report increasing poverty and hunger at exactly the same time as they experience vigorous growth in agricultural exports. In Thailand, for example, agricultural exports were up by 65 percent between 1985 and 1995, but the percent of the population below the poverty line increased during that period to 43 percent. In Bolivia from 1985 to 1990, there was spectacular growth of exports, but 95 percent of the rural population still earned less than a dollar per day. In the Philippines, there has been an enormous increase in the acreage devoted to growing cut flowers for export, with a corresponding decline in acreage for food staples like rice and corn. Approximately 350,000 rural livelihoods have been destroyed by the shift. The Philippines, which had long been self-sufficient with rice, saw rice imports leap tenfold in the late 1990s, increasing dependency and hunger.

In Brazil during the 1970s, when soybean exports increased phenomenally—to be shipped to Japanese and European markets for animal feed—hunger also increased from one-third to two-thirds of the population. During the 1990s, Brazil actually became the world's third largest agricultural exporter, with the area devoted to industrial farming of soybeans growing by 37 percent from 1980 to 1995, displacing millions of small farmers in the process. Meanwhile, per capita production of the staple rice fell by 18 percent, increasing hunger and poverty.

Vandana Shiva summarized the situation at the 2002 People and Planet conference in Kingston, Ontario, remarking that the root causes of hunger and poverty are by now obvious: "A combination of loss of land and loss of control of local resources like water, seeds, and biodiversity. All of these are basic to farming communities but are now in the hands of global corporations." She adds with irony, "The food security of the United States and other wealthy food-importing countries depends largely on the destruction of other people's security."

~

The shattering of established social arrangements and cultures also leads to tribal and ethnic hostilities, as people are thrown into competition for scarce lands and resources. In the Indian state of Punjab, for example, Hindus and Muslims were traditionally cooperative and peaceful. But they turned to violence against each other partly because of the pressures of the so-called Green Revolution—the World Bank–backed, corporate-driven shift to chemical- and machine-intensive production of the 1960s and 1970s. This mode of production required massive increases in use of fresh water, which was already scarce, thus creating competition for its availability. Similar conflicts have taken place in Africa over resource scarcities exacerbated by World Bank–inspired industrial monocultural production for export using vast amounts of water for irrigation.

Industrial agriculture is one of the world's greatest consumers of the planet's scarce freshwater. Commercial hybrid seeds for wheat require twenty times more water than traditional wheat varieties developed and grown in India. The massive infrastructure needed to divert water to industrial agriculture farms also has devastating environmental impacts, and chemical fertilizers and pesticides degrade water and soil, contribute to loss of species, poison air, and have other dire results. According to the U.K.-based International Society for Ecology and Culture (ISEC), governments subsidize water used in industrial agriculture, either directly or by paying for massive irrigation projects. This has, for example, encouraged the growth of water-intensive monocultures in such formerly desert areas as California's San Joaquin Valley, where industrial farms could not exist without water subsidies.

As for efficiency, global industrial agriculture can be called efficient only if the long list of hidden and overt subsidies that industrial societies provide agribusinesses are ignored. In ISEC's report *Bringing the Food Economy Home,* authors Helena Norberg-Hodge, Steven Gorelick, and Todd Merrifield cite a long list of subsidies in the large industrial nations, including export promotional supports as well as massive funding for research, education, and application of biotechnology and chemical- and energy-intensive monocultures. According to the report, many governments "directly subsidize pesticides and chemical fertilizers as a means of encouraging large-scale agriculture for export." Most of these countries are doing this at the urging of World Bank and IMF policies and because of pressure from global corporations. During the 1980s, for example, China's annual pesticide subsidies averaged some $285 million, Egypt's $207 million, and Colombia's $69 million. Pakistan devoted about 75 percent of its total agricultural budget to subsidize chemical fertilizers. But little support was given for smaller-scale organic methods.

Industrial agriculture also depends upon huge infusions of largely subsidized energy for operation of farm machinery and production of pesticides and fertilizers. Present estimates are that three times more energy is used to produce food in the industrial agriculture model than is derived from consuming it. In Canada, on-farm energy use grew by 9.3 percent between 1990 and 1996. In developing countries, during the height of the Green Revolution—1972 to 1982—total use of energy for agricultural production rose by 30 percent, not counting energy used for transport, marketing, or packaging of agricultural products.

Mechanized, modern tools of farming that require expensive hybrid seeds, biotech seeds, fertilizers, chemicals and pesticides, tractors, and other energy-rich systems have been pushed by the World Bank, the IMF, and the WTO but have been a main cause of the desperate situation of small and peasant farmers worldwide, leading to rising debt, increased hunger, the abandonment of small farms, and an epidemic of farm suicides.

In addition, there are gigantic hidden subsidies from the "externalization" of cleanup costs resulting from industrial agricultural processes: poisoned soils, rivers, estuaries, wildlife habitats, and so on. Industrial agriculture is also a major contributor to climate change because it depends on long-distance shipping to distant markets. The average plate of food eaten in Western industrial food-importing nations is likely to have traveled fifteen hundred miles from its source. Each one of those miles contributes to the environmental and social crises of our times. Shortening the distance between producer and consumer has to be one of the crucial reform goals of any transition away from industrial agriculture.

"If these subsidies for the large and global were redirected toward appropriate smaller-scale, more localized producers," says the ISEC report, "the shift toward more ecological and equitable food economies would be given a major boost."

Globalization has exacerbated this situation immeasurably, as global trade and investment rules strongly favor global agribusinesses. WTO rules also permit subsidies to exporters and commodity traders but not to the small-scale production that is characteristic of the South. The scales are strongly tipped in favor of the largest corporations. These circumstances and policies at the national and international bureaucratic levels have brought about a degree of corporate mergers and concentration in agriculture that is equal to any industry, including oil. For example, according to the Rural Advancement Foundation (RAFI), by 2000, five grain-trading companies controlled 75 percent of the world's cereal commodity market (and its pricing). In the United States, four cattle processors controlled 80 percent of the U.S. market (double their share in 1980), whereas five food retailers controlled nearly 50 percent of retail food sales.

All of this leaves small producers and farmers caught in a terrible trap, as both their inputs for farm production and their outlets for distribution are controlled by an ever-smaller number of giant corporations, which also control commodity price markets. Any system that deliberately sets out to separate from their lands farmers who have been feeding their families and local communities, replacing them with ecologically unsustainable export production from absentee landowners, is absurd on its face—and tragic for millions of people. In the name of "progress," family farms and rural communities are being driven to extinction. Millions of people are being pulled off the land and moved into ever-expanding cities. This process must be reversed, and it can be.

ACTIONS AND POLICIES TOWARD ALTERNATIVE SOLUTIONS

Millions of people around the world are mobilizing to reverse the globalization of industrial agriculture. Millions of farmers in India alone have protested corporate biopiracy of their biodiversity and their seeds, and the eventual commercial patenting of indigenous varieties. (See chapter 3 for more on biopiracy.)

The movement also includes tens of thousands of farmers in Japan, the Philippines, Bolivia, Germany, and most significantly, the growing international movement of landless peasants throughout the Third World who are demanding a meaningful land reform process. In Brazil, for example, the landless peasant movement (Movement of Landless Rural Workers, or MST) has won actual title to over fifteen million acres of farmland that are able to serve 250,000 families. The Brazilian government has recognized that legalizing MST land occupations—especially when lands were formerly idle—is far less costly (even including compensatory payments to prior landowners) than to have millions of people in abject poverty, without food, without work, edging toward violence, terrorism, and public health disasters, and filling overcrowded cities even further. A veritable land reform from below, the actions of MST are being duplicated in other countries. The success story in Brazil has been an inspiration to activists everywhere.

Nor is the movement against globalized industrial agriculture confined solely to the poorest nations. Western industrial nations are also seeing small farmers and artisanal producers increasingly sacrificed to production and distribution rules and standards that favor large, monocultural, industrial producers while inhibiting the options of small farmers. For example, French farmer José Bové has become an international leader protesting these rules in Western countries. Together with leaders of Southern movements, he has been joined by public health officials and environmentalists around the world in a common cause—seeking new policies that favor small-scale diversified farming and healthier food.

~

The campaign to achieve meaningful change must be simultaneously carried forward on the international, national, and local levels. We frame our discussion around six central convictions:

- Access to land for self-reliant food growing is a fundamental human right; it cannot be denied to communities or nations by global trade regimes or in the interests of international trade processes.

- Loss of small holders' farmlands to highly concentrated large corporations is a primary cause of poverty and hunger in the world, as well as of environmental devastation.
- Wherever people are still living and working on their traditional lands, incentives and policies should help them remain in place, working for their families and communities not the global market. Where communities have been deprived of their lands, *distributive land reform* is crucial.
- The bias of international bureaucracies like the World Bank, IMF, and WTO toward large-scale, export-oriented monocultural production must be reversed. Invigorating small farms and indigenous agricultural practices that protect local biodiversity and innovation devoted to sustainable use for local populations must be encouraged.
- Solutions must serve to shorten the distance between producer and consumer.
- The ultimate sustainable agriculture solution is transition to noncorporate, small-scale organic farming as practiced for millenia.

EIGHT KEY CHANGES

Here, then, is a partial list of policies and actions that can help produce the needed changes.

1. Permit Tariffs and Import Quotas That Favor Subsidiarity

Most international trade rules now favor export production and the global corporations that dominate it. These must be replaced by rules that emphasize support for local production, local self-reliance, and real food security. This means applying the principle of *subsidiarity:* whenever production can be achieved by local farmers, using local resources for local consumption, all rules and benefits should favor that option, thus shortening the distance between production and consumption. We are not suggesting that there should be no trade at all in food products but only that trade should be confined to whatever commodities cannot be supplied at the local level, rather than export trade being the primary driver of production and distribution—its raison d'être.

New rules must permit the judicious use of trade tariffs and import quotas to regulate imports of food that can be produced locally. For example, a country like South Korea, which can easily be self-sufficient in its staple food, rice, should never be forced to open its market to U.S. rice exports. Such policies destroy the livelihoods of Korean farmers and their communities while rendering American farmers vulnerable to the volatility of the global pricing system. In both Korea and the United States, the bias should invariably be toward local production for local consumption and the reduction of long-distance food shipments.

2. Reverse the Present Rules on Intellectual Property and Patenting

The World Trade Organization attempts to impose the U.S. model of intellectual property rights protection on all countries of the world. This model strongly favors the rights of global corporations to claim patents on medicinal plants, agricultural seeds, and other aspects of biodiversity, even in cases where the biological material has been under cultivation and development by indigenous people or community farmers for millennia. Most of these communities have traditionally viewed such plants and seeds as part of the community commons, not subject to ownership and fee structures imposed by outside corporations. (For more on this, see chapter 3, "The Commons.")

These new global patent regimes have become important issues in such countries as India, which has always had a patent regime based on sui generis ownership—that is, community patenting of the biodiversity of each community. Other countries have similar systems that protect local commons from outside expropriation. Many countries, led by India, are battling to retain their domestic systems against the enormous pressures of the WTO and global corporations. In Mexico, thousands of peasant farmers protested against an American company that patented an indigenous bean variety that had long been grown by local farmers; the community is now asked to pay the patent holder $69 million annually to grow this traditional local bean!

Some aspects of this issue recently reached the boiling point when poor nations like South Africa, Thailand, and Brazil attempted to circumvent the WTO rules on intellectual property to make inexpensive generic versions of medical treatments for AIDS; each of these countries is in the midst of a medical crisis made worse by the fact that most of the victims are extremely poor. Millions of people have taken to the streets to protest such unjust rules. They have finally succeeded in gaining negotiated reduced rate settlements with global corporations that had been making windfall profits from the disease. But at this time, the intellectual property rights rules (TRIPs) still remain in the WTO. These rules should be abandoned to permit reassertion of rules that favor the needs of local and domestic communities and the protection of innovations and knowledge developed over centuries, as well as to deal with public health crises. Placing profits of global corporations before local food sustainability and public health defies logic and justice.

3. Localize Food Regulations and Standards

In the name of food safety, many international rules, such as the WTO's Agreement on the Application of Sanitary and Phytosanitary Standards (SPS) and the Codex Alimentarius, have enforced a kind of processing of foods that works directly against local and artisanal food producers while favoring the global food giants. Among other things, they require irradiation of certain products, pasteurization, and standardized shrink-wrapping of local cheese products.

Such rules as these tremendously increase costs for small producers and also negatively affect taste and quality. In fact, the greatest threats to food safety and public health do not come from small food producers but from industrial farms and distributors whose practices have accelerated the incidences of salmonella, *e. coli* infection, *listeria* and other bacteria in foods, as well as Mad Cow disease, hoof and mouth disease, and others. Industrial processes make it impossible for food producers to observe food quality closely, whereas small and artisanal food producers can more easily stop disease outbreaks. Ironically, while describing themselves as working for food safety, the SPS agreement and Codex permit even higher levels of pesticide residue (including DDT) on food, and set firm ceilings on every member nation's health, safety, and environmental standards. Other aspects of the WTO have also effectively prevented governments from introducing labeling of genetically modified foods. These homogenized global standards are exquisitely attuned to the primary goal of benefiting global corporate producers. Food production standards should be localized and every nation permitted to set high standards for food safety.

4. Allow Farmer Marketing—Supply Management Boards

Currently disallowed by the WTO and NAFTA, these price and supply regulations let farmers negotiate *collective* prices with domestic and foreign buyers to help ensure that they receive a decent price for their commodities. Less than two years after NAFTA went into effect, Mexican domestic corn prices fell by 48 percent as a flood of cheap U.S. corn exports entered the country. Stable prices for Mexico's domestic corn growers could have been achieved by the government price regulation agencies dismantled by NAFTA. Without these, thousands of farmers have been forced to sell their lands.

5. Eliminate Direct Export Subsidies and Payments for Corporations

Although the WTO has eliminated direct payment programs for most small farmers, they allow export subsidies to agribusinesses. For example, the U.S. Overseas Private Investment Corporation, supported by U.S. taxpayers, provides vital insurance to U.S. companies investing overseas. Even loans from the IMF to Third World countries have been channeled into export subsidies for U.S. agribusinesses. Such subsidies help multinational corporations dominate smaller local businesses both domestically and abroad. These export subsidy policies should be eliminated, and programs that permit and encourage low-interest loans to small farmers, creation of domestic seed banks, and emergency food supply systems should be allowed.

6. Recognize the Failure of WTO Market Access Rules

Many Southern countries were originally persuaded to join the WTO and to open their markets because of the promise that Northern countries would do likewise, in a fair exchange. But while Southern countries *have* opened markets, most Northern countries have not matched them. This, combined with the technological advantages and greater wealth and subsidies already enjoyed by Northern agricultural producers, has led to even greater imbalance in the system. Subsidized Northern imports have destroyed rural communities and self-sufficient livelihoods throughout the South, and many people now working for poverty wages at Nike subcontractors are refugees from self-sufficient farming regions. Many in the South are furious about this turn of events.

Some activists strongly argue that developing countries *must* have market access as promised, to level the playing field. But others believe that the entire export model is doomed because it is destructive to basic self-sufficient traditional farming. These divergent viewpoints have led to a partial rift among activists, depending upon whether one feels the situation is now so desperate that market access can provide the only quick fix or whether one takes a longer view toward a paradigm of community self-sufficiency. Still, most activists who advocate for agricultural self-sufficiency acknowledge that in the short term, many Southern nations remain dependent on agricultural exports to the North. Hence, they recognize that transition strategies are needed to help nations that often feel trapped in colonial trade patterns to shift toward greater food security and self-sufficiency.

The International Forum on Globalization has hosted several debates on this point, and we will continue to do so, although most of our members feel the WTO is probably an unsustainable institution (see chapter 7) and that these issues would be better dealt with by a less corporate-oriented bureaucracy—one that embraces the ten principles for sustainable societies.

7. Promote Redistributive Land Reform

History shows that the *redistribution* of land to landless and land-poor rural families is an effective way to improve rural welfare. Dozens of successful land reform programs were carried out after World War II. According to a report by Food First, "When a significant portion of quality land was distributed to a majority of the rural poor, with policies favorable to successful family farming, and when the power of rural elites was broken, there have been measurable poverty reduction and improvement of human welfare. The economic success of Japan, South Korea, Taiwan, and China has partly resulted from such reforms."

According to a report by Food First co-director Peter Rossett, "Our research shows that small farmers are more productive and more efficient, and contribute more to broad-based regional development than do the larger corporate farmers. Given secure tenure, small farmers can also be much better stewards of natural resources, protecting long-term productivity of their soils and conserving functional biodiversity."

So effective has serious land reform been that even the World Bank has grudgingly accepted the principle that it is a fundamental requirement to help offset the grossly inequitable ownership of reproductive resources in many countries and that this maldistribution of land is negatively effecting meaningful economic development. The bank has now begun to include land reform among the requirements in some policy packages when dealing with Third World countries. Unfortunately, however, as Rossett has written, "What the bank calls land reform is essentially privatization and 'market-led' mechanisms of redistribution. These are a far cry from what Via Campesina, Food First, and others are calling for. But at least the bank is making it legitimate again to call for land reform and to struggle over its definition."

When communal lands are privatized, as has happened among Mexico's *ejidos* and as current World Bank policies promote, systems of individual land titling, registries, and land market schemes can result in mass sell-offs of small holders' plots. This increases landlessness, land ownership concentration, and migration to urban areas. Even when lands are not sold off under these schemes, the privatization of small holdings negatively affects the sense of community management and the construction of community-style agricultural systems like terracing and small-scale irrigation. The usual community approaches give way to a new individual profit motive that undermines collective activity and community welfare.

As for "market-led redistribution"—the current favorite of the World Bank—it is fraught with risks, says Rossett. He notes: "Landowners often choose to sell only the most marginal plots (steep slopes, dense rainforests, desert margins, and so on) often at exorbitant prices." Trying to farm these kinds of lands can often lead to ecologically unsustainable practices to attempt to eke out some productivity. Also, loans offered to purchasers under World Bank financing schemes may leave poor farmers with high debts on marginal lands, thus leading to deeper poverty and land degradation, as with many of the failed reforms of earlier decades. In addition, World Bank loan packages often require a commitment to pesticide and chemical production and to the use of nontraditional export crops.

All of these policies have been prescriptions for failure, as was the case with market-led reforms in Brazil, which the World Bank is still trying to duplicate in the Philippines and elsewhere.

Food First and other activist groups oppose that kind of land reform and are fighting for a truly redistributive land reform that has worked where it has been fully supported by government policies. Food First lists several crucial ingredients that must apply if land reform is to be successful:

- Government grants of land must be debt free.
- Women must have full rights of title and use.
- Only good quality land should be used (past failures have often resulted when lands were of poor quality).
- There must be a highly supportive policy environment—reasonable credit terms and good infrastructures for sound local environment technologies.
- There must be easy access to markets.
- The power of rural elites must be broken so they can no longer block and distort policies, subsidies, and profits in their favor.
- Reforms must apply to the majority of the rural poor so they have sufficient strength in numbers to be politically effective.
- Most important, a new farm economy should be the centerpiece of a country's entire economic development model. When land reform is viewed as welfare, failure is inevitable.

8. Change at the Grassroots

There are many opportunities for local communities, too, to assist the transition away from globalized agriculture. The International Society for Ecology and Culture lists several of these opportunities, already well under way in some places:

- *Buy-local campaigns.* These campaigns help local food businesses thrive and prevent money from "leaking" from the local economy. This protection of the local is also expressed by hundreds of regional campaigns against the entry of global franchises like McDonald's and Wal-Mart.
- *Farmers' markets.* Thriving in many parts of the world, farmers' markets are now also being rediscovered and supported throughout industrial countries. These markets are ways of directly connecting consumers with local producers, often organic farmers, who can keep prices down by avoiding distribution costs.
- *Local food co-ops.* These are small retail outlets, similar to farmers' markets but where financial benefits are shared by producers and consumers.
- *Community banks and loan funds.* Run by community boards, these increase capital available for local residents and businesses and allow people to invest in their neighborhoods rather than in distant corpora-

tions. Such banks favor small-scale local activity over global corporate activity.

- *Local currencies.* Growing in popularity, these alternative scrips used only in communities enable people to avoid the dominant currencies and keep money within the local community. Local currency schemes are similar in intent to Local Exchange Trading Systems (LETS), which are large-scale barter systems for local communities, often facilitated by a central credit and debit accounts system. Among the leading examples of a successful LETS program is the Berkeley Regional Exchange and Development (BREAD). (For further information about this movement, see www.breadhours.org.)

- *Urban gardens.* Urban gardens are one of the most original and revitalizing movements among urban dwellers, especially in Northern countries

---

BOX M: CUBAN ORGANIC AGRICULTURE

*By Helena Norberg-Hodge, Todd Merrifield, Steven Gorelick,
International Society for Ecology and Culture*

In the past few decades, an important shift has taken place in Cuban agriculture—away from chemical-intensive monoculture for export and toward the production of diverse, organic food for local consumption.

Until 1990, the majority of agricultural land in Cuba was devoted to a vast monoculture of sugarcane for the world market (and after the Cuban revolution in 1959, for the Soviet bloc countries). With earnings from sugar, Cuba imported chemicals and oil needed to support its agriculture, as well as much of its food; before 1990, the country imported an estimated 57 percent of its caloric intake. With the collapse of the Soviet market and the tightening of the U.S. embargo, Cuba experienced an 80 percent drop in pesticide and fertilizer imports and a 50 percent decline in food imports. Remarkably, the government responded by adopting a range of innovative strategies to diversify production, lessen dependence on chemical inputs and fossil fuels, encourage popular participation in farming, and enhance national food security.

These strategies included the breakup of huge state-controlled farms into smaller worker-owned and managed farm collectives, as well as reorientation of agriculture toward basic food needs. Cuba encouraged diversification of crops, crop rotation, intercropping, manuring, and soil conservation. The country's agricultural

CONTINUED

where access to natural sites may be difficult. Making use of empty lots, small patches of private property, and public parks, urban gardens enable city dwellers to grow their own organic foods. Such projects are helpful in educating urban children about where food comes from. Many schools are initiating such gardens on their own property, teaching a survival skill that can bring confidence, self-reliance, and joy.

IV. Manufacturing Systems

A major development over the last half-century is that manufacturing processes in just about every country in the world have become ever more interconnected within a global production system that is increasingly complex, geographically far-flung, and in the control of relatively few global

---

BOX M: CONTINUED

research sector also reoriented itself toward low-input ecological methods, giving rise to biofertilizing and biological pest control. Oxen have been bred to replace tractors that cannot be used for lack of fuel. To meet the new demand for agricultural labor, the government improved rural services and incentives for people to remain on the land. It also relaxed price controls and restrictions on the direct sale of produce, which led to new farmers' markets around the country.

Urban gardens have also had an important role. An Urban Agriculture Department oversees these efforts, and by 1998, there were over eight thousand gardens in Havana, cultivated by over thirty thousand people. The Ministry of Agriculture replaced its front lawn in Havana with a garden of lettuce, bananas, and beans, and many of the ministry's employees work in the gar-

den. These urban gardens have reduced the burden on rural areas and led to a reduction in food transport and storage while increasing quality and variety of produce in cities.

Although Cuba made these changes out of necessity and may abandon some of them when the nation is not as isolated, its experience is nonetheless encouraging. It shows the possibilities of a more ecologically and socially sensitive agriculture on a national scale, and demonstrates that, with political will, governments can shift from a focus on global food to local food and implement policies that are good for people, communities, and the environment.

SOURCE: Adapted from Helena Norberg-Hodge, Todd Merrifield, and Steven Gorelick, "Is a Shift in Direction Possible? Lessons from Cuba," in Helena Norberg-Hodge, Steven Gorelick, and Todd Merrifield, *Bringing the Food Economy Home.* West Hartford, CT: Kumarian Press and London: Zed Books, 2002.

corporations. Manufacturers around the globe employ hundreds of millions of people in sectors as diverse as apparel, automobiles, and shipbuilding. But in any given product line, each country's involvement has tended to be only one cog in a larger "global assembly line."

Few countries carry production from start to finish. In the United States, for example, textiles, autos, electronics, food manufacturing, and many other industries are constructed as part of a long process, where discreet parts are shipped back and forth across the world in ships, processed or assembled in different places—often on different continents—and then finally sold in markets thousands of miles from their material sources or the factories where they were built. A car, for example, may contain production elements from as many as sixteen countries. A large apparel company usually subcontracts to hundreds of manufacturing facilities in dozens of countries. As we have already discussed, the amount of global shipping that such a system requires represents a major social, public health, and environmental threat in itself.

This shift in production away from traditional local systems, where countries were able to produce products from start to finish, has had a tremendous impact on domestic governance systems and prerogatives. Under globalization, countries' laws may be subordinated to WTO trade and investment rules that assist global corporations to operate efficiently in this new manner. The shift has also had effects on labor and the environment.

Workers of the world find this new arrangement unfortunate from many perspectives. With corporate mobility accelerated by globalization rules, and with manufacturers now free to roam from country to country and to invest freely in resources and production facilities, workers in every industry in every country have lost some of the leverage provided by once powerful domestic labor unions. As unions have weakened relative to global corporations, workers have been pushed into wage competition with workers in other countries, bringing a downward spiral of wages and working conditions everywhere. Under a globalized manufacturing system, labor unions are daily threatened with pressures to allow worker "givebacks" and wage concessions for people trying to keep jobs on this global assembly line, often managed thousands of miles away. In fact, the existence of strong labor unions in a country can often be sufficient reason for global corporations to stay away altogether, since there are many other countries that are less worker-friendly. The net result is to create a greater power imbalance between corporations and workers than ever before, making it more difficult to counter sweatshop conditions or abusive practices. However, the rising global justice movement has supported unions and other worker movements through a series of public campaigns against apparel, footware, and other firms that have abused sweatshop labor. (Many IFG associates are participating in a more intense investigation of labor and globalization issues in a dialogue organized by Focus on the Global South, which brings together union and NGO leaders from around the world.)

Chapter 4 describes the principle of *subsidiarity*—bringing power and economic activity toward the local. Subsidiarity can help correct at least some of the injustices of a production system in which power imbalances are inherent in the design of large-scale, stateless corporate manufacturing that functions without any transparency or accountability. Corporations that are more locally rooted, as chapter 5 describes, would need to face the fact that the workers are also customers and neighbors—a far different arrangement than the global one.

But if democracy and workers' rights are directly affected by the present global manufacturing system, there is an even larger context to consider. Present global manufacturing processes are also a direct threat to all life on earth, and to sustainability. The rest of this section will focus on those issues.

⁓

In 1981, Lester Brown defined a sustainable society as one that is able to satisfy its needs without diminishing the chances of future generations. The same definition was used by the World Commission on Environment and Development (in the Brundlandt report). By that definition, current manufacturing processes are leading society in exactly the opposite direction than it should be headed.

At present, global manufacturing and production processes consume more than 220 billion tons of resources annually, all taken from the earth's "natural capital"—oceans, forests, plants, plains, soils, mines, and all other aspects of biodiversity.

Standard production practice today is for resources to be gathered wherever on earth they are, then processed, formed into usable products, and shipped back and forth across the planet. A high percentage of the materials are wasted in the mining and manufacturing parts of the cycle, as well as through shipping, and again when the finished products are discarded. We call this whole process the "take-make-waste" cycle.

Physicist Fritjof Capra, in his new book *The Hidden Connections: A Science for Sustainable Living*, offers a comprehensive argument for why it does not have to be this way. He asserts that new concepts of systemic practice have the potential to convert nearly 100 percent of the present waste production into raw materials for further economic activity, in a continuously beneficial cycle that does not deplete the planet. The new view suggests that "all waste is food" for further technical activity or, if it is organic matter and properly handled, for recycling back to nature's own processes.

Many of the ideas that Capra and others propose are entirely compatible with the primacy of subsidiarity as applied to manufacturing. A far more localized, democratic, community-oriented system would avoid most of the social and environmental pitfalls now inherent in the global system.

The following is a short list of some of the principles now being proposed for a more sustainable manufacturing process.

FULL COST ACCOUNTING

The depletion of forests and topsoils, overfishing of the oceans, and the dissemination of toxic wastes into soils, rivers, and oceans are currently being accounted for in two misleading ways. First, resource depletion and mining are measured as being *beneficial* to Gross National Product (GNP) and Gross Domestic Product (GDP) because they are indicators of increased economic activity. In fact, however, they ought to be considered negative factors because they decrease the long-term ability of societies to sustain themselves. (See further discussion on this subject in the last section of this chapter, "Measurements of Economic Progress.") Second, these depletions and toxic outfalls bring significant costs for cleanup or renewal, costs that are invariably externalized. That is, corporations creating these costs do not pay for them; taxpayers pay through government cleanup programs. These amount to government subsidies of wasteful practices by corporations. It is little wonder, therefore, that natural resources corporations make billions in profits: their resources are essentially free.

Nor do corporations have to pay for the external social costs that derive from their activities—costs of health care from toxic processes and pollutants, costs of welfare for people driven from farmlands or forests. Bringing externalized costs back where they belong, into the operating costs and balance sheets of corporations and into the prices of products they produce, might do more than any other single change to create a realistic measure of impacts and costs on the earth, people, and communities.

But as this volume goes to press, President George W. Bush has announced that the U.S. government will no longer require corporations to pay their share of the cleanup costs—amounting to many billions of dollars—for toxic Superfund sites in the United States. Either taxpayers will pay, or the environment will not be cleaned at all. Sadly, this approach is typical in the United States and in most other countries too.

A transition to full cost accounting is a crucial component of a socially or ecologically sustainable society.

CLOSE THE LOOP DESIGN: ZERO WASTE

New industrial models are now being developed that attempt to mimic nature's fundamental design principle—no longer a cycle of "take-make-waste" but one that approaches production as a whole system, leaving no waste at all. This is sometimes called a "closed-loop system." Fritjof Capra puts it this way: "The principle 'waste equals food' means that all products and materials manufactured by industry, as well as the *wastes* generated in the manufacturing process, must eventually provide nourishment for something new. A sustainable business organization would be embedded in an 'ecology of organizations,' in which the waste of any one organization would be a resource for another. In such a sustainable industrial system, the total outflow of each organization—its products and wastes—would be perceived and treated as resources cycling through the system."

"To realize how radical an approach this is," Capra says, "we need to realize that our current businesses throw away most of the resources they take from nature. For example, when we extract cellulose from wood to make paper, we cut down forests but use only 20 to 25 percent of the trees, discarding the remaining 75 to 80 percent as waste. Beer breweries extract only 8 percent of the nutrients from barley or rice for fermentation; palm oil is a mere 4 percent of the palm tree's biomass; and coffee beans are 3.7 percent of the coffee bush."

Capra says that new ecological "clusters" of industries have already sprung up in many parts of the world and are actively being promoted by such organizations as Zero Emissions Research and Initiatives (ZERI), founded in Europe by Gunter Pauli in the 1990s. "Taking nature as its model," says Capra, "ZERI tries to eliminate the very idea of waste." That is, it tries to achieve zero net material consumption and therefore causes virtually no pollution or resource depletion. It also brings a major reduction in health problems that result from incineration and dumping.

Amory and Hunter Lovins and Paul Hawken make a distinction between two kinds of waste, biological and technical. *Biological nutrients* must always be put back into nature to be consumed by microorganisms and naturally enrich soil processes. Many production elements can be converted into biologically degradable materials, notably packaging, which now accounts for about half of the planet's solid waste disposal. Meanwhile, *technical nutrients* must be designed to be recovered and put back into technical cycles. "Every output of manufacturing should be either composted into natural nutrients or remanufactured into 'technical nutrients,'" say the Lovinses and Hawken—in other words, either flowed back into nature or flowed into becoming raw material ("food") for the next manufacturing cycle. There should never remain a necessity to dispose of industrial wastes because all waste should be incorporated into new resources as part of the basic design of the system. Using closed-loop models, there would be no materials thrown away, no toxic dumping, no smokestacks or emission pipes causing pollution downstream. This may sound expensive or difficult, but it is a form of whole-system engineering that is already being effectively applied in many parts of the world and is becoming big business.

In 1996 in the United States, the so-called remanufacturing industry showed revenues of $53 billion, far more than many durable goods sectors. Many other countries are providing incentives for industries to think along these lines; Germany and Japan both require manufacturers to be responsible for their products and processes *forever*—a policy exactly opposite to President Bush's policy cited here. And at least one international agreement, the Basel Convention, has prohibited any transboundary shipment of hazardous waste materials. (The United States has refused to sign.) In any case, the ban should be extended to all exporting of wastes through encouraging systemic designs that include reintegration of wastes.

The ZERI organization has already initiated more than fifty projects on five continents in very diverse settings. Its work among Colombian coffee farmers helps illustrate the method.

The global market has recently left coffee farmers in deep trouble as prices have dropped dramatically. But because coffee farmers have until now only used about 3.7 percent of the plant and wasted most of the rest as wastewater and caffeine-contaminated compost, there was an opportunity to put the waste to work. Coffee biomass can be used profitably to cultivate tropical mushrooms, feed livestock, compost organic fertilizer, and generate energy.

Capra explains as follows: "When the coffee beans are harvested, the remains of the coffee plant are used to grow shiitake mushrooms (a high-priced delicacy); the remains of the mushrooms (rich in protein) feed earthworms, cattle, and pigs; earthworms feed chickens; cattle and pig manure produces biogas and sludge; the sludge fertilizes the coffee farm and surrounding vegetable gardens; while the energy from the biogas is used in the process of mushroom farming."

So rather than concentrating on the global coffee market, local farmers generate several revenue streams in addition to producing locally used produce and animals, while creating new jobs in the community. Only the shiitake mushrooms are grown for export. The net results are beneficial to the environment and the local community; there are no high investments and no need for farmers to give up their livelihoods based on the volatility of the export markets.

"Technologies in the typical ZERI clusters are small-scale and local," remarks Capra, and "the places of production are close to those of consumption, thereby radically reducing transportation costs."

Paul Hawken adds an interesting illustration of a systemic approach to manufacturing design by the Tunweni Brewery in Namibia:

> This is a beer made from local sorghum, the only such beer in the world. Three times each day sewage and plant effluents are washed out, and then used to flush nearby pigpens into a "biodigester," thus eliminating any breeding of flies, while also producing a clean humane environment for pigs. Caustic soda from the washdown neutralizes the acidic manure. Meanwhile, the solid waste and spent grains are used to cultivate mushrooms. Not only does this help produce a new valuable crop, but the cultivation process converts the ligno-cellulose into carbohydrates, increasing the economic value of the spent grains. Part of the residue is then fed to pigs, and part is held back

for earthworm farming, an eventual source of protein for the pigs. Meanwhile, the biodigester creates methane gas that will help diminish the fuel costs of the brewery, while the partially mineralized water released from the biodigester is used to grow algae that can also be fed to livestock. From the algae basins, the water goes to fishponds. Because of the high level of nutrients in this enriched water, there is no longer a need to buy fish food. Later, water from these fishponds can be used to irrigate crops.

What is also important about this example—in addition to the 100 percent elimination of waste in the production cycle—is that every step of the way, the use of waste cuts costs, provides "food" for new processes and products, and increases employment. It also encourages a full cycle of small-scale economic activity and its benefits within the local community.

REINVESTMENT IN NATURAL CAPITAL

Until society is able to institute a universal closed-loop design, manufacturers must face the fact that global resource depletion is endangering their own continued functioning. Ironically, a shift in manufacturing policy toward active replenishment of resources is actually proving profitable to companies that try it because it ensures long-term supply and viability at far less cost than dependency on long-distance supply lines.

Among recent examples is a power company that plants trees to offset carbon emissions from its power plants. A ranching company in New Mexico adopted New Zealand's so-called management-intensive rotational grazing; this requires that cattle be kept on the move, thereby not overgrazing any single area and mimicking the natural behavior of plains animal herds before industrialization. In California, rice farmers flood their fields after harvest to create seasonal wetlands, supporting millions of wild fowl, replenishing groundwater, and improving fertility. In addition, the farmers are able to bale and sell rice straw rather than burn it because its high silicon content makes it a useful construction material.

These companies, among dozens of others, are finding that profits often increase from restorative methods, though too few companies yet follow the practices, and governments do not provide sufficient incentives for this approach. Perhaps as more economic activity localizes, where impacts are more visible and easily experienced, where the local commons is the economic base of the community, such ecologically and financially viable approaches will gain increased practice.

CHANGES IN MANUFACTURING SCALE

Changes in energy, transportation, and agriculture systems will make them more compatible with local economies and eliminate the wasteful resource uses that go with long-distance supply lines, marketing, and travel. Localizing production and manufacturing will also serve ecological and democratic goals.

Paul Hawken has described recent changes in the Emilia-Romagna region of Italy, "where a sharp loss of mass-production jobs (geared to an export-oriented economy) since 1970 has been countered by a phenomenal growth in small businesses." In this region of four million people, there are 325,000 registered businesses. A combination of small artisanal firms, local labor unions, governments, and trade associations have cooperated to jointly purchase materials, share services, and market assessments while also instituting common standards and quality assurances.

This activity is a further expression of the efforts of small manufacturers to "cluster" into "horizontal networks" to share resources. Firms that might have been competitive with one another come together for mutual benefit and to effectively combat the scale or size of much larger external corporations seeking to make inroads in the local market.

CHANGES IN TECHNOLOGICAL SCALE

Megatechnologies require megainvestments and megamanagement. They are invariably biased toward absentee, usually global, ownership and operation, run by principles that are anathema to communities and democratic governance. If manufacture is to be more community based and designed to be smaller, then all technological systems and infrastructures need to be appropriately designed and scaled. Local infrastructures for reuse, recycling, and recovery of materials are mandatory, as well as a strong emphasis on local energy systems, including solar, small-scale electrical generation, wind, and local hydro, operating on a scale that fits the needs of small, flexible manufacturing processes.

A shift is required in the types and scale of technology at every level of economic activity. The essential issue should always be whether the technology is suited to megascale operation or whether it is better suited to local application, household use, and community-based systems. By such measures, technologies like nuclear power and long-distance delivery of oil for energy would be at the bottom of a list of energy systems topped by such local systems as those named earlier. The same could be said for transport or agricultural technologies.

Shifts in technological scale must also be accompanied by the principle that polluters must pay for damages they cause—no more externalization. And the *precautionary principle* described in chapter 2 should apply to every technological intervention. All technologies should be assumed potentially guilty of harms until proven innocent, a reversal of present standards.

Insurance liability coverage is a crucial indicator for precautionary standards: if the insurance industry refuses coverage, that is a clear signal of danger and unsustainability. At present, the risks endemic to nuclear power, genetic engineering, and large-scale chemical production, for example, have all been *externalized*, with governments and taxpayers assuming all the risk for insurance companies that refuse to cover losses beyond a certain amount. The nuclear and genetic engineering industries are specifically protected by law from the full risk of coverage of their inventions. Now the insurance industry itself is seeking government support to make up for the failure of "reinsurance" industries (those that insure insurers) to go beyond certain amounts.

The argument given for governments assuming the risks of catastrophic events is that losses might be so enormous that no corporation or insurer could possibly cover them. The cost of a nuclear catastrophe, for example, could be in the hundreds of billions of dollars. However, it is part of the central logic of a reformed, decentralized, and localized economic system that if catastrophic risk is a possibility from any industrial process, the precautionary principle should apply. If the risk is beyond the means of the perpetrators, then it should not be permitted.

GREEN PROCUREMENT

Other helpful changes would be the aggressive promotion among local governments of green procurement and so-called ecologically preferable purchasing programs at every level of economic activity. These would stand in direct opposition to the current rules of the World Trade Organization, the World Bank, and the IMF, each of which discourages local preferences as well as preferences for certain production processes, even in the name of ecological sustainability, such as eco-labeling for sustainably harvested forest products.

~

Finally, it is worth noting that many of the principles indicated here—recycling, zero waste, small scale, local control—already are standard economic practice in the less developed world, often bringing significant local successes. The major problems with these systems have emerged largely because of the global bureaucracies that try to *undermine* traditional local production systems to favor global corporations, and because of the inherent unsustainable nature of globalized industrial production.

V. Measurements of Economic Progress

So far in this chapter, we've talked about four of the key economic systems of our society—energy, transportation, agriculture, and manufacturing—to help us all think through the kinds of shifts needed for our society to break the hold that corporate globalization has on our options. We discussed some changes that would help set us on the path in a more democratic, equitable, environmentally sustainable direction. In this final section of the chapter, we discuss a related matter, how society measures the success of these systems and its overall economic performance.

Not surprisingly, the primary unit that currently measures our success—Gross Domestic Product (GDP)—does so in terms that are compatible with the expansive goals of corporate-driven globalization while marginalizing all other ways of judging how we are progressing as a society. This gives corporate globalization a powerful tool to convince us that the direction we are going in is a good one when it isn't. By other standards, we are doing poorly.

GROSS NATIONAL PRODUCT AND GROSS DOMESTIC PRODUCT

The GDP came into use in the mid-1980s, when it replaced the previous Gross National Product (GNP). We will come back to that important difference a little later in this section.

Both measurements are rooted in the World War II period, when U.S. economists were trying to find a way to measure the speed at which productive capacity in the country was increasing to meet war production needs. It was a useful measure at that time for that purpose, but its continued application is leading to distorted analyses and conclusions that exacerbate all the problems described in the earlier sections of this chapter.

GDP measures societal performance by one economic standard, the market value of the aggregate of all economic production—that is, the rate at which resources are converted to commodities and sold, the activities that go into that process, and all other paid services and activities in the formal economy. The assumption is that as GDP grows, society is better off: GDP growth brings progress and national well-being. Politicians run for office promising to increase GDP, and most domestic and international agencies use it as their standard of success.

However, the system is tragically flawed because it measures the wrong things and does not measure what it should measure. Clear-cutting of forests, strip-mining of mountaintops, construction of toxic dumpsites: all show up in GDP as positive indicators. So does expansion of military hardware and activities, prison construction, war, crime (and resources devoted to prevent it), as well as reconstruction from natural disasters.

Long-distance shipping of goods across oceans is seen as a good thing because it adds many layers of economic activity, from production to port to shipment to delivery. Local production for local consumption, involving less shipment (and less environmental impact), is seen as less productive because it does not contribute as much to GDP.

Unpaid household labor, care for the sick and elderly, self-sufficient food growing within communities—activities often carried out by women—do not contribute to GDP because little money changes hands, so they do not get counted. The same is true when anyone decides to keep land, forests, or other pristine areas as biodiversity preserves. This does not show up as a positive act. Razing the forests or putting copper mines on that land or converting it to mechanized agriculture or housing developments would add to GDP.

As David Korten likes to point out, using GDP as the standard of economic or social health "makes no more sense than taking the rapid expansion of one's personal girth as an indicator of improved personal health.

Applying such a standard to society's economic priorities has led to a gross distortion of economic priorities and resource allocation that is helping to lead the world toward social and environmental collapse."

In their article "The Need for New Measurements of Progress," which appears in Jerry Mander and Edward Goldsmith's *The Case Against the Global Economy,* authors Clifford Cobb and Ted Halstead (then of Redefining Progress, an organization that has been a leading voice critiquing the GDP measurement) point out: "GDP is the statistical distillation of the worldview of conventional economics. It basically assumes that *everything* produced is good by definition. It is a balance sheet with no cost side of the ledger; it does not differentiate between costs and benefits, between productive and destructive activities, or between sustainable or unsustainable ones. It is a calculating machine that adds but does not subtract. It treats everything that happens in the market as a gain for humanity while ignoring everything that happens outside the realm of monetized exchange regardless of its importance to well-being." The authors conclude: "To do otherwise, economists generally say, would be to make 'value judgments.' But refusing to make such judgments is a judgment in itself."

THE IMPORTANCE OF INCLUDING THE NEGATIVE

GDP not only excludes beneficial nonmonetized economic activity but conveniently (for corporations) leaves out the actual costs to society of some activities—now and in the future—of this growth. Most alarming is the failure of GDP to account for the *depletion* of natural capital—topsoil, minerals, forests, rivers, life in the seas, the atmosphere—whose diminishment impoverishes the future of any society. Herman Daly of the University of Maryland, a former World Bank official, bemoans this failure of GDP and points out that natural capital is the basis of all real wealth in the world.

Cobb and Halstead agree: "When a timber company harvests an ancient redwood forest, the GDP rises by the market value of the wood. But it takes no account of the economic, environmental, and social costs involved in the loss of the forest." GDP actually treats resource overuse as *income* rather than *depletion*, thus creating a spectacular distortion in any effort to make judgments about the long-term health of any economy.

Similarly, the changeover of food-growing activity from small-scale, local, organic systems to industrial agriculture has increased pesticide use and fossil fuels and the need for long-distance transport. All are positive indicators for GDP. But they have serious health effects, causing illnesses of all kinds. Amazingly, however, these health effects also show up as positives in the GDP because they increase doctors' fees, hospital services, ambulances, medical machinery, drugs, and so on. (The messes created by the use of pesticides and oil require expensive cleanup operations, but these too are positive for GDP.) So from the point of view of GDP, public health problems are a good thing, not a bad one.

Particularly in higher-income countries, a significant portion of economic growth (increased GDP) comes from sales of such things as bottled water, which is actually a response to the *decline* in the purity and safety of water supplies. Another example is the increased demand for security systems to compensate for what is also a negative trend in society.

In the perverse world of GDP accounting, even a strong, stable family life contributes nothing to the economy. A divorce, however, generates lawyers' fees and probably means that at least one more new household will need to be furnished and fitted with commodities—a plus for GDP. A woman who bears her own child counts for nothing to GDP, but if she hires a surrogate to bear her child, that fee adds to GDP—as do the commissions and fees for lawyers, doctors, and other intermediaries. A parent who stays home to care for his or her own children counts for nothing. Parents who take a job to pay for day care add to GDP. All too often, GDP growth is actually a measure of social or environmental deterioration, not progress.

There are also countless cases of mining companies that extract gold and other minerals from the lands of indigenous peoples, using methods that kill topsoil, poison local water, and dump enormous piles of rocky waste into riverbeds. Human and natural losses can be enormous, and the sources of livelihood of the local people may be destroyed for generations to come, but GDP accounts record only the returns from the sale of the ore and the costs of mining it.

Military activity provides the supreme example. All additions to military hardware or personnel salaries or university research on weapons systems add to GDP, though they surely also add to the instability and insecurity in society. Once this hardware is actually used in war, then great destruction takes place, which requires later redevelopment and reconstruction—yet another plus for GDP, although the entire cycle of activity has been negative from start to finish. Death and destruction and pollution from this activity are not measured at all. So a country that becomes warlike may be assumed to be in better economic health as a result, receiving increased investment and other financial benefits.

GDP'S BIAS AGAINST THE THIRD WORLD AND THE POOR

The Gross Domestic Product Index is designed to be helpful in measuring economic growth from year to year, and most economists argue that growth is crucial to lifting the world's poorest countries and peoples. We believe that this assumption is false and misleading. Ecological degradation of the kind that is measured as positive by GDP actually has devastating impacts on the poor because it reduces the resources—forests, lands, water, biodiversity—that poor people depend on, reducing their ability to live self-sufficiently and increasing their poverty. In any case, GDP reveals nothing about *who benefits* from growth, which is an essential question.

GDP makes no distinction between the production of goods and services that might actually help the poor—basic foods, health services, water, housing, education, job training, and so on—and the production of more luxuries for the rich—fancy foods, hotels, golf courses. This is yet another way in which GDP is useless as an indicator for society's performance. It is all too common for the deprivation of the poor to actually *increase* during periods of rapid economic expansion, because such growth often results from a systematic transfer of productive resources from the weaker elements of society to the rich and powerful. This is a common experience in low-income countries today, where many development projects—often financed with loans from the World Bank and its regional sister development banks—involve appropriating the lands on which poor people depend for their livelihoods and converting them to use for dams, tourist resorts, industrial agriculture and forestry estates, housing developments, and so on, which are designed to benefit people already better off than those displaced. Through this process, control of productive assets is consolidated in the hands of the capital-owning classes, and wages are depressed as the pool of wage labor expands among the displaced peoples. By the logic of economic growth and the GDP index, all this counts as progress.

The numbers clearly bear this out. In a recent report by the International Forum on Globalization, titled *Does Globalization Help the Poor?* more than one hundred quotes from economists, researchers, scholars, and journalists show that during the thirty-year period of the world's most accelerated economic growth (1960 to 1990), the gap between the rich and poor within countries and among countries greatly increased. (See Box D in chapter 1.) Many of the sources for these data were actually from the institutions that have pushed for rapid economic growth via globalization, including the World Bank, the IMF, the United Nations, and even the CIA.

~

GDP measurements have another direct negative impact on the South. Much of the production there takes place in the informal sector—community and household collaboration and exchange—and in subsistence agriculture. None of it appears in national accounting ledgers. The net effect of the invisibility of this activity is to open the door to development agencies that can argue for more "productive" economic approaches, such as increased foreign investment for capital-intensive infrastructures, industrial agriculture, high-tech assembly operations, and the like. All of these might create better numbers for GDP purposes and add to the illusion of progress, but they directly undermine traditional economies, cultures, and self-reliant systems. A type of small-scale financial support for local activities would make less of a splash for World Bank development figures but be far more beneficial for local people.

Finally, we mention an even more subtle though insidious manipulation that occurred in the mid-1980s, when the official measurement system switched from Gross National Product (GNP) to GDP. According to Clifford Cobb and Ted Halstead, this switch produced a "fundamental shift that exaggerated the contributions of multinational corporations. Under the old GNP, the profits of multinationals were attributed to the nation in which the corporations were based. If Goodyear owned a factory in Indonesia, the profits generated there were included in the U.S. GNP figures. Now, however, under GDP, the profits are included in Indonesia's figures, *even though the profits come back to the U.S.*"

This shift in strategy has made it seem as if Southern countries were growing in wealth, when actually the multinationals have been walking off with the profits for the benefit of their Northern investors. Southern countries get nothing. According to Cobb and Halstead, "Suddenly, multinationals seemed an unqualified boon. . . . It has brought an even greater social and ecological cover-up for the social and ecological costs of globalization."

MEASURING WHAT MATTERS

Recently there has been a trend toward using indices like the Dow Jones Industrial Average and the Nikkei Index; in some quarters they are replacing GDP as the most closely watched economic indicators. TV and radio stations in some countries issue hourly reports on market fluctuations, with significant commentaries. However, stock prices are an even less meaningful indicator of human well-being than GDP. Only a tiny portion of the world's people own stock (although roughly half do in the United States), and as the recent collapse of the stock bubbles along with corporate scandals have revealed, there may be little connection between stock prices and substantive value. A rise in share prices increases the financial power of those who own the shares relative to the financial power of those who don't, but this is largely negative for society—a source of growing injustice—if there is no corresponding increase in productive capacity.

But we have also had a burst in very promising new efforts to develop new and better sets of indicators that would more accurately measure the things that matter. Readers can learn more details about some of them by contacting the International Institute for Sustainable Development of Canada, Environment Canada, the United Nations Development Program, or Redefining Progress (U.S.). These organizations have also joined with the World Bank and the U.N. Division for Sustainable Development in a comprehensive listing of some of these initiatives. (See http://iisdl.iisd.ca/measure/compindex-asp.) We offer a brief review of their suggestions here.

Genuine Progress Indicator

This is one of the better-known alternatives to the GDP, developed by Redefining Progress, of Berkeley, California. The GPI would include many factors now left out of GDP: resource depletion, pollution, long-term environmental damage, housework and nonmarket transactions, positive adjustments for growth in leisure time, negative adjustments for unemployment and underemployment, income distribution (positive adjustment for greater equity in the system, negative adjustment for greater disparity), positive adjustment for greater life span of durables and infrastructure, negative adjustment for defensive expenditures (those that try to maintain a given level of service without adding anything, such as pollution control devices and medical and material costs of auto accidents), and sustainable investment (which encourages domestic over foreign investment and investment from savings rather than borrowing).

Results from the GPI index compared with the GDP index vary from country to country but generally show that GPI rose more or less in tandem with GDP until about 1980. Then it sharply declined. The GPI is a big improvement over conventional GDP accounting because it begins to make visible the negative consequences of pursuing growth without accounting for costs and depletions.

Community Accounting Systems

Building on the work of Philippine economist Sixto Roxas, his country has become an important center of efforts to create true community accounting systems that take the household, rather than the enterprise, as the basic accounting unit. The differences are fundamental because in many instances the interests of the individual firm are at odds with the interests of the household and community. For example, a business benefits economically by hiring the fewest possible workers at the lowest possible wage. In contrast, the household benefits economically from having its members fully employed at the highest possible wage. The business benefits from selling its products at a high price, the household from buying at a low price.

Many investment projects may be highly profitable to a firm or individual yet very costly for the community—clear-cut logging for export, for example, or so-called export processing zones. The latter expropriate land, dominate local government decision making, enjoy tax holidays, demand fully developed infrastructure that must be paid for by local taxpayers, make priority claims on local water supplies and power generation, have few linkages to the local economy other than hiring labor at low wages, and contaminate local land and water supplies with their toxic wastes. Firms that operate in export-processing zones generate handsome profits that immediately go abroad, without compensating the community for the costs it incurs.

In contrast, community accounting systems take the household and community as the basic accounting unit and assess the costs and benefits of economic activity from a community perspective. At all levels, the community-based accounting system defines an economy that is inseparable from its habitat and corresponds to a local government responsible for managing the economy and its natural resource base.

The community balance sheet shows local natural resource stocks as *assets*. Production processes, such as in agriculture, forestry, mining, fisheries, trade, and services, create flows between asset accounts, firms, and households to reveal the consequences in terms of resource depletion and the distribution of benefits. Clear-cutting a forest is reflected immediately in the reduction of relevant community asset accounts. Unmet household needs are identified; resource flows into and out of the community are revealed; and the link between the community's well-being and the health of its local ecosystem is highlighted. This results in a perspective on investment decisions that is very different from the one provided by conventional methods of project assessment. Communities can more accurately assess the impact of proposed investments on the community balance sheet and negotiate with outside investors and trade interests accordingly.

Community-based accounting systems are also an important tool for implementing the principle of subsidiarity, because they allow local jurisdictions to see more clearly when trade offers real advantages to the community over local production—and when it does not. A substantial degree of self-reliance is encouraged, yet the community also remains open to beneficial trade and outside investment.

Local Indicators Initiatives

Many communities around the world have undertaken local initiatives to compile indicators of community social and environmental health. Redefining Progress identifies more than two hundred such efforts in the United States alone. Citizen led, they tend to focus on the kinds of communities in which people want to live. Recognizing the complexity of the human and natural systems involved, these initiatives make no effort to arrive at a single indicator. Many of those chosen reflect a highly sophisticated appreciation of the interplay between natural and human systems. Rarely do they include economic growth.

For example, the main indicator of social and environmental health chosen by Sustainable Seattle is the size of the seasonal spawning run of wild salmon. There is an almost primordial recognition that the condition of the wild salmon is a measure of the health of the watersheds on which all of the region's life depends. Toxic chemicals, loss of forest cover, disruption of stream flows, and urban sprawl all contribute to diminishing the salmon runs.

Sustainable Seattle's measure of stream quality is equally sophisticated. Rather than using a conventional test of the presence or absence of contaminants, it uses what is known as a benthic index of biological integrity, a measure of the diversity and density of bottom-dwelling (benthic) invertebrates. These are the mayflies, stoneflies, worms, mussels, and other groups of insects and invertebrates on which fish, birds, amphibians, and others rely for their food. The cleaner the water, the more they thrive.

Indicators of the number of pedestrian- and bicycle-friendly streets, open spaces near urban villages, reduction of fuel consumption and vehicle miles traveled, increased participation in gardening, and library and community center use all reflect a concern with the physical and social quality of urban life. Indicators of local farm production, employment concentration, and community reinvestment reveal the value placed on economic diversification and local ownership. A strong equity thrust is revealed in the decision to include indicators of unemployment, personal income distribution, number of hours of work required to meet basic needs, and the prevalence of low birthweight infants, children living in poverty, adult literacy, and racial equity in justice (disparities in the rate of arrests by race, for example).

～

All of the new indicators described here, and others, reject the argument that the well-being of society depends mainly on economic growth. Only the interests of economists, financiers, corporation heads, and others like them are served by economic expansion. When the poor speak for themselves, they speak of their need for secure rights to the land and waters on which they depend for their livelihoods, decent jobs that pay a living wage, and health care and education for their children. Some say they need money, but rarely, if ever, do they say, "We need economic growth and rising share prices."

One of the best ways to assess the health of any society may be with indicators that show the condition of the most vulnerable among us—children, the poor, the elderly. When infant mortality rates are low, everyone is literate, the poor and elderly are nourished and housed, crime rates are low, voter turnout is high, and community events are well attended, then we are probably looking at a healthy society—no matter the GDP, GNP, or Dow Jones average.

CHAPTER SEVEN

From Bretton Woods to Alternatives

THOSE OF US WHO HAVE CONTRIBUTED to this volume have all faced variations on a nagging question from journalists, pundits, and government officials as we debate economic globalization around the world. "Isn't economic globalization, along with the key global institutions that underlie it, inevitable?" That this question persists for institutions that have existed from merely a decade (the World Trade Organization) to a half-century (the World Bank and IMF) is a tribute to the power of the forces that have backed and benefited from economic globalization during this period.

But as this volume goes to print, the grip of inevitability is loosening. With colossal failures by the Bretton Woods institutions in Asia, Africa, Eastern Europe, and most recently Argentina, coupled with the confidence-shattering collapse of Enron Corp., WorldCom, and others, the notion is spreading that perhaps the guardian institutions of economic globalization are not guarding so well—or are guarding only the few. And perhaps more important, the array of forces rising in opposition to economic globalization have begun making a convincing case for the replacement of the Bretton Woods institutions with alternatives that could better serve humanity and the planet.

It is the subject of this chapter to outline a number of these alternatives. We start by analyzing the need for change, then outline the essential elements of a more just and sustainable international system and its institutions. We go on to make the argument for decommissioning the core multilateral economic institutions and unifying global economic governance under a restructured United Nations system. We end with proposals on what new institutions might do the job better.

A Review of the Current Situation

The experience of the Southern countries is instructive of the need for alternatives. As earlier chapters described, when the traditional institutions of colonialism were phased out, the newly liberated nations sought a pathway to economic development. Seeking to create a demand for its services, the World Bank stepped forward with a simple formula: Development is synonymous with economic growth. Economic growth depends on investment. Poor countries have little to invest, so foreign borrowing would be their salvation. The more the foreign borrowing, the more rapid the growth and the faster the development.

It is true that foreign borrowing can be a sound choice *if* the borrowed funds are used to buy essential capital goods from abroad that are not available domestically *and* those capital goods are used in ways that generate sufficient export earnings to repay the foreign loans. Unfortunately, such conditions were rarely met. To this day, most foreign borrowing pays for the import of luxury goods and military arms or finds its way into the foreign bank accounts of privileged elites.

Unpayable debts accumulated under the World Bank programs until the IMF stepped in to protect the interests of creditors. Domestic economies were reoriented to produce for export to earn the foreign exchange to repay the debts. Whether from ignorance or malice, the World Bank and the IMF favored policies that stripped governments of their ability to manage the movement of goods and money across their borders. When import controls were relaxed, many countries experienced a dramatic increase in imports but no increase in their ability to pay for them. Firms producing for domestic markets suffered. Concurrent relaxation of foreign exchange controls unleashed waves of foreign borrowing, capital flight, and financial speculation. This added to already high foreign claims (including foreign debt) against the country's current and future foreign exchange earnings and created further pressure to increase exports and attract yet more foreign funds—including speculative portfolio investments that contribute nothing to productive capacity but add significant volatility and instability to the financial system.

Because many countries lacked the capacity to produce manufactured or service exports, they came under strong pressure from the World Bank and IMF to devote still more of their national resources to producing shrimp, cotton, timber, coffee, and other primary commodities for export. The World Bank and the regional development banks commonly financed such expansion with loans to pay for the infrastructure that subsidized the projects of foreign corporate investors. But because many countries were doing the same thing, a flood of coffee, cocoa, and other commodities onto world markets depressed prices. Foreign debt continued to grow as a result of new borrowing, but falling export earnings reduced capacity to repay. Falling commodity prices also resulted in downward pressure on wages in the commodity-producing sectors. This in turn placed downward pressures on wages in other sectors, including the industrial sector, thus giving foreign corporations greater incentives to export jobs from the North to take advantage of exploited workforces in the South.

The World Bank and IMF are leading advocates of markets unfettered by the distortions of subsidies and government intervention—except when the distortions favor corporate interests. The artificial depression of commodity prices is a market distortion that in turn artificially depresses wages in both South and North, creates the illusion that environmental resources are abundant at a time of growing scarcity and encourages their wasteful consumption, undermines the South's terms of trade with the North, and favors returns to investors at the expense of labor and the public treasury. That corporate profits are enhanced at the expense of equity and environmental security is not a random inevitability; like all of today's globalization rules, it is based on a set of subjective policy choices.

The pundits who dismiss antiglobalization protestors as know-nothings and economic illiterates, depriving the poor of an opportunity for a better life, would do better to apply such labels to the World Bank and IMF ideologues who advocate and defend the policies that have had such disastrous consequences.

As discussed in chapter 1, the General Agreement on Trade and Tariffs (GATT) and the World Trade Organization (WTO) have exacerbated the imbalances and distortions. A key to understanding the failure of the globalists' free market ideology is that it views economic policies from the perspective of returns to the corporation rather than to the community. Thus,

---

BOX N: UNEMPLOYMENT
The Role of Monetary Policy

By Martin Khor, Third World Network

There has been much concern in Northern countries about the impact on domestic employment and wages of the corporate export of jobs to lower-wage countries. Less attention has been given to the extent to which high unemployment and falling wages in the Northern countries themselves are an intentional consequence of the monetary policies of central bankers. Many Northern countries base their monetary policies on a formula known as NAIRU—the nonaccelerating inflation rate of unemployment—on the theory that keeping unemployment above a particular level will maintain sufficient downward pressure on wages to prevent inflation. For those who read the business press, it is public knowledge that in most Northern countries the explicit goal of the central bankers responsible for monetary policy is to keep wages low and stock prices rising, which assures a steady increase in the economic power of those who hold shares in the financial markets relative to those who live from their labor. A new approach to monetary policy is needed, with the goal of maintaining full employment and living wages everywhere while keeping a lid on speculative bubbles in share prices and land values.

---

there is no conflict between corporate and community interests. By their reckoning, increased profits for corporations mean increased wealth for the community. But as chapter 5 explained, this is a false assumption.

Global corporations are driven by stock markets to maximize short-term financial profits without regard for the health of individuals, the social fabric, or the environment, even though these are all essential to the well-being of people and communities. Global corporations maximize profit by employing the smallest possible number of people at the lowest possible wage; in contrast, the healthy community seeks living wage jobs for all who need employment. A global corporation can obtain a quick return by clear-cutting a forest and then moving on to another; in contrast, communities prosper by sustaining productive yield of their natural resource base.

Markets need rules. Because the purpose of the market is to serve people, these rules should favor community interests. This can happen only if the rules are made by people acting in their capacity as citizens of communities.

When corporations make the rules, corporate interests are inevitably given priority over community interests. Corporations will seek to capture economic gains for themselves while shifting costs to communities. They will seek to increase their own rule-making power while weakening their accountability to people. The legal boundaries that define the corporation's assets will be well protected. The political boundaries that define the assets of communities—the commons—will be weakened or erased. This is exactly what has happened in the global economy as rule-making power shifted from people to corporations.

It is useful to look at the corporate concept of free trade from this perspective. In the name of free trade, corporate globalists call for the virtual elimination of the boundaries that define communities and nations. Local efforts to regulate or manage exchanges with other communities and countries are dismissed as protectionism, an infringement of market freedom. Corporate globalists effectively dismiss the very existence of community interests that might actually merit protection.

These same individuals take a very different position, however, when it comes to matters relating to trade among or within corporations—insisting that it is the right of the individual corporations to regulate and manage the most minute details of their trade relations with other subsidiaries or other corporations as they see fit. They reserve the right to do business only with others of their choice and on terms of their own choosing. Thus, in the world of the corporate globalist, when private interests are at stake, the rules of free trade do not apply: borders are well defended and trade is carefully managed. And because the largest corporations command internal economies larger than those of most countries, this is not a trivial matter.

Yet public interests are real, and it is an essential responsibility of governments to protect them. Just as corporations demand the right to manage trade among themselves in the defense of private interests, communities and nations must manage trade and investment relationships among themselves in defense of the public interest.

One essential reason why a community must manage its trade relations with its neighbors is to keep the value of its imports and exports in balance. If it is paying more for imports than it earns from its exports, it is living beyond its means and building up debt to its neighbor. Usually the beneficiaries are those who hold power while the burden of repayment falls to future generations and the weaker elements of the society. If a country is exporting more than it is importing, then people are not enjoying the benefits of their own labor and resources. Usually the primary burden of producing the export surplus is borne by the poorer members of society while the financial surplus finds its way into the foreign accounts of the rich and powerful. Such imbalances create instability in the international system and do not serve the public interest.

In the press to expand trade for its own sake, a simple but obvious truth has been forgotten: the primary reason for a country to export is to generate foreign exchange to pay for the import of goods it cannot reasonably produce for itself. But as the Bretton Woods institutions have forced Southern countries to open their borders to the free flow of goods across their borders, the result has been a surge in imports with no corresponding increase in the ability to pay for them. Many of the imports are nonessential goods that subsidized producers are able to sell at less than full cost. This creates unfair competition for domestic producers that do not enjoy comparable subsidies, and a growing external debt that can only be repaid by shifting the balance of the domestic economy from import surplus to export surplus—thus diverting resources away from meeting domestic needs and requiring a decrease in domestic consumption. The result is a downward spiral of dependency and impoverishment that contradicts the claim of free market ideology, that trade liberalization leads to accelerated economic growth.

There is a wealth of evidence to document this contradiction. The United Nations Conference on Trade and Development (UNCTAD) *Trade and Development Report, 1999* found that for developing countries, excluding China, the average trade deficit in the 1990s was higher than in the 1970s by 3 percent of GDP, whereas the average growth rate was down by 2 percent. Inappropriate trade liberalization contributed to this negative phenomenon.

A 1994 UNCTAD study of forty-one least developed countries (LDCs) came to a similar conclusion. It found that over a ten-year period there was "no clear and systematic association" between trade liberalization and devaluation, on the one hand, and the growth and diversification of output and growth of output and exports of LDCs, on the other. In fact, it found that in many LDCs, trade liberalization had been accompanied by deindustrialization.

Disturbing evidence of post-1980 liberalization episodes in the African and Latin American regions have also been documented. For example, Senegal experienced large job losses following liberalization in the late 1980s; by the early 1990s, employment cuts had eliminated one-third of all manufacturing jobs. The chemical, textile, shoe, and automobile assembly industries virtually collapsed in the Ivory Coast after tariffs were abruptly lowered by 40 percent in 1986. Similar problems have plagued liberalization attempts in Nigeria. In Sierra Leone, Zambia, Zaire, Uganda, Tanzania, and the Sudan, liberalization in the 1980s brought a tremendous surge in consumer imports and sharp cutbacks in foreign exchange available for purchases of intermediate inputs and capital goods, with devastating effects on industrial output and employment. In Ghana, liberalization caused industrial sector employment to plunge from 78,700 in 1987 to 28,000 in 1993, mainly because "large swaths of the manufacturing sector were devastated by import competition," according to UNCTAD. Adjustment programs introduced in the 1990s have also been difficult for much of the manufacturing sector in Mozambique, Cameroon, Tanzania, Malawi, and Zambia. Import competition precipitated sharp contractions in output and employment in the short run, with many firms closing down operations entirely.

Some developing countries outside Africa have experienced similar problems. According to a 2001 study, "Liberalization in the early nineties seems to have resulted in large job losses in the formal sector and a substantial worsening in underemployment in Peru, Nicaragua, Ecuador, and Brazil. Nor is the evidence from other parts of Latin America particularly encouraging." The regional record suggests that the normal outcome is a sharp deterioration in income distribution, with no clear evidence that this shift is temporary in character.

A responsible national trade policy depends on calibrating national trade rules to achieve a balance between imports and exports. Many Southern countries are unable to increase imports because of production constraints on their ability to increase export earnings. Moreover, the main exports of many developing countries are primarily commodities, the prices of which have declined significantly over time. Also, the products exported by Southern countries face trade barriers imposed by Northern countries. If import liberalization proceeds while the conditions for successful export growth are not yet in place, there can be adverse results—such as increases in the trade deficit and balance-of-payments difficulties—which then add to the level of external debt and greater debt-servicing burden, leading to slowed economic growth and increased unemployment.

Similar problems have arisen in the area of finance. Since 1997, a continuous series of devastating financial and economic crises has hit Mexico, Thailand, Indonesia, South Korea and Malaysia, Russia, Brazil, Turkey, and Argentina. There have been conflicting reasons given for these crises, the dominant one (propagated by the IMF, the World Bank, and the developed countries) is that the affected countries suffered from bad political and economic governance. This is quite remarkable because most of the affected countries had been lavishly praised just prior to their crises as shining examples of good economic management.

A more accurate and credible explanation is that these crises were caused by the financial liberalization and deregulation that has swept the world since the early 1970s. As a result, there has been an explosive increase in financial speculation as investment funds and speculators move rapidly across borders in search of profits. In recent years, many developing countries were also advised to deregulate and liberalize their financial systems. The controls over the inflow and outflow of funds, which these countries previously had, were significantly relaxed. This led to excessive short-term borrowing by local firms and banks, as well as the entrance of international funds and players that invested, speculated, and manipulated currencies and stock markets.

IMF action to impose financial liberalization is a violation of Article VI of its own articles of agreement, which specifically sanctions the right of a nation to adopt capital controls. This is integral to a nation's right to economic self-determination, and it is inappropriate for outside parties to pressure a national government to abandon them. The crucial question of *when* or *how* a state wishes to liberalize its capital account—or *whether* it wishes to embark on such liberalization at all—is properly left to its sole determination, without outside pressure.

The IMF, the World Bank, and the rich countries involved in these institutions that want access to the emerging markets for their financial institutions have for years promoted the idea that liberalization is beneficial and poses little danger. When the crisis struck, the IMF made it worse by misdiagnosing the cause and promoting even further financial liberalization as part of its loan conditionality, as well as a policy package (high interest rates, tight monetary policies, and closure of local financial institutions) that converted a financial-debt problem into a structural economic recession. The IMF also denied that hedge funds and other highly leveraged institutions had played a destabilizing role. It took the near collapse of a giant private hedge fund, Long-Term Capital Management (LTCM), to expose the risks posed by these highly leveraged speculative funds.

Essential Rules of a Just and Sustainable International Trade and Finance System

The global trade and finance system and its primary rule-making institutions—the Bretton Woods institutions—have come to a crossroads. Decisions made in the next few years will have important effects on which direction the system will go. There is no question of the need for a multilateral system of rules for international trade and finance. A proper system of rules is essential to stability, predictability, and fairness for all participants; the present system is unstable, unpredictable, and extremely unfair.

Rules are essential, but they must be determined democratically to serve the public interest.

In addition to being stable, predictable, and fair, a suitable international system should support the following four goals.

DEMOCRATIC SELF-DETERMINATION

The democratic right of all people to establish their own economic priorities and policies must be protected as long as their actions do not infringe on the rights and freedoms of those in other localities and nations. This means that people, communities, and nations should own the productive assets on which their livelihoods depend, be free from illegitimate foreign debts, and have the right and ability to manage the flow of goods and money across their borders that is essential to setting their own economic priorities and to maintaining high social and environmental standards consistent with community well-being. In a just and sustainable system, stronger and more affluent countries would not be able to demand access to the markets or resources of weaker and less affluent countries against their will and interests. Nor would any corporation have such rights. If a corporation wishes to do business in a jurisdiction other than the one in which it is chartered, it could be required to apply for a charter in that country subject to its requirements, laws, and taxes. The most pressing restraints on Southern countries are their lack of control over their own economic resources, their inability to determine their own economic priorities, and the limits on their access to essential technologies.

BALANCED TRADE

Every country, both Northern and Southern, has a responsibility to its international neighbors to maintain a balance between imports and exports. It has been a basic premise of trade theory, going back to David Ricardo, that in a fair and mutually beneficial international system, each country maintains stable, balanced trade relations with its neighbors (imports equal exports), and investment is national. International debts accrue when the value of a country's exports is greater than its imports. When a country's trade is balanced, it has no reason to accumulate foreign debts, eliminating a major potential source of economic instability, domination, and exploitation.

FAIR COMMODITY PRICES

Economic theory has long recognized the inherent instability of commodity markets because of the interplay between short-term price sensitivity and long-investment lead times. As a result, there are periodic swings between an artificial scarcity that drives market prices far above real production costs and an artificial oversupply that depresses market prices below true production costs. As we elaborated earlier, there is a need for international commodity agreements and mechanisms among countries to maintain fair and stable commodity prices that reflect the full costs of production, including a living wage and all environmental costs. There should be institutional mechanisms at the international level through which nations can coordinate their policies to achieve fairness and stability in international market prices. The appropriate international concern here is to insulate international markets from the consequences of domestic subsidies or price supports that may artificially depress international market prices at the expense of efficient producers in other countries.

OPEN ACCESS TO INFORMATION AND KNOWLEDGE

Intellectual property rights should be limited to measures necessary to stimulate innovation and creativity. Restrictions undermine the public interest when used to enforce corporate monopolies over information and technology. Information and technical knowledge are among the few resources that can be infinitely reproduced and freely shared without negative environmental impacts or depriving anyone of their use. Open access to information and beneficial technology is a key to a just and sustainable human future. Every contemporary human invention necessarily builds on the common knowledge accumulated over countless generations—the information commons. The proper use of intellectual property rights is to ensure acknowledgment and reward for those who contribute to that pool, not to establish publicly defended information monopolies. It is revealing that the same corporate globalists who eagerly promote the free movement of goods and money, which tends to undermine community self-determination and self-reliance, are adamantly opposed to the free movement and sharing of information and knowledge that has the potential to increase self-determination and self-reliance. The international interest, particularly of Southern countries (and the former Soviet Union and Eastern Europe), is best served by international regimes that seek to minimize barriers to the free flow and sharing of information and technology. Indeed, a commitment by Northern countries to share their capital stock of information and technology with Southern countries might be considered partial compensation to the people of the South for the wealth the North has extracted from them over the past five hundred years.

If public policy is to serve community interests, countries of both South and North need adequate policy space and freedom to choose trade and investment policies consistent with the interests of their people and domestic enterprises. This principle should be central to any system of international rules on trade and finance. Its application should accomplish the following:

- Help countries prevent debt and financial crises by implementing measures that regulate and control the type and extent of foreign loans that the public and private sectors are allowed to obtain and that prevent speculation and manipulation in stock and currency markets.

- Enable affected countries to manage financial crisis effectively so that debtors and creditors share the burden equitably, including the option of a debt standstill arrangement and recourse to an international debt arbitration court or panel, which would then arrange for a debt workout.
- Permit countries to establish systems of control over the inflow and outflow of funds, particularly the speculative variety, without fear of attracting penalties.
- Obligate governments of countries that are sources of internationally mobile funds to discipline and regulate their financial institutions and players to prevent them from causing volatility and speculation abroad.
- Provide for international regulation of hedge funds, investment banks, and other highly leveraged institutions, offshore centers, currency markets, and derivatives trade.
- Stabilize currency exchange rates.
- Give poor countries a fair say in the policies and processes of international institutions like the WTO and IMF by increasing the transparency of decision processes and increasing their voting shares.

Essential reforms to restore the integrity of the international financial system are closely related to essential reforms in other areas, such as trade. When a country liberalizes its imports even though its local sectors are not prepared to compete, and it has no capacity to increase its export revenue, its trade and balance-of-payments deficits and therefore its international debt burden will inevitably worsen. A nation must have the right and capacity to manage flows of both money and goods across its borders.

Under assault from predatory corporations and financial speculators, developing countries have no choice but to institute domestic measures to protect themselves. In particular, they should have regulations that control the extent of public and private sector foreign loans (for example, restricting them to projects that yield the capacity to repay in foreign currency), prohibit manipulation of their currencies and stock markets, and treat foreign direct investment in a selective way that avoids buildup of foreign debt.

The array of national policy instruments should include capital controls that would allow the country to avoid an excessive buildup of external debt, curb volatility of the flow of funds, and provide scope to adopt macroeconomic policies that can counter recession (such as lower interest rates or budget expansion) while reducing the risks of volatility in the exchange rate and flow of funds.

As a first step toward creating a just and sustainable global system, the processes of liberalization should be halted. All proposals to expand the scope and authority of the IMF and the World Trade Organization should be rejected, including these:

- Proposals to amend the IMF Articles of Agreement to give it jurisdiction over capital account convertibility, which would give the IMF additional authority to force developing countries to remove remaining controls over their capital accounts and markets.
- Efforts by the OECD countries to revive negotiations on a multilateral agreement on investment that would give unfettered freedom of mobility to all types of capital flows.
- Proposals for giving the WTO new authority over international investment, government procurement, ownership of public services, and environmental and social standards that would be used to eliminate capital controls, standards for foreign investments, public ownership of essential services, and the ability of governments to give preference to local procurement and to set social and environmental standards appropriate to local conditions and public interests. (These are not trade issues, and to the extent that there is a need for global rules, there are more appropriate venues in which to address them.)

There is a related need to review and roll back provisions of existing trade agreements that distort development, the environment, public health, and labor and are otherwise contrary to important public interests. Particular attention should go to the following:

- The existing WTO TRIMs and specialized financial services agreement that open domestic finance to foreign corporate control, and the TRIPs agreement on intellectual property rights that supports corporate monopolization of essential information and technology. Serious consideration should be given to transferring responsibility for these agreements from the WTO to more suitable forums.
- IMF and World Bank structural adjustment provisions that impose harmful liberalization policies on Southern countries.

- United Nations Conference on Trade and Development could take a lead role in these reviews and in calling for a moratorium on proposals to expand the authority and mandates of the Bretton Woods institutions.

Restructuring the Institutional Framework

In addition to these immediate interim measures to prevent further damage and begin to reframe the problem, there is a need for a basic restructuring of the institutions of international economic governance to create a system that is accountable to the needs and preferences of people, communities, and nature. Our recommendations follow.

UNIFY GLOBAL GOVERNANCE
UNDER A RESTRUCTURED UNITED NATIONS

Global governance functions today are divided between the United Nations system—including the U.N. secretariat; its specialized agencies, such as the World Health Organization, the International Labor Organization, the Food and Agriculture Organization; and its various development assistance funds, such as UNDP, UNFPA, UNICEF, and UNIFEM—and the Bretton Woods system. (Although the Bretton Woods institutions are commonly included in lists of United Nations organizations and may, when it is to their advantage, claim themselves to be part of the United Nations system, the relationship actually has no substance. The Bretton Woods institutions have their own governing boards and budgets and acknowledge no accountability or subordination to the United Nations or its governing bodies.) The U.N. system has by far the broader mandate and, despite its considerable flaws, is more open and democratic. In practice, it has given much greater weight to human, social, and environmental priorities than have the more secretive Bretton Woods institutions.

Erskine Childers and Brian Urquhart, in their 1994 report *Renewing the United Nations System,* point out that the founders of the United Nations intended that the responsibility for global economic affairs—including the overall supervision and policy direction of the Bretton Woods institutions— would fall under the jurisdiction of the Economic and Social Council of the

U.N. General Assembly. The scope of its intended role in this regard is spelled out in Article 55 of its charter, which provides that the United Nations shall promote the following:

- Higher standards of living, full employment, and conditions of economic and social progress and development
- Solutions for international economic, social, health, and related problems
- International cultural and educational cooperation
- Universal respect for, and observance of, human rights and fundamental freedoms for all without distinction as to race, sex, language, or religion

But the United States and other corporate-dominated Western governments—the same ones that took the lead in creating both the United Nations and the Bretton Woods systems after World War II—allowed and even encouraged the Bretton Woods institutions to act as a global government with the ability to impose their will on nation-states in disregard of U.N. conventions and treaties.

Also, throughout most of the 1980s and 1990s, the U.S. Congress refused to pay the full dues owed by the United States to the United Nations, starving it of the financial resources necessary to carry out its mandate and creating a permanent crisis atmosphere in what should be the most important, influential, and stable international body. In contrast, the World Bank, the IMF, the WTO, and the global corporations they faithfully serve have been flush with resources. Underfunded, understaffed, and bypassed by the United States and other Northern governments in most economic matters, the United Nations largely ceded to the Bretton Woods institutions the power to shape global economic policies and relationships.

Dividing governance of the global affairs of one world between two competing governmental systems is not wise policy. The complexity of labor, health, food, human rights, environmental, trade, and investment issues is now much greater than in 1945, and the need for coherent global-level policies is far more urgent.

A choice must now be made either to expand the power and mandate of the Bretton Woods system to provide the leadership at the global level or to reaffirm the mandate of the United Nations and build its capacity to fulfill its intended function. Expanding the mandate of the Bretton Woods system appears to be a grave error from both a human and a planetary perspective.

It is true that these institutions have been far more effective in implementing well-defined agendas than has the United Nations. Yet although the United Nations has been less effective, its more open and democratic decision processes and greater responsiveness to the will of the people have often resulted in more consensual agendas aligned with human and planetary interests.

True democracy rests not on application of brute force but on consent of the governed. Force is the instrument of the self-interested tyrant. The poor and the weak are generally better served by less coercive regimes. As the coercive power of the corporate-dominated Bretton Woods institutions has grown, they have increasingly chosen to impose rules that serve the strong at the expense of the weak.

Clearly, there is a need for international rules. To serve the whole of humanity, however, they must be based on the consent of the governed, and enforcement must be left primarily to democratically elected local and national governments. The decision processes of the United Nations largely align with these principles. Limiting the powers and mandates of the IMF, the World Bank, and the WTO will create a greater space for a reformed United Nations to fulfill its intended functions and for people to act through their national and local governments to establish a policy framework consistent with the healthy, authentic development of people and communities.

We are the first to acknowledge that the United Nations has been greatly weakened and compromised over the past two decades. From the time Ronald Reagan became president of the United States in 1981, the U.S. government has actively undermined those U.N. agencies it viewed as interfering with market freedom. The United States has continued to use its great power status in the wake of the Cold War to manipulate the United Nations to serve a number of narrow U.S. political and economic interests. In addition, the United Nations inevitably suffers from the democratic deficits of many of its member states. The fact that many governments poorly represent the will of their people is likewise reflected in flawed decision making.

A related threat to the capacity of the United Nations to perform its intended functions on behalf of humanity is the increasingly successful effort by corporate interests—led by the International Chamber of Commerce and the World Business Council on Sustainable Development—to establish a presence in the United Nations to ensure that its resources and policies align with the corporate agenda and that there is no meaningful and enforceable call for corporate accountability in U.N. forums. Starved of financial resources and bullied by the U.S. government, the United Nations has been actively solicitous of corporate engagement. The July 2000 Global Compact that the United Nations launched with forty-four global corporations increases the corporate influence, placing at risk the U.N.'s legitimacy and credibility with the civil society groups that have launched increasingly effective campaigns to immobilize and eventually close the Bretton Woods institutions. Civil society generally has been highly supportive of the United Nations, but a corporate-dominated United Nations would not be immune to similar attacks.

The United Nations is an institution of governments and people. There is no legitimate place in its deliberations and decision processes for corporations that represent only the narrow financial self-interests of a small, wealthy elite. If the United Nations takes on a larger role in reforming and democratizing economic relations among and within nations, it will be more important than ever that it is freed of corporate influence and serve as a fully open and democratic body, solely accountable to its member governments and the people these governments presume to represent.

We believe that the time has come to reshape the system of global economic governance under the auspices of the United Nations, providing it with the human and financial resources to fulfill its original mandate and introducing reforms intended to strengthen its function as a democratic governing body.

DECOMMISSION THE BRETTON WOODS INSTITUTIONS

The larger goal is to replace a governing system that serves the needs of global financiers and transnational corporations with one that serves the needs of people and communities. The Bretton Woods institutions, the cornerstones of the former system, thus need to be dismantled.

As this volume has explained, these institutions have persistently advanced the economic interests of powerful corporations and the economic advantages of the rich countries. They embrace an ideology that denigrates the right of a country to pursue policies consistent with the interests of its own people and radically dilutes the right of low-income countries to special and differential treatment. They have raised inequality to a principle of decision making. Finally, they are staffed by economists so indoctrinated in free market ideology that they are unable to accept even the possibility of more equitable and sustainable alternatives. It would be unrealistic to turn to these institutions for leadership in resolving the crisis that they have played such a major role in creating.

A number of Southern countries achieved important social and economic progress between 1950 and 1980, before centralized power was institutionalized in a set of all-encompassing and powerful multilateral organizations. Much of the momentum was lost between 1980 and 2000 as the World Bank and the IMF consolidated their power and began imposing their ideological policy prescriptions. Many of the poorest countries suffered reversals.

It is a tragic truth that much of the work ahead centers on repairing the enormous damage caused by the Bretton Woods institutions. Debts must be cancelled, commodity prices stabilized, control established over the goods and money flowing across borders, anti-trust measures implemented to break up concentrations of corporate power, corporations with repeat criminal convictions dechartered, national economies rebuilt and redirected with proper regulatory regimes to meet local needs, the environment healed, the power of corporations curbed, financial speculation brought under control, wealth redistributed to create a semblance of equity, and the democratic accountability of governments established.

An ongoing debate in civil society concerns whether the triumvirate of Bretton Woods institutions can be reformed or should be closed. Institutional reform is a viable strategy when the institutions in question are fundamentally fair and aligned with a legitimate purpose but have simply been corrupted, as is the case with many national governments. It is not a viable strategy when a system is in its structure, mandate, purposes, principles, and processes so fundamentally at odds with the human interest, as is the case with the Bretton Woods institutions.

To borrow a phrase applied to aging nuclear power plants, it is time to begin a decommissioning process. Developing countries' governments and international civil society ought not allow their energies to be hijacked into reforming these institutions. The best they could hope for would be to administer a facelift to fundamentally flawed institutions.

The World Trade Organization

The WTO is often promoted as a "rules-based" trading framework that protects the weaker and poorer countries from unilateral actions by the stronger states. But the opposite is true. The WTO, like many other multilateral institutions and agreements, institutionalizes and legitimizes inequality. It serves as an instrument by which stronger countries can impose a discipline of their own choosing on weaker countries at less cost than would be possible in a more fluid, less structured international system.

The GATT had limited power and was more flexible and sympathetic to the special status of developing countries. Furthermore, what power the GATT did have was counterbalanced by a variety of other international actors, including UNCTAD, the International Labor Organization (ILO), evolving trade blocs such as Mercosur in Latin America, SAARC in South Asia, SADCC in Southern Africa, and ASEAN in Southeast Asia, many of which actively sided with Southern interests. This flexibility and active support allowed countries in East and Southeast Asia to craft successful development strategies of their own design in which activist states promoted exports on the one hand and protected domestic industries on the other.

The claim made that the only alternative to a powerful WTO is chaos constitutes pure fear-mongering by those who profit from the current situation. If anything, the international system has become less stable and has suffered more serious trade imbalances and disputes since the WTO was established in 1995. The return to a more fluid, less structured, more pluralistic world with multiple checks and balances will again allow developing nations and poor communities worldwide the opportunity to carve out the space they need to put themselves on a positive path based on their values, their rhythms, and the strategies of their choice.

Any plan for a new round of WTO negotiations or an expansion of the WTO mandate or membership should be firmly rejected. So too should attempts to shift the WTO expansion agenda to regional negotiations, such as the Free Trade Area of the Americas. The focus of the WTO member countries should instead be on negotiating an orderly rollback of many of the rules put in place by and following the GATT Uruguay Round and the orderly phaseout of WTO operations, including its staff and assets. After such a rollback, what remains of the original GATT framework would need to be updated to ensure transparency and accountability. Some aspects of the original International Trade Organization, first proposed after World War II, should be reexamined. This rollback will clear the way for the many other actions required to repair the damage of the Bretton Woods era.

The IMF and the World Bank

As for the IMF and the World Bank, we recommend the appointment of an international "decommissioning commission" for each institution, to oversee phasing out its operations and disposing of its assets and liabilities. Certainly, half the members of these bodies should come from the civil society organizations that have been instrumental in bringing to light their destructive impact.

This decommissioning commission would mandate an immediate rollback of all structural adjustment programs in the Third World and the former socialist world. It would implement a concurrent reduction in the IMF professional staff from over a thousand to a few hundred, with commensurate cuts in IMF capital expenditures and operational expenses. Most of the group's economists are today employed in micromanaging adjustment programs. Because their functions will be eliminated along with these programs, their services will no longer be needed. The commission would coordinate with the International Insolvency Court (described in the next section) to determine the proper disposition of outstanding debts owed to the IMF. The decommissioning should be completed within a few years. At the end of this time, the remaining staff would be released. All buildings and facilities would be turned over to the United Nations as they become available for use by the new institutions to be created under the U.N. jurisdiction. We recommend that the commission model the termination benefits that will be provided to IMF staff on the benefits typically offered to persons terminated from public employment under IMF structural adjustment programs.

The World Bank decommissioning commission would take similar steps with regard to its staff and assets, with the goal of releasing all World Bank staff and turning over all remaining assets to the United Nations within a few years of its appointment.

International civil society will need to act quickly and forcefully. With their credibility and legitimacy in tatters, the IMF and the World Bank are in severe crisis. We may expect, however, that rather than taking decisive action, the powers that be will attempt to wait for the storm to blow over while talking about reform. With the IMF and the World Bank sidelined and ultimately removed, the way will be open to move ahead with putting in place an international financial system that favors long-term productive investment over short-term speculation, stability over volatility, and local over foreign investment and ownership.

Strengthening the Countervailing Powers of the U.N. System

As the Bretton Woods institutions are dismantled, the countervailing institutional power required to reform the global trade and financial systems and end global corporate rule can come from strengthened states and a reformed United Nations. We hasten to note that though we believe the United Nations should be strengthened in its mandate and resources, we continue to believe that international institutions should have responsibility and authority for only those functions that cannot be reasonably carried out at national and local levels. Wherever possible, the primary responsibility of international institutions should be to support effective and responsive democratic local governance.

There are strong arguments for upgrading the capacity of the World Health Organization, the International Labor Office, and the United Nations Environment Program to address trade-related health, labor, and environmental issues. Trade-related standards should come under the jurisdiction of the U.N. agencies, with the primary responsibility and expertise on the related standards. Good health is an end. Worker rights, dignified wages, and safe working conditions are ends. A healthy environment is an end. In contrast, international trade and investment are merely means and should be dealt with accordingly. Appropriate programs will need to be worked out for each relevant U.N. agency. This next section of the chapter takes UNCTAD as an example of the kind of strengthened roles these agencies might play in global economic governance under a new regime.

THE ROLE OF UNCTAD

The United Nations Conference on Trade and Development (UNCTAD) was created in 1964. Over the next decade, it became the principal vehicle used by Third World governments to restructure the global economy to support their national development efforts. Subsequently, as the Bretton Woods institutions gained power, UNCTAD became increasingly marginalized along with the concerns of Southern countries.

If trade is to serve a process of just and sustainable development, with a bias toward the needs of the poor and workers as well as low-income countries, there is a strong argument for making a strengthened UNCTAD the primary United Nations rule-making body for international trade. The failing credibility of the Bretton Woods institutions has created a moment of opportunity for UNCTAD to position itself as a contender. An appropriate first step would be to raise a serious challenge to the premise that the full integration of developing countries into the world economy is the way to prosperity, and to position itself as chief advocate in the international system for a true alternative based on the principles outlined in this volume.

UNCTAD's former influence came primarily from serving as a voice of Southern governments and an advocate for their development interests. Debt relief and a rollback of structural adjustment are two of the most immediate and widely recognized needs of Southern countries. They are also issues high on the civil society agenda. There is the basis here for a natural alliance between Southern governments and civil society groups working on these issues that would strengthen the hands of both. UNCTAD is well positioned to be a broker of this alliance.

It should also be of interest to Southern governments that civil society's call for debt relief and a rollback of structural adjustment is part of a much larger agenda that seeks to dismantle a global system that is arguably little more than a re-creation of the institutions of colonialism with a more friendly face, and to put in its place a system designed to strengthen the role of national governments in facilitating national development based on democratic self-reliance and self-determination in a supportive global framework. This agenda is strongly aligned with the interests of Southern countries. Again, UNCTAD can take the lead in brokering dialogue on such possibilities in the U.N. system.

We urge UNCTAD to also take a lead role in challenging the hegemony of the WTO as the ultimate arbiter of trade and development issues. It should propose an arrangement whereby the relevant expertise of organizations such as UNCTAD, the ILO, the WTO, UNEP, and the implementing bodies of multilateral environmental agreements and regional economic blocs is brought to bear on these issues, participating as equals to clarify, define, and implement international economic policies in service to people and planet.

It took five hundred years of colonialism and fifty years of Bretton Woods to put the existing system in place. The need for an alternative is urgent, but realistically it will take several decades to establish it fully and bring global economic relationships into an equitable and sustainable balance. In the meantime, there is an urgent need for new international agreements that begin the process of transition to a new economy. UNCTAD can and should initiate the transition. Here are three transitional international agreements that UNCTAD might initiate to begin to move the world toward a more just, sustainable, and democratic system:

- *An agreement on economic self-determination.* Such an agreement would accord Southern countries "special and differential treatment" in global trade, investment, and finance. It would acknowledge the perils posed for Southern countries from indiscriminate liberalization and guarantee their right to give priority to their domestic development needs in their economic relationships with the North, including their right to establish controls over financial flows across their borders, set the terms of foreign investment, give preference to domestic finance and ownership, place limits on resource extraction, and favor local value-added processing of export commodities. It would also establish a framework for creating an international system of commodity price supports and for securing preferential access to Northern markets to the extent required to generate the foreign exchange to repay international debts and pay for imports from Northern nations.
- *An agreement on trade claims.* UNCTAD could also play a key role in addressing the critical nexus of trade and the environment. Together with the U.N. Environment Program and UNDP, UNCTAD could lead in drafting an agreement specifying broad but binding guidelines and a pluralistic mechanism involving civil society actors that would resolve the conflicting claims of trade bodies, multilateral environmental agreements, governments, and NGOs.
- *A "New Deal" for agriculture in developing countries and for small farmers in developed countries.* UNCTAD could lead in forging such a program. The

emphasis would not be the integration of agriculture into world trade but the integration of trade into a development strategy that puts the emphasis on raising incomes and employment in the agricultural sector, achieving food security through a significant degree of food self-sufficiency, and promoting ecologically sustainable production.

It is wholly appropriate for UNCTAD, as the U.N. voice of the South, to assume a leadership role as we move to a new economy. Southern countries know best the reality and consequences of the present unjust, unsustainable, and undemocratic system and have the most immediate stake in achieving rapid progress toward an alternative.

These proposals would also put Southern countries on the leading edge of bringing the new economy into being. For example, the agreement on economic self-determination would address the particular needs of Southern countries. It would also create a prototype for a new approach to international economic relationships ultimately as appropriate to the North as to the South.

UNCTAD does not have the material resources of the Bretton Woods institutions, but it has something that their economic power cannot buy—legitimacy among Southern countries and their governments.

Creating New Global Institutions

In addition to reforming and strengthening existing U.N. bodies, a small number of new institutions at the global level need to be created under U.N. authority and oversight. Here are ideas on five such bodies.

U.N. INTERNATIONAL INSOLVENCY COURT

Debt relief is the appropriate response to the continuing debt crisis of poor countries. People cannot be both free and in debt. We therefore endorse recommendations to create an International Insolvency Court (IIC) that have already come from UNCTAD, the Jubilee 2000 Coalition, and the Canadian government. The IIC would comprise a conciliation panel and an arbitration panel. The former would facilitate negotiated settlements between debtors and creditors. Where parties failed to reach a settlement, the arbitration panel would make a legally binding final ruling. Debtor countries might be supported in the preparation and presentation of their cases by UNCTAD and by the International Finance Organization, proposed in the next section. We envisage the following essential elements of the IIC:

- It must be an independent body insulated from the influence of the IMF and the World Bank—so long as they exist—and have balanced representation from debtor and creditor nations.
- Privately incurred debts, unless originally guaranteed by a government in an open democratic process consistent with established law, should remain private. Where repayment of a private debt is in dispute, it should be a matter between the private contracting parties to be settled in the appropriate civil courts.
- Its work must be fully transparent and open to public observation and review.
- A debtor government that determines that its debt obligations have reached a critical level and cannot be repaid without impairing the well-being of its citizens would voluntarily initiate the procedure by presenting its case to the court.
- After a preliminary assessment, the debtor country would be granted a stay on its repayments for a period sufficient to complete the court's review and decision process. In the meantime, it would also agree to incur no new debt.
- An assessment process would determine how much a country owes and is able to pay over time without compromising its ability to perform essential governmental functions, including the delivery of necessary social services. The court would also review the debt portfolio to identify odious debts subject to legal repudiation, including debts to the World Bank and IMF that were not legitimately contracted or were used for purposes that yielded no public benefit. The latter would include debts incurred for bank-designed projects that failed as a result of faulty design and negligent bank oversight.
- On the basis of the assessment, a debt-relief plan would be negotiated to cover any amounts a country owes after repudiation of odious debts, with adequate allowance for necessary government functions and the delivery of essential services. The plan would provide for necessary debt

rescheduling, reduction, and cancellation—taking into account the implicit debt owed to debtor countries in the South by creditor countries in the North for wealth extracted without proper compensation.

- Debt-relief plans would seek to leave a country with its international accounts balanced and free of international debt. Debt-relief agreements should include strict limits on incurring new international debts and provide guidelines for financial regulation and trade management intended to keep current accounts in balance.

The IIC can become operational as the World Bank and the regional development banks are decommissioned, with any remaining assets of the decommissioned institutions applied to debt relief.

U.N. INTERNATIONAL FINANCE ORGANIZATION

The proposed International Finance Organization (IFO) would work with U.N. member countries to achieve and maintain balance and stability in international financial relationships, free national and global finance from the distortions of international debt and debt-based money, promote productive domestic investment and domestic ownership of productive resources, and take necessary actions at the international level to support nations and localities in creating equitable, productive, sustainable livelihoods for all. The IFO would replace the IMF but with full accountability to the United Nations. Lacking either lending capacity or enforcement powers, its functions would be to maintain a central database on international accounts, flag problem situations, and facilitate negotiations among countries to correct imbalances. It would also provide advisory services on request. Its charter would mandate that it favor human, community, and environmental interests over the interests of global corporations and financiers in all its activities. More specifically, IFO functions would include the following:

- Monitor and publish regular statistical compilations on national trade and current account balances and facilitate negotiations toward agreement on corrective action where a country's import and export accounts are in consequential and persistent imbalance.
- Maintain a central information facility on practices and experiences of

different governments relating to capital controls, foreign borrowing, and the management of trade balances. In cooperation with UNDP, provide advisory services, on request, to assist national governments in establishing appropriate and adequate capital controls that strengthen domestic employment, investment, ownership, and technical capability; discourage financial speculation; and keep international accounts balanced.

- Facilitate the negotiation and implementation of international agreements by which national governments will take coordinated action to prevent the use of offshore banks and tax havens for money laundering and tax evasion.
- Carry out policy studies relating to measures intended to dampen speculative financial movements, facilitate the negotiation of appropriate agreements, and provide support as requested for implementing actions.
- Carry out policy studies on the feasibility of shifting money creation from banks to governments, develop implementing proposals, and provide advisory support to interested governments.

The International Financial Organization and the regional monetary funds recommended in the following paragraph may be phased in as the IMF is decommissioned. Any remaining IMF assets could be applied to debt relief and to capitalizing the regional funds.

REGIONAL MONETARY FUNDS

Recognizing the legitimate need for access to short-term emergency foreign exchange loans, while also recognizing that finance should be local to the extent possible, we endorse the creation of regional monetary funds accountable to the member countries of their region. These regional funds would provide quick-response, short-term emergency loans in the event of an unanticipated foreign exchange shortfall. Accountable to their region's governments, these funds would reflect regional sensibilities and interests. Although all countries would be welcome to send representatives to their meetings as observers, no country should be allowed to be a voting member of more than one regional fund.

U.N. TRADE DISPUTES COURT

Steps toward the localization of production and consumption recommended in this volume would lead to a reduction in the movement of goods between countries. Even so, the world will continue to need a system of rules to maintain the stability and fairness of the international trading system, because so long as there is trade among nations there will be disputes and the potential for abuse and coercion of the weak by the strong. The world has no need, however, for a World Trade Organization that regulates democratic governments to prevent them from setting and enforcing rules and standards to protect the public interest.

Trade is a means, not an end; the expansion of trade per se is not a goal; and responsibility for negotiating and enforcing trade rules should rest with agencies that understand this distinction. Thus, we are inclined to the view that the jurisdiction for trade issues should be distributed among the U.N. agencies concerned with such matters as development, health, food, labor, and the environment. The responsibility should rest with the same agencies responsible for the outcomes that trade should support.

As suggested earlier, UNCTAD might have a lead in the rule-setting process. The U.N. International Finance Organization would track current account balances and raise a warning when international intervention is required.

There remains the need for a body to mediate and arbitrate trade disputes. To meet this need, we propose the creation of a U.N. Trade Disputes Court. It would have a structure similar to that of the U.N. International Insolvency Court, with a conciliation panel to facilitate negotiated settlements between trading partners and an arbitration panel to make legally binding rulings based on the provisions of relevant international agreements—including treaties and declarations on human rights, labor, health and safety, and the environment—where parties fail to reach a voluntary settlement.

What might require the intervention of a trade disputes court? Say, for example, a country's trade accounts are seriously and persistently out of balance. Here is an important case in point. The United States has a massive and persistent import surplus, which suggests it is living beyond its means, supporting wasteful and environmentally destructive lifestyles by expropriating the labor and resources of others with far greater need. China, in contrast, has a large and persistent export surplus based on a large supply of exploited labor. The losers in this instance include other low-wage countries that are unable to compete in world markets against China's low wages and marginal working conditions. The debt of the United States to the rest of the system is cumulative so long as the imbalance exists. To bring itself back into balance with the rest of the system, the United States must export more or import less. China must import more or export less. Ideally, the United States would embrace the challenge of learning to live within its means. China should direct more of its productive capacity to meeting the needs of its own people. In both cases, there will be a long and difficult process of adjustment with impacts on the trade relations of both China and the United States with many countries. These are not simple matters and appropriately involve complex dialogue and negotiations with all consequential trading partners.

Another example would be a country that believes a trading partner has taken a precipitous trade action for purely political reasons to extort some concession, such as access to oil or a particular vote in the United Nations. In general, a country should have the right to reorient its social, environmental, and economic priorities from time to time and to adjust its trade relationships as appropriate. But this should be done in an orderly, phased manner, undertaken in agreement with trading partners and giving all parties time to adjust to the change. Member countries could turn to the U.N. Trade Disputes Court if bilateral negotiations to resolve the situation fail.

U.N. ORGANIZATION FOR CORPORATE ACCOUNTABILITY

Second only to financial speculation, the greatest economic threat to the well-being of people and planet is the growth and abuse of unchecked corporate power. There are virtually no mechanisms in place at the international level for dealing with this threat, and the Bretton Woods institutions regularly seek to block corrective actions at national levels. Giant corporations move freely around the world, buying off politicians and playing states, communities, and people against one another in competition for the jobs, finance, and access to technology that corporations control. Eliminating the Bretton Woods institutions, rescinding structural adjustment programs, and canceling provisions in international trade agreements that place the interests of global corporations and financiers ahead of human interests would be important steps toward restoring the right and responsibility of governments to hold corporations accountable to public interests.

The primary function of the proposed U.N. Organization for Corporate Accountability would be to support national initiatives on corporate accountability through the provision of information and advisory services, facilitating negotiation of relevant bilateral and multilateral agreements and coordinated bilateral and multilateral implementing actions. Although enforcement authority would lie entirely at the national and local levels, the OCA would provide both governments and the general public with comprehensive and authoritative information on corporate practices as a basis for legal action and for investor and consumer action. More specifically, the OCA would do the following:

- Compile and publicize periodic reports on corporate concentration in major sectors and produce special studies on monopolistic practices, including strategic alliances and cartels contrary to sound market principles. Focus international attention on the implications of corporate concentration in key sectors such as banking, media, and agribusiness to encourage appropriate anti-trust actions by national governments.
- Monitor pricing practices in international trade to document and publicize unfair competitive practices, such as export subsidies or pricing goods below cost to unfairly drive competitors from the market.
- Maintain comprehensive and readily accessible public records for all corporations with consequential transnational operations, of regulatory infractions and civil and criminal prosecutions and convictions. Publish an international watch list of corporations that exhibit persistent patterns of illegal activity, which might serve as a trigger for consumer boycotts or legal actions at the national level to decharter or decertify.
- Maintain comprehensive and readily accessible public records for the one thousand largest global corporations, listing by corporation all identified direct and indirect subsidies, including special tax concessions and the public costs of substandard wages and working conditions, the sale of harmful products, the discharge of harmful wastes, and other externalized costs.

- Coordinate the negotiation and implementation of international agreements assuring the right of those harmed by the actions of a reckless corporate subsidiary in one country to sue and recover damages from the parent corporations, wherever they may be located.
- Coordinate the negotiation of a recommended uniform code of standards for corporations operating in more than one country. This code would serve as a recommended model for use by governments in framing national and local laws regulating the activities of global corporations operating within their jurisdiction. Such standards should assure a consistent bias in favor of smaller, locally owned enterprises. For example, corporations with operations in more than one country should be expected to adhere to the highest of international, local, or home country standards on human rights, labor, environment, health, and safety wherever they operate; decline any special concessions, subsidies, or tax breaks not generally available on equal or more attractive terms to local businesses; obey all national and international laws; provide no payments or gifts to public officials or politicians and refrain from any attempt to influence elections and public policies; deal in good faith with unions; provide at least a living wage to all employees; provide full and accurate labeling of products; and publicly disclose all toxic releases. Global corporations commonly claim that they adhere to the highest international standards wherever they operate. Those corporations that in fact live by this principle have no reason to object to the public being informed about their actual records. Although the OCA would have no actual enforcement powers, it would monitor and publicize compliance or noncompliance with these standards as guides to governmental and public action.
- Assist U.N. member countries in establishing and enforcing anti-trust legislation and other legislation related to setting and enforcing standards for corporate accountability.
- Convene an international panel to recommend national legislation to limit the political influence of global corporations on government policymaking, including limits or prohibitions on corporate financial contributions to political parties and candidates, and corporate spending on advertising and public relations campaigns related to legislation and public issues.

CHAPTER EIGHT

Conclusions

A FEW YEARS AGO, such proposals as we have advanced in these pages might have seemed wildly unrealistic to some. From 1980 to the late 1990s, corporate globalization was so ascendant that many forgot that during the 1960s and 1970s the development debate was still very vibrant. Local, national, and global alternatives flourished. During that period, civil society joined with Southern governments to sketch out alternatives that were implemented on the ground in many countries.

History is likely to view the 1980s and 1990s as historical anomalies, a time when a single dominant model was promoted despite its inherent unsustainability and its failures.

But since the mid-1990s, the political scene has undergone a dramatic change. The World Bank and IMF have come under sharp criticism by civil society, governments, even a bipartisan commission of the U.S. Congress. In the wake of the Enron and WorldCom scandals, global corporations have lost a great deal of public trust. Global citizen alliances have found new strength in the growing size and success of demonstrations around the world that have brought millions of people onto the streets. Tens of thousands of representatives of civil society organizations around the world now gather annually at the World Social Forum to strengthen their alliances and share a new vision of a world that can thrive if it is freed from the grip of corporate globalization.

There is also the potential for yet another explicit alliance between civil society groups in the world and some governments of the Group of 77

(G-77), a coalition of over 130 Southern countries that was formed to articulate and promote their collective economic interests and enhance their joint negotiating capacity on international economic issues. The protests that contributed to a breakdown of the 1999 WTO meeting in Seattle emboldened some governments of Southern countries to be more forthright in their challenge to WTO procedures and proposals harmful to their national interests. The subsequent April 2000 protests in Washington, D.C., against the World Bank and the IMF called for debt relief and a rollback of structural adjustment. These protests coincided with a meeting of the G-77 heads of state in Cuba, where several government representatives issued statements sharply critical of the World Bank and IMF, expressed support for the Washington protesters, and called for a transfer of some responsibilities for global economic policies from the Bretton Woods institutions to the United Nations.

The G-77 countries have much to lose from business as usual under the Bretton Woods regime and much to gain from new procedures like those proposed in this volume—especially debt relief, removal of structural adjustment conditions, and controls on speculative financial movements. These countries also account for a majority of the votes in the United Nations General Assembly, a power they have previously been reluctant to use in defiance of the powerful Northern industrial countries. But growing alliances with civil society are strengthening popular support in both North and South for taking an *independent* stand in the interests of democracy, the environment, and the well-being of the poor.

That a grand alliance of some G-77 leaders, global civil society, and sympathetic politicians from the North might emerge with sufficient power to achieve sweeping institutional reform at the global level has a precedent in similar alliances between progressives in the North and popular leaders in the former colonies, which resulted in the dismantling of the trans-Atlantic slave trade and later of colonial empires, following World War II. Recent events give credence to the view that a new cycle of change is under way.

~

Fifty years of development experience demonstrate conclusively the failures of the policies and institutions of corporate globalization. The legacy of exclusion and inequality find current expression in the violence, loss of institutional legitimacy, and collapsing environmental systems that threaten the foundations of societies and even life on earth. The crisis cannot be solved by the very same institutions and policies that established these practices. Using the police and military powers of the state to suppress dissent and contain a rage born of hopelessness and despair will only deepen the despair and intensify the rage.

There is an alternative. The failing legitimacy of the institutions of global corporate rule combined with the political force of an enlivened civil society have created an unprecedented moment of opportunity to rethink and transform the institutions of economic life, advance the democratic project, and realize the ageless human dream of liberty, justice, and prosperity for all.

What we write here should lay to rest the claim by corporate globalists that the goal of those of us who resist is the elimination of all institutions of global governance. This has always been a serious misrepresentation. The goal of civil society is to replace the autocractic institutions of corporate rule with democratic institutions, as earlier generations replaced the institutions of monarchy with those of political democracy.

Over the past decade, to make this point, Ralph Nader and Public Citizen's Lori Wallach have developed their upper-body strength by lugging around copies of the thousands of pages that constitute the agreements establishing the World Trade Organization and NAFTA. By crashing them down on podiums around the world, they remind their audiences that these institutions are the creations of men and a few women whose vision of governance begins and ends with the short-term needs of companies like Enron, ExxonMobil, and Monsanto. As the creations of humans, these institutions can be replaced.

The time has come to create democratic institutions of global governance that will end corporate rule, secure the human rights and democratic sovereignty of people everywhere, and restore control of national economies and resources to their own governments. All of this can be achieved through a framework of international agreements that support economic justice, food security, full employment, environmental sustainability, and financial stability. Consistent with the ten principles for sustainable societies that we outlined in this volume, such a system would support national and local jurisdictions in controlling and using their own resources to meet their own needs in ways that are appropriate to their own circumstances and cultures. Rule making, standard setting, and enforcement functions would be predominantly local and national. Global-level rule making and intervention would be reserved primarily for matters of compelling international interest, such as maintaining stable, balanced economic relationships among nations or stopping climate change. Trade and investment agreements would embody a strong bias for the poor in all countries and would seek to secure weak nations against predatory actions by strong nations and global corporations.

Now is the time to join the growing political struggle that will embrace new pathways such as those we describe here. Over the next few years, the International Forum on Globalization will be working with hundreds of other civil society organizations on every continent to discuss, refine, and introduce into public policy many of these and other ideas. We hope you will join in this crucial process.

Sources

Anderson, Ray. *Mid-Course Correction.* Atlanta: Peregrinzilla Press, 1998.

Anderson, Sarah, ed. *Views from the South: The Effects of Globalization and the WTO on Third World Countries.* San Francisco: International Forum on Globalization, 2000.

Anderson, Sarah, and John Cavanagh. *Top 200: The Rise of Corporate Global Power.* Washington, DC: Institute for Policy Studies, December 2000.

Anderson, Sarah, John Cavanagh, Chris Hartman, and Betsy Leondar-Wright. *Executive Excess 2001: Layoffs, Tax Rebates, and the Gender Gap.* Washington, DC: Institute for Policy Studies and United for a Fair Economy, May 2001.

Anderson, Sarah, John Cavanagh, and Thea Lee. *A Field Guide to the Global Economy.* New York: New Press, 2000.

Barker, Debi, and Jerry Mander. *Invisible Government: The World Trade Organization, Global Government for the Millennium?* San Francisco: International Forum on Globalization, 1999.

Barlow, Maude. *Blue Gold: The Global Water Crisis and the Commodification of the World's Water Supply.* San Francisco: International Forum on Globalization, 2001.

———. *The Free Trade Area of the Americas: The Threat to Social Programs, Environmental Sustainability, and Social Justice.* San Francisco: International Forum on Globalization, 2001.

———. *Profit Is Not the Cure.* Toronto: Stoddart, forthcoming.

Barlow, Maude, and Tony Clarke. *Blue Gold: The Battle Against Corporate Theft of the World's Water.* New York: New Press, 2002.

———. *Global Showdown: How the New Activists Are Fighting Global Corporate Rule.* Toronto: Stoddart Publishing, 2002.

Barnes, Peter. *Who Owns the Sky?* Washington, DC: Island Press, 2001.

Barnet, Richard J., and John Cavanagh. *Global Dreams: Imperial Corporations and the New World Order.* New York: Simon & Schuster, 1994.

"Barshefsky on U.S. Trade Agenda for 2000." Presentation by Charlene Barshefsky to the United States Mission to the European Union, Brussels, Belgium, February 8, 2000. http://www.useu.be/Issues/barsho208.html.

"Basic Call to Consciousness: The Hau de no sau nee Address to the Western World." *Akwesasne Notes.* Rooseveltown, NY: Mohawk Nation, 1978.

Bello, Walden. *The Future in the Balance: Essays on Globalization and Resistance.* San Francisco: Food First and Focus on the Global South, 2001.

Bello, Walden, Nicola Bullard, and Kamal Malhotra, eds. *Global Finance: New Thinking on Regulating Speculative Capital Markets.* London: Zed Books, 2000.

Bello, Walden, Shea Cunningham, and Li Keng Poh. *A Siamese Tragedy: Development & Disintegration in Modern Thailand.* London: Zed Books, 1998.

Bello, Walden, Shea Cunningham, and Bill Rau. *Dark Victory: The United States, Structural Adjustment, and Global Poverty.* London: Pluto Press, 1994.

Bello, Walden, with David Kinley, and Elaine Elison. *Development Debacle: The World Bank in the Philippines.* San Francisco: Institute for Food and Development Policy, 1982.

Bello, Walden, and Stephanie Rosefeld. *Dragons in Distress: Asia's Miracle Economies in Crisis.* San Francisco: Institute for Food and Development Policy, 1990.

Book of Knowledge: Investing in the Growing Education and Training Industry. New York: Merrill Lynch, Global Securities Research & Economics Group, Global Fundamental Equity Research Department, 1999.

Braun, Henry. *The Phoenix Project: An Energy Transition to Renewable Resources.* Phoenix: Research Analysts, 1990.

Brecher, Jeremy, Tim Costello, and Brendan Smith. *Globalization from Below: The Power of Solidarity.* Cambridge, MA: South End Press, 2000.

Broad, Robin, ed. *Global Backlash: Citizen Initiatives for a Just World Economy.* Lanham, MD: Rowman & Littlefield, 2002.

Brown, Lester. *Building a Sustainable Society.* New York: W. W. Norton, 1981.

———. *Eco-Economy: Building an Economy for the Earth.* New York: W. W. Norton, 2001.

Brown, Lester R., and others. *State of the World 1988.* Washington, DC: Worldwatch Institute, 1988.

Brown, Lester, Christopher Flavin, Hilary French, and others. *State of the World 2001.* Washington, DC: Worldwatch Institute, 2001.

Bruno, Kenny, Joshua Karliner, and China Brotsky. *Greenhouse Gangsters Versus Climate Justice.* San Francisco: Transnational Resource and Action Center, 1999.

Capra, Fritjof. *The Hidden Connections: A Science for Sustainable Living.* London: HarperCollins, 2002.

———. *The Hidden Connections: Integrating the Biological, Cognitive, and Social Dimensions of Life into a Science of Sustainability.* New York: Doubleday, 2002.

Carstensen, Michelle, and David Morris. *Biochemicals for the Automobile Industry.* Washington, DC: Institute for Local Self-Reliance, 1997.

Cashman, Ty. "Fuel from Water." *Whole Earth Review,* Spring 1994, pp. 50–53.

———. "Hydrogen Energy." *Whole Earth Review,* Winter 2001, p. 46.

———. "Jump-Starting Renewables: What It Takes to Enter the Hydrogen Era." *Whole Earth Review,* Winter 2001, p. 57.

Cavanagh, John, ed. *South-North: Citizen Strategies to Transform a Divided World* (pamphlet). San Francisco: International Forum on Globalization, November 1995.

Central Intelligence Agency. *Global Trends, 2015.* Langley, VA: Central Intelligence Agency, 2000.

Childers, Erskine, and Brian Urquhart. *Renewing the United Nations System* (special issue of *Development Dialogue*). Uppsala, Sweden: Dag Hammarskjold Foundation, 1994.

Chomsky, Noam. *World Orders Old and New.* New York: Columbia University Press, 1994.

Chossudovsky, Michel. *The Globalisation of Poverty: Impacts of IMF and World Bank Reforms.* Penang, Malaysia: Third World Network, 1997.

Clarke, Tony. *Silent Coup: Confronting the Big Business Takeover of Canada.* Ottawa: Canadian Centre for Policy Alternatives, 1997.

———. *By What Authority!* San Francisco: International Forum on Globalization, 1999.

Clarke, Tony, and Maude Barlow. *MAI: The Multilateral Agreement on Investment and the Threat to Canadian Sovereignty.* Toronto: Stoddart, 1997.

Commoner, Barry. *Making Peace with the Planet.* New York: New Press, 1992.

Daly, Herman E. *Beyond Growth: The Economics of Sustainable Development.* Boston: Beacon Press, 1996.

Daly, Herman E., and John B. Cobb, Jr. *For the Common Good: Redirecting the Economy Toward Community, the Environment, and a Sustainable Future.* Boston: Beacon Press, 1989.

Danaher, Kevin. *10 Reasons to Abolish the IMF & World Bank.* New York: Seven Stories Press, 2001.

———, ed. *Democratizing the Global Economy: The Battle Against the World Bank and the IMF.* Monroe, ME: Common Courage, 2001.

Doniger, David, David Friedman, Roland Hwang, Daniel Lashof, and Jason Mark. *Dangerous Addiction: Ending America's Oil Dependence.* New York: Natural Resources Defense Council and the Union of Concerned Scientists, 2002.

Douthwaite, Richard. *The Growth Illusion.* Dublin: Lilliput Press, 1992.

———. *Short Circuit: Strengthening Local Economies for Security in an Unstable World.* Dublin: Lilliput Press, 1996.

Dunn, Seth. "Micropower: The Next Electrical Era." Worldwatch Paper No. 151. Washington, DC: Worldwatch Institute, 2000.

————. "Decarbonizing the Energy Economy." In *State of the World 2001*, eds. Lester Brown, Christopher Flavin, Hilary French, and others, Washington, DC: Worldwatch Institute, 2001.

————. "Hydrogen Futures: Toward a Sustainable Energy System." Worldwatch Paper No. 157. Washington, DC: Worldwatch Institute, 2001.

"Eight Benefits of Micropower." *Whole Earth Review*, Winter 2001, p. 20.

"Energy Innovations: A Prosperous Path to a Clean Environment." Cambridge, MA: Union of Concerned Scientists, 1997. www.ucsusa.org/energy/find.ei.html.

Estes, Ralph. *Tyranny of the Bottom Line: Why Corporations Make Good People Do Bad Things*. San Francisco: Berrett-Koehler, 1996.

Faux, Jeff, and Lawrence Mishel. "Inequality and the Global Economy." In *Global Capitalism*, eds. Will Hutton and Anthony Giddens. New York: New Press, 2000.

Gardner, Gary, and Payal Sampat. "Mind Over Matter: Recasting the Role of Materials in Our Lives." Worldwatch Paper No. 144. Washington, DC: Worldwatch Institute, 1998.

Garrett, Laurie. *The Coming Plague: Newly Emerging Diseases in a World Out of Balance*. New York: Farrar, Straus & Giroux, 1994.

Gates, Jeff. *The Ownership Solution: Toward a Shared Capitalism for the Twenty-First Century*. Cambridge, MA: Perseus, 1999.

George, Susan. *A Fate Worse Than Debt*. London: Penguin Books, 1988.

————. *The Debt Boomerang: How Third World Debt Harms Us All*. London: Pluto Press, 1992.

George, Susan, and Fabrizio Sabelli. *Faith and Credit: The World Bank's Secular Empire*. London: Penguin Books, 1994.

Global Energy Technology Strategy. *Addressing Climate Change*. Washington, DC: Battelle, 2000.

"Globalization, Inc. Concentration in Corporate Power: The Unmentioned Agenda." *ETC Group Communique*, 71, July–August 2001.

Goldsmith, Edward. *The Way*. Athens: University of Georgia Press, 1998.

Goldsmith, Sir James. *The Trap*. New York: Carroll & Graf, 1993.

Gorelick, Steven. *Small Is Beautiful, Big Is Subsidized*. Berkeley, CA, and Devon, UK: International Society for Ecology and Culture, 2002.

Gray, John. *False Dawn*. New York: New Press, 1998.

Greider, William. *One World, Ready or Not: The Manic Logic of Global Capitalism*. New York: Touchstone, 1998.

Grossman, Richard L., and Fran T Adams. *Taking Care of Business: Citizenship and the Charter of Incorporation*. Cambridge, MA: Charter Ink, 1993.

Hancock, Graham. *Lords of Poverty: The Power, Prestige, and Corruption of the International Aid Business*. New York: Atlantic Monthly Press, 1989.

Hartman, Thom. *Unequal Protection*. Emmaus, PA: Rodale Press, 2002.

Hawken, Paul. *The Ecology of Commerce: A Declaration of Sustainability.* New York: HarperBusiness, 1993.

Hawken, Paul, Amory Lovins, and L. Hunter Lovins. *Natural Capitalism: The Next Industrial Revolution.* Boston: Back Bay Books, 2000.

Hemispheric Social Alliance. "Alternatives for the Americas," 2001. www.asc-hsa.org.

Henderson, Hazel. *Paradigms in Progress: Life Beyond Economics.* Indianapolis: Knowledge Systems, 1991.

———. *Creating Alternative Futures: The End of Economics.* West Hartford, CT: Kumarian Press, 1996.

———. *Beyond Globalization: Shaping a Sustainable Global Economy.* West Hartford, CT: Kumarian Press, 1999.

Hertsgaard, Mark. *Earth Odyssey.* New York: Broadway Books, 1998.

Hines, Colin. *Localization: A Global Manifesto.* London: Earthscan Publications, 2000.

Hoffman, Peter. *Tomorrow's Energy: Hydrogen Fuel Cells and the Prospects for a Cleaner Planet.* Cambridge: MIT Press, 2001.

International Forum on Globalization. *Does Globalization Help the Poor?* San Francisco, 2001.

International Network for Cultural Diversity. "Draft Convention on Cultural Diversity." March 2002.

Karliner, Joshua. *The Corporate Planet.* San Francisco: Sierra Club Books, 1997.

Kaul, Inge, Isabelle Grunberg, and Marc A. Stern. *Global Public Goods: International Cooperation in the 21st Century.* New York: United Nations Development Program and Oxford University Press, 1999.

Kelly, Marjorie. *The Divine Right of Capital: Dethroning the Corporate Aristocracy.* San Francisco: Berrett-Koehler, 2001.

Khor, Martin. "The Revolt of Developing Nations." *The Seattle Debacle* (special issue of *Third World Resurgence*), December 1999–January 2000.

———. *Globalization and the South: Some Critical Issues.* Penang, Malaysia: Third World Network, 2000.

———. *Globalization and the Crisis of Sustainable Development.* Penang, Malaysia: Third World Network, 2001.

———. "The WTO, the Post-Doha Agenda and the Future of the Trade System: A Development Perspective" (special paper from Third World Network) 2002. www.twnside.org.sg

Kimbrell, Andrew. *The Human Body Shop: The Engineering and Marketing of Life.* San Francisco: Harper San Francisco, 1993.

———. "Defending the Genetic Commons." *UTNE Reader*, January–February 2002, p. 44.

———, ed. *Fatal Harvest: The Tragedy of Industrial Agriculture.* Washington, DC: Island Press, 2002.

Klein, Naomi. *No Logo: Taking Aim at the Brand Bullies.* New York: Picador, 1999.

Korten, David C. *The Post-Corporate World: Life After Capitalism*. San Francisco: Berrett-Koehler and West Hartford, CT: Kumarian Press, 1999.

———. *When Corporations Rule the World*. 2d ed. West Hartford, CT: Kumarian Press and San Francisco: Berrett-Koehler, 2001.

Lang, Tim, and Colin Hines. *The New Protectionism: Protecting the Future Against Free Trade*. London: EarthScan Publications, 1993.

Lappé, Frances Moore. "Meet the P7." *Guerrilla News Network*, 2001. www.guerrillanews.com/globalization/doc243.html, December 18, 2001.

Lappé, Frances Moore, Joseph Collins, and Peter Rosset. *World Hunger: Twelve Myths*. New York: Grove Press, 1998.

Lappé, Frances Moore, and Anna Lappé. *Hope's Edge: The Next Diet for a Small Planet*. New York: Jeremy P. Tarcher/Putnam, 2002.

Lasn, Kalle, and Tom Liacas. "Corporate Crackdown." *Adbusters*, August–September 2000, pp. 36–48.

Lovins, Amory B., Michael Brylawski, David Cramer, and Timothy Moore. *Hypercars: Materials, Manufacturing, and Policy Implications*. Snowmass, CO: Rocky Mountain Institute, 1996.

Lovins, Amory B., and L. Hunter Lovins. "Frozen Assets?" *RMI Solutions* (newsletter of the Rocky Mountain Institute), Spring 2001, pp. 1–3, 20–21.

Lovins, Amory B., L. Hunter Lovins, and Paul Hawken. "A Road Map for Natural Capitalism." *Harvard Business Review*, May–June 1999, pp. 145–158.

Luttwak, Edward. *Turbo Capitalism: Winners and Losers in the Global Economy*. New York: HarperCollins, 1999.

MacArther, John R. *The Selling of "Free Trade": NAFTA, Washington, and the Subversion of American Democracy*. New York: Hill & Wang, 2000.

Madeley, John. *Big Business, Poor Peoples: The Impact of Transnational Corporations on the World's Poor*. London: Zed Books, 1999.

Mander, Jerry. *In the Absence of the Sacred: The Failure of Technology & the Survival of the Indian Nations*. San Francisco: Sierra Club Books, 1991.

Mander, Jerry, and Edward Goldsmith. *The Case Against the Global Economy: And for a Turn Toward the Local*. San Francisco: Sierra Club Books, 1996.

McDonough, William, and Michael Braungart. "The Next Industrial Revolution." *Atlantic Monthly*, October 1998, pp. 82–92.

McLaren, Deborah. *Rethinking Tourism and Ecotravel: The Paving of Paradise and What You Can Do to Stop It*. West Hartford, CT: Kumarian Press, 1998.

Meadows, Donella, Dennis L. Meadows, and Jorgen Randers. *Beyond the Limits*. Post Mills, VT: Chelsea Green, 1992.

Menotti, Victor. *Free Trade, Free Logging: How the World Trade Organization Undermines Global Forest Conservation*. San Francisco: International Forum on Globalization, 1999.

Mishel, Lawrence, Jared Bernstein, and John Schmitt. *The State of Working America, 1998–99*. Washington, DC: Economic Policy Institute, 1999.

"Model Sustainable Energy Statute Summary." Global Resource Action Center for the Environment, 2002. www.gracelinks.org/nuke/sustainable_energy-summary2.html], .

Monks, Robert A. G. *The Emperor's Nightingale: Restoring the Integrity of the Corporation in the Age of Shareholder Activism.* Reading, MA: Addison-Wesley, 1998.

Morris, David. *Getting from Here to There: Building a Rational Transportation System.* Washington, DC: Institute for Local Self-Reliance, 1992.

———. *Seeing the Light: Regaining Control of Our Electricity System.* Washington, DC: Institute for Local Self-Reliance, 2001.

Nader, Ralph, William Greider, Margaret Atwood, David Philips, and Pat Choate. *The Case Against Free Trade: GATT, NAFTA, and the Globalization of Corporate Power.* San Francisco: Earth Island Press, 1993.

Norberg-Hodge, Helena. *Ancient Futures: Learning from Ladakh.* San Francisco: Sierra Club Books, 1991.

Norberg-Hodge, Helena, Peter Goering, and John Page. *From the Ground Up: Rethinking Industrial Agriculture.* London: Zed Books, 2001.

Norberg-Hodge, Helena, Steven Gorelick, and Todd Merrifield. *Bringing the Food Economy Home.* West Hartford, CT: Kumarian Press and London: Zed Books, 2002.

Northrup, Michael. "Addressing Global Warming: A Way Forward." *Environmental Grantmakers Association: News and Updates* VI(I), Winter 2002, pp. 1, 21–22.

Pauli, Gunter. "Industrial Clustering and the Second Green Revolution." Lecture presented at Schumacher College, Devon, United Kingdom, May 1996.

Payer, Cheryl. *Lent and Lost: Foreign Credit and Third World Development.* London: Zed Books, 1991.

Perkins, Logan R. R. "Why Reduce Automobile Dependence." *Livable Cities,* 1, November 1997.

Perlas, Nicanor. *Shaping Globalization: Civil Society, Cultural Power, and Threefolding.* Quezon City, Philippines: CADI and GlobeNet3, 2000.

For a Sustainable Chile: A Citizen's Agenda for Change. Santiago: Sustainable Chile Program, 1999.

Posey, Darrell Addison, ed. *Cultural and Spiritual Values of Biodiversity.* London: Intermediate Technology Publications, 1999.

Program on Corporations, Law & Democracy. "By What Authority?" *Challenging Empire's Story* 4(2), Spring 2002, pp. 1–7.

Raghavan, Chakravarthi. *Recolonization: GATT, the Uruguay Round, and the Third World.* Penang, Malaysia: Third World Network, 1990.

Real Price of Gasoline. Washington, DC: International Center for Technology Assessment, 2002.

Register, Richard. *Ecocity Berkeley: Building Cities for a Healthy Future.* Berkeley: North Atlantic Books, 1987.

————. *Ecocities: Building Cities in Balance with Nature.* Berkeley: Berkeley Hills Books, 2002.

Retallack, Simon. *Climate Crisis: A Briefing for Funders.* London: Think Publishing, 2001.

Rich, Bruce. *Mortgaging the Earth: The World Bank, Environmental Impoverishment, and the Crisis of Development.* Boston: Beacon Press, 1994.

Rifkin, Jeremy. *Biosphere Politics: A New Consciousness for a New Century.* New York: Crown, 1991.

————. *The Hydrogen Economy.* New York: Tarcher/Putnam, 2002.

Ritz, Dean, ed. *Defying Corporations, Defining Democracy: A Book of History and Strategies.* New York: Apex Press, 2001.

Robertson, James. *Future Wealth: A New Economics for the 21st Century.* London: Mansell Publishing, 1989.

Roddick, Anita. *Take It Personally.* London: HarperCollins, 2001.

Rodrik, Dani. *Has Globalization Gone Too Far?* Washington, DC: Institute for International Economics, 1997.

Rosset, Peter. "Access to Land: Land Reform and Security of Tenure." *World Food Summit/Five Years Later, Civil Society Input/Case Studies.* Oakland: Institute for Food and Development Policy, October 2001.

Rowe, Jonathan. "The Hidden Commons." *Yes! A Journal of Positive Futures* 18, Summer 2001, pp. 12–17.

————. "Fanfare for the Commons," *UTNE Reader,* January–February 2002, pp. 40–44.

Sachs, Wolfgang, ed. *The Development Dictionary: A Guide to Knowledge as Power.* London: Zed Books, 1992.

Sale, Kirkpatrick. *Dwellers in the Land: The Bioregional Vision.* San Francisco: Sierra Club Books, 1985.

Sands, Phillipe, ed. *Greening International Law.* Law and Sustainable Development Series. Sterling, VA: Stylus, 1996.

Sassen, Saskia. *Globalization and Its Discontents: Essays on the New Mobility of People and Money.* New York: New Press, 1998.

Seabrook, Jeremy. *The Myth of the Market: Promises and Illusions.* Devon, UK: Green Books, 1990.

Shiva, Vandana. *The Violence of the Green Revolution: Third World Agriculture, Ecology, and Politics.* Mapusa, Goa, India: The Other India Press, 1991.

————. *Biopiracy: The Plunder of Nature and Knowledge.* Boston: South End Press, 1997.

————. *Stolen Harvest: The Hijacking of the Global Food Supply.* Boston: South End Press, 1999.

————. "U.S. Patent System Legalizes Theft and Biopiracy." *The Hindu,* July 28, 1999.

————. *Water Wars: Privatization, Pollution, and Profit.* Boston: South End Press, 2002.

Shiva, Vandana, Afsar H.Jafri, Gitanjali Bedi, and Radha Holla-Bhar. *The Enclosure and Recovery of the Commons.* New Delhi: Research Foundation for Science, Technology and Ecology, 1997.

Shuman, Michael. *Towards a Global Village: International Community Development Initiatives.* London: Pluto Press, 1994.

————. *Going Local: Creating Self-Reliant Communities in a Global Age.* New York: Routledge, 2000.

Simms, Andrew. *The Environmental War Economy.* London: New Economics Foundation, 2001.

Soros, George. *Open Society: Reforming Global Capitalism.* New York: Public Affairs, 2000.

————. *On Globalization.* New York: Public Affairs, 2002.

Stiglitz, Joseph E. *Globalization and Its Discontents.* New York: W. W. Norton, 2002.

Stone, Michael K. "The Hypercar." *Whole Earth Review,* Winter 2001, p. 53.

Sustainable Energy and Economy Network. *The World Bank and the G-7: Still Changing the Earth's Climate for Business, 1997–98.* Washington, DC: Institute for Policy Studies and the International Trade Information Service, December 1998. www.seen.org.

Suzuki, David, and Holly Dressel. *Good News for a Change: Hope for a Troubled Planet.* Toronto: Stoddart Publishing, 2002.

Tellus Institute. *Halfway to the Future: Reflections on the Global Condition.* Boston: Tellus Institute, 2001.

Transnational Resource and Action Center. "Tangled Up in Blue: Corporate Partnerships at the United Nations." San Francisco: Transnational Resource and Action Center, September 2000. www.corpwatch.org.

United Nations Conference on Trade and Development. *International Monetary and Financial Issues of the Nineties.* Geneva: United Nations, 1992.

————. *Trade and Development Report, 1997.* Geneva: United Nations, 1997.

————. *Trade and Development Report, 1999.* Geneva: United Nations, 1999.

United Nations Department of Economic and Social Affairs. *World Economic and Social Survey, 2001.* New York: United Nations, 2001.

United Nations Development Program. *Human Development Report, 1999.* New York: United Nations Development Program and Oxford University Press, 1999.

————. *Human Development Report, 2001.* New York: United Nations Development Program and Oxford University Press, 2001.

Vallette, Jim, and Daphne Wysham. *Enron's Pawns: How Public Institutions Bankrolled Enron's Globalization Game.* Washington, DC: Institute for Policy Studies, 2002.

Wallach, Lori, and Michelle Sforza. *Whose Trade Organization? Corporate*

Globalization and the Erosion of Democracy. Washington, DC: Public Citizen, 1999.

Wallach, Lori, Michelle Sforza, and Ralph Nader. *The WTO: Five Years of Reasons to Resist Corporate Globalization.* New York: Seven Stories Press, 2000.

Warshall, Peter. "An Electric Dragon Mantles the North American Continent." *Whole Earth Review,* Winter 2001, pp. 12–19.

Wasserman, Harvey. *The Last Energy War: The Battle Over Utility Deregulation.* New York: Open Media/Seven Stories Press, 1999.

Welton, Neva, and Linda Wolf. *Global Uprising: Confronting the Tyrannies of the 21st Century.* Gabriola Island, British Columbia: New Society Publishers, 2001.

"Whole Systems Thinking." *Annual Report, 2000–01.* Snowmass, CO: Rocky Mountain Institute.

Williamson, Thad, David Imbroscio, and Gar Alperovitz. *Making a Place for Community: Local Politics in a Globalized World.* New York: Routledge, 2002.

World Bank. *World Development Report, 2000–01.* Washington, DC: World Bank and Oxford University Press, 2001.

———. *Global Development Finance: Financing the Poorest Countries, 2002.* Washington, DC: World Bank, 2002.

The Drafters

JOHN CAVANAGH is director of the Washington-based Institute for Policy Studies, vice-president of the IFG Board, and coauthor of eleven books on the global economy, including *Global Dreams: Imperial Corporations and the New World Order.*

JERRY MANDER is president of the IFG Board, senior fellow at the Public Media Center, and the author or coeditor of the best-selling books *In the Absence of the Sacred, The Case Against the Global Economy and For a Turn Toward the Local,* and *Four Arguments for the Elimination of Television.*

SARAH ANDERSON is director of the Global Economy Project at the Institute for Policy Studies and coauthor of *A Field Guide to the Global Economy.*

DEBI BARKER is executive director of the IFG and coauthor of *Invisible Government: The World Trade Organization, Global Government for the Millennium?*

MAUDE BARLOW is national chair of the Council of Canadians, an IFG Board member, and author or coauthor of fourteen books, including *Blue Gold, The Battle against Corporate Theft of the World's Water*—published in ten countries—and the forthcoming *Profit Is Not the Cure.*

WALDEN BELLO is executive director of the Bangkok-based Focus on the Global South, an IFG Board member and author or coauthor of eleven books, including *The Future in the Balance: Essays on Globalization and Resistance.*

ROBIN BROAD is a professor at the School of International Service at the American University and author of *Global Backlash: Citizen Initiatives for a Just World Economy.*

TONY CLARKE is the director of the Polaris Institute of Canada, vice-chair of the Council of Canadians, an IFG Board member, and author or coauthor of six books, including *Blue Gold: The Battle against Corporate Theft of the World's Water,* published in ten countries.

EDWARD GOLDSMITH is the founding editor of *The Ecologist,* an IFG Board member, author of twenty books, including *The Way: An Ecological World View,* and coeditor of *The Case Against the Global Economy and for a Turn Toward the Local.* He was awarded the Right Livelihood Award in 1991.

RANDALL HAYES is president of Rainforest Action Network, U.S. director of Destination Conservation, commissioner on the City of San Francisco's Commission on the Environment, an IFG Board member, author of numerous works, and producer of the award-winning documentary film *The Four Corners, A National Sacrifice Area?*

COLIN HINES is founder and coordinator of the Middlesex-based Protect the Local, Globally and an IFG associate. He is coauthor of *The New Protectionism—Protecting the Future against Free Trade* and *Localization: A Global Manifesto.*

ANDREW KIMBRELL is founder and director of the Center for Food Safety, an IFG Board member, author of numerous books and articles, including editor and contributing writer of *Fatal Harvest: the Tragedy of Industrial Agriculture,* and a featured guest on television programs, including *The Today Show,* the *CBS Morning Show, Crossfire,* and *Good Morning America.*

DAVID KORTEN is founder of the People-Centered Development Forum, an IFG associate, and author of numerous publications, including the now-classic *When Corporations Rule the World* (1995) and its sequel, *The Post-Corporate World* (1999).

SARA LARRAIN is cofounder of the Chilean national political party, the Partido Alternative de Cambio, coordinates the Chilean Ecological Action Network, founded the Chilean office of Greenpeace International, and is an

IFG Board member. She was the leading independent candidate in the 1999 Chilean presidential election.

HELENA NORBERG-HODGE is founder and director of the International Society for Ecology and Culture, an IFG Board member and winner of the Right Livelihood Award. She is author of numerous publications, including the international classic *Ancient Futures: Learning from Ladakh,* translated into more than thirty languages.

SIMON RETALLACK is managing editor of *The Ecologist* magazine's special issues, codirector of the Climate Initiatives Fund, and an IFG associate. Among his many publications, he is a contributing editor and writer for the IFG publication *Environmental Impacts of Globalization* (2002).

VANDANA SHIVA is founder and director of the Research Foundation for Science, Technology, and Natural Resource Policy and an IFG Board member. She received the Right Livelihood Award in 1993 and in 2001 was named among the top five "Most Important People in Asia" by *AsiaWeek* magazine. Shiva is author of more than 300 papers in leading journals and numerous books, including *Monocultures of the Mind: Biodiversity, Biotechnology and the Third World.*

VICTORIA TAULI-CORPUZ is an indigenous activist of the Kankanaey peoples of the Cordillera region in the Philippines. She is director of the Philippines-based Indigenous Peoples' International Centre for Policy Research and Education and an IFG associate. She is also a member of the World Commission on the Social Dimensions of Globalization and chairperson of the United Nations Voluntary Fund for Indigenous Populations.

LORI WALLACH is director of Public Citizen's Global Trade Watch and an IFG Board member. Dubbed the "Trade Debate's Guerrilla Warrior" by the *National Journal,* she is coauthor of *Whose Trade Organization? Corporate Globalization and the Erosion of Democracy.*

Index